# Dream League™

# A GUIDE TO SUCCESS
# 1992-1993

Peter Wroe

Cover Design: Panico Theodesiou
© 1992 Peter Wroe and Dream League Limited

Published by Football Directories/Dream League
North Curry, Taunton, Somerset TA3 6DU
Consultant: Tony Williams

All rights reserved. No part of this publication may be produced, stored in a retrieval system, or transmitted in any form or by any means, electronic, mechanical, photocopying, recording or otherwise, without prior permission in writing of the author.

Typeset in 9/10pt Caxton Book
Typeset by R & D Graphics
Unit 3, Willow Business Centre, 17 Willow Lane, Mitcham, Surrey CR4 4NX
Printed by Brightsea Press
Exeter Airport Business Park, Fairoak Close, Clyst Honiton, Exeter EX5 2UL

'Dream League' is a registered trade mark of Dream League Limited

British Library Cataloguing in Publication Data
    Wroe, Peter 1953–
    Dream League a Guide to Success 1992-1993

    ISBN 1-869833-60.0

*For
Sara and Dino*

# Dream League™

# CONTENTS

| | |
|---|---|
| 1. So who would you have in your team? | 1 |
| 2. Reviews | 7 |
| 3. National Cup Tournaments 91/92 | 25 |
| 4. National Dream League 91/92 | 35 |
| 5. How to play Dream Team | 43 |
| 6. How to play Dream League | 47 |
| 7. The Rules | 53 |
| 8. Auction Guide | 65 |
| 9. Scorecheck | 73 |
| 10. Player & Goalie Guide<br>Including Quick Reference | 99 |

# Dream League

## SO WHO WOULD YOU HAVE IN YOUR TEAM?

— 1 —

Welcome to the future of sports in Britain. Fantasy Sports and in this case Dream League Football. I warn you now that Dream League will change your views on a lot of things. Teletext for one and the countless football results that you have ignored over the years will now become vitally important at the weekends. Searching for who got the winner at Stoke on Friday night or did Mark Carter score for Barnet in that rearranged fixture last Sunday?

Fantasy Sports grew out of New York in the early eighties and being a sports fan resident in Manhattan, during those heady times, I didn't fail to take notice.

Dream League could even boast some roots in Nepal where I met a Stanford graduate from Los Angeles called Don Brunsten who regaled me, and whoever else was prepared to listen on the foothills overlooking Annapurna, with stories of American Sports and in particular baseball. It was years later, when I moved to New York chartering Concorde for major sporting events, that I got to learn more about baseball and the ways in which the Americans are totally besotted with sports statistics.

My first visit to Shea Stadium was to see the New York Mets, my second was to see the Rolling Stones, but the creative use of statistics surrounding baseball still interested me.

# DREAM LEAGUE – CHAPTER 1

In New York my work was primarily built around golf and I toured across the country attending the majors and other big golf tournaments regularly returning to Britain for more golf tournaments. Don and I met up often and fantasy baseball was always a talking point, but the problem was converting it to my first love, football.

Born in green bus country, St. Albans, the only red buses went to Arnos Grove and from there to Tottenham High Road and White Hart Lane. At Spurs I was lucky to enjoy what was to become my real passion, international football, through the UEFA Cup and Cup Winners' Cup campaigns. Wednesday nights watching mysterious talent from the eastern bloc trying to get to grips with a super fast formation of wingers and half-backs. I suppose that all started when my parents splashed out and purchased a package of nine tickets for the World Cup Finals in 1966. Seeing grown men cry, especially Germans, was quite an experience for a 12 year old, amongst the euphoria of what was then the biggest footballing event ever to be held in Britain.

I have now been to three World Cup tournaments since and witnessed two more finals. Spain was troublesome as the organisation seemed to be well off the boil compared with my coddled experience at Wembley in '66. Mexico was the opposite, delightfully easy with pesos millionaires buying anything for $10 including the odd wedding reception here and there.

Then Italia 90 and the sheer delight of being paid to be there with a client company picking up the tab for the hotels, meals and match tickets and, thank goodness, the phone bills.

Italia 90 was a fabulous experience and reading some of the more indepth accounts that surfaced after the event it was fascinating to note how many incalculable hours of executive time and millions of dollars in marketing effort were reduced to side shows of fun fair proportions. Mind you when you see some of the characters that are actually running around with the multi million dollar budgets and still good seats go empty, it's criminal. Goals were the only thing that mattered, of course, and they were very very precious.

For a number of years I had struggled with how best to hash football statistics to create a fantasy sport for football in Britain. It was not as easy as it first seemed as I wanted to ensure that anybody who 'owned' a team could look at the scores in a paper (and now on Ceefax) and know instantly how they were doing and how their competitors were faring at the same time. I did not wish to have a controling influence that would reduce the game to fiction.

On the morning after the World Cup final in Rome, enjoying a damn fine cup of expresso in the hotel restaurant overlooking the city I found I had the basics of Fantasy Football. Goals - For and Against but using full backs, half backs and forwards to make up a team. The good old 2-3-5. The W formation.

I sat next to Gary Lineker that afternoon on the British Airways flight back

## SO WHO WOULD YOU HAVE IN YOUR TEAM?

to London. Well I had to be sitting next to somebody famous as the whole aircraft was packed with football writers, TV personalities, working press, sponsors, officials and the new 'cognescenti' of English football and me.

In London I called up the lads, Crystal Palace fans, Arsenal, Maidstone, Tottenham and Leeds supporters. The class of '74 who joined British Airways nearly twenty years ago to see the world and what it had to offer. Plenty. Hence the free tickets to get us all to Nepal for a month and working in British Airways Reservations the 'other' airlines simply rained tickets on you. New York for a weekend? Oh no, not again. How about Alaska then? JAL need some people to try their new Business Class. Try nine hours of Sake tasting at 42000 feet followed by a visit to a glacier at minus 20 and some very dubious watering holes with Eskimos hanging onto the chicken wire protecting the Band.

They all responded and the Original Dream League was formed topped up by Jim Tuck's court from the Railway Bell in South London. Off we went, a committee of ten and in as many directions. We held the auction for players in my West End office sharing a crate of cheap Portuguese beer and the overwhelming desire to show that each was better than the other in creating a team to outscore all of the others over ten months of the football season.

Having had the benefit of the more recent computer training I got the job of collating the scores, not that that gave me any leverage. I was astonished how every team owner simply got into it in such a big way so quickly. Monday mornings were a totally different day. The phone calls, How exactly did you do? Where does that put you in the League? I was seven and three, how can Beasant do that to me? I see your boy got a couple, interested in letting him go to a better team? I'll sell you David Speedie for Steve Lovell.

The admin was a pain so I gave it to one of my staff who was not really au fait with football, which proved one didn't have to be a fanatic to follow the game and she liked all the phone calls from the lads. The real stuff was to outmanouvere the other team owners and snap up hot players in wicked and devious transfer deals. Totally within the rules, of course. As the season unravelled there was the crowing of Not Very Athletic as they opened up a 20 point lead by Christmas. Then their capitulation in the winter schedule and the Libero Party's emergence as a serious contender despite all the rabbit. The Three G's consistency at third place with players nobody had heard of. In The Net FC's award for sense of humour as their team got referred to as Where's The Net? and What's A Net? The sheer tightness of some team owners (we were of course playing for real money, Dream League Dollars came later) expecting ridiculous sums for their star forward as late as February whose team was already out of both cup competitions.

By the time we made it to the Spring of 91 conversations were in shorthand and sounded like a coded language for eavesdroppers at the bar. It got silly

3

sometimes and that was the fun. We each owned a football team and it was pure fantasy. Friends and aquaintances asked if they could join but ten teams was the limit in the Original Dream League as we called it. Meetings went on and on with fine banter about wether to include European goals, the size of the squads, cup competitions and where to have the end of season gathering.

We settled on the Chicago Pizza Pie Factory and the Libero Party were promptly handed the majority of the kitty that built up over the season. And in the true spirit of a winning team owner immediately bought the bottles of bubbly and we schemed our way through the night. I need a new midfield, what about that lad at Birmingham who came good late this season? Spend more money on a goalkeeper, push their spending up at the next auction.

More enquiries came because something was right. Going to matches and telling anybody who was listening that you owned the midfielder, got him for $10 no less, a good buy. It was all the more enjoyable when couples and families started owning teams and letters started arriving stating "We have moved ground and would like you to note our new address" or "How come I didn't get a mention in the newsletter after I drubbed the Stinky Rabbits 4-1?" A few breweries took an interest as landlords and licencees started creating Dream Leagues at their pubs and clubs. The correspondence grew and there seemed only one way to go and that was to write the book. And here it is, a complete self contained game system and the opportunity to do cerebral battle with your fellow football followers and then of course, there is the big time, to compete in the National Dream League Challenge Cups and Leagues.

I have thoroughly enjoyed getting this book together and that is because of the great team that has built up at Dream League HQ, giving up time, providing expertise and in some cases, chipping in real money for the good of the game, the fantasy game that is Dream League Football.

My sincere thanks go to......

**The Management** (and the teams that they own)

| | | |
|---|---|---|
| Jeff Thomas | – | East Sussex Bytes FC |
| Mike Street | – | Fisher Pathetic |
| David Owen | – | Facts & Figures FC |
| Bob Warren | – | Warren's Wizards (Original Dream League) |
| Simon Newlyn | – | Shandwick's All Stars |

## SO WHO WOULD YOU HAVE IN YOUR TEAM?

and special thanks...

### The Committee

| | | |
|---|---|---|
| Simon Crisp | – | Crispy Duck FC |
| Richard Flintham | – | FC Madchester |
| Andy Goodsell | – | Pembury Pirates |
| Peter Hurn | – | Screaming Alice |
| David Loader | – | Richmond Vikings |
| Andy McLeod | – | FC Madchester |
| Alasdair McNabb | – | Macca's Muckers |
| Mike Parsons | – | Golden Wonders |
| Ross Williams | – | Real Newcassel |
| Paul Woodhall | – | Barnsley Bargettes |

### Supported by

| | | |
|---|---|---|
| Terry Chapman | – | Sheffield Steel FC |
| Tony Diston | – | Diston's Disasters |
| Paul Hammerton | – | Hammerton Academicals |
| Frank Lyons | – | Dynamo Chernobyl |

### And the pioneering members of the Original Dream League

| | | |
|---|---|---|
| Russell Gilbey | – | The Gay Blades |
| Andy Lee | – | New Kentonia |
| Dave Littlejohns | – | In The Net FC |
| Des McCarthy | – | Scooby & Shaggy United |
| Stuart Pepper | – | The Red Hot Peppers |
| Jules Rastelli | – | Not Very Athletic FC |
| Tony Robinson | – | The Three G's |
| Jim Tuck | – | The Libero Party |

*Peter Wroe*

# Dream League™

## REVIEWS

## — 2 —

Style and imagination are two of the finest attributes a football team can adopt unless you are of the afflication that work rate and running is what it is all about. In Fantasy Sports your team adopt the perfect style and class because you give it to them. If you fancy five towering haircuts upfront, you've got them. Just because Graham Taylor didn't fancy putting Lineker alongside Wright because "they had similar playing styles" it doesn't mean you cannot pair Aldridge with McClair or Hughes with Rush.

When you study the real football clubs and the items that they produce for sale to fans it thows up some rather odd changes of direction. Take Sheffield Wednesday, they have a logo dated circa 70's of a stylised owl, what happened to the marvellous corporation crest that was on everything around the 1966 Cup Final? Across town United have held onto the Yorkshire rose and the 'Blades'. An eagle perched on the Palace. Wimbledon has a fine crest that is far removed from the football that achieved their recent success. We realised when Dream Team logos first started arriving at Dream League HQ that they can say so much about the team or alternatively, fuel the old alter ego to say something the team owner would like to say but normally doesn't.

Out went the Dream League Review and a wealth of Dream League experience instantly came back. With management strategies like "stitch up as many of the others (Dream Team Owners) as possible" and team mottos like "Back Door Son" there was obviously more to fantasy football than simply building a well oiled goalscoring machine.

## DREAM LEAGUE - CHAPTER 2

What strip would your team play in? Some team owners go back to their favourite strip worn by their real life club in the 60's or 70's. I remember Tottenham wearing Navy Blue V-neck Short Sleeved Shirts in a European Cup Tie due to a colour clash of white in the days before away strips, infant strips and the ultimate disco version home strip. You could make a statement with your strip. The Body Shop's ECO-ROVERS would line up in say, Green Shirts with Natural Collar and Cuffs, Socially Aware Shorts and Earthy Socks wearing boots made of a natcha-rool material invented by football mad Brazilian Indians and totally shin bone friendly.

Then there is the management style. Second only to referees, managers with the possible exception of chairmen, get the most criticism so 'Buddy Management' is becoming more popular to carry the burden on four shoulders rather than just two. And in Dream League you have the full backing of the board, because you are the board!

> *We have had an offer to sponsor the best Dream Team File to include Logo, Motto, Strip etc. The company would then like to make up the winning strips for real. We are considering it, so look out for more news in the Dream League HQ newsletter.*

# REVIEWS

League Name – Gilbert & Sullivan Dream League
Team Name – Pembury Pirates
*Team Owner(s)* – Andy Goodsell
*Team Motto* – Persistance Wins
*Team Colours* – Shirts: Chelsea Blue
– Shorts: Chelsea Blue
– Socks : Chelsea Blue
*Team Logo* – Footballing Pirate
*Description of League:*
10 regulars from Gilbert & Sullivan pub in Covent Garden

## AUCTION

*Management Strategy*
– Stitch-up as many of the others as possible
*Managerial Acumen*
– Lineker and Grobbelaar formed base of my team. Outbid at the end for Aldridge
*Player* – Costliest: Gary Lineker
– Cost: $36
– Worth it: Every cent

## THE SEASON

*Best player & why*
– Can't separate Lineker, Holdsworth, Bamber or Grobbelaar
*League highs & lows*
– Good start to the season saw me at the top. Went third after a "sticky" patch but climbed back through tough winter campaign and Easter games
*League Ambition(s)*
– I've achieved winning The Gilbert & Sullivan, now I really want to challenge for national glory in League or Cup competition.
*Transfers*
– Holdsworth and Bamber kept the fans happy. If only I had had them at the begining.
*Experience gained*
– Lower Division players are more likely to produce the goods. Study the form of the teams and go for their best striker(s)

## COMMENTS

A great excuse for a regular booze up with the other team owners and increases your football knowledge no end.

## 4th National Dream League

DREAM LEAGUE – CHAPTER 2

## PEMBURY PIRATES F.C.

Dave Bamber
7/10/91
Blackpool

Steve Bull
8/9/91
Wolverhampton W.

Dean Holdsworth
7/10/91
Brentford

Gary Lineker
8/9/91
Tottenham Hotspur

David Speedie
8/9/91
Blackburn Rovers

Paul Baker
8/9/91
Hartlepool United

Craig Shakespeare
8/9/91
West Bromwich Albion

John Sheridan
2/12/91
Sheffield Wednesday

Phil Babb
8/9/91
Bradford

Eli Roger
23/3/92
Burnley

Bruce Grobbelaar
8/9/91
Liverpool

**PLAYERS SOLD**
Andy Jones, Andy Sussex, John Morrissey, Tony Dorigo

## GILBERT & SULLIVAN DREAM LEAGUE

|  | Goals for this period | Goals against this period | Points this period | Points Season to date | |
| --- | --- | --- | --- | --- | --- |
| PEMBURY PIRATES | 8 |  | 8 | 119 | 1 |
| ALPHA ALPHA FC | 3 | 1 | 2 | 68 | 2 |
| MARYLAND MEMBERS ELEVEN | 6 | 2 | 4 | 66 | 3 |
| TARDIS ELEVEN | 6 | 1 | 5 | 63 | 4 |
| C.C. FC | 2 | 1 | 1 | 55 | 5 |
| KREMLIN KICKERS FC | 8 | 1 | 7 | 54 | 7 |
| DEEPS FC | 3 | 2 | 1 | 52 | 6 |
| LOSERS FC | 5 | 1 | 4 | 45 | 8 |
| LUMPY JUMPERS FC | 3 |  | 3 | 36 | 9 |
| NONSENSE ELEVEN | 3 | 7 | −4 | −21 | 10 |

# REVIEWS

League Name – Pia Zadora Dream League
Team Name – Screaming Alice F.C.
*Team Owner(s)* – Peter Hurn
*Team Motto* – Back Door Son
*Team Colours* – Shirts: White, with Claret & Light Blue facings
– Shorts: Black; Socks: White with Black hoops
*Team Logo* – Pink Ribbon in Hair
*Description of League:* – 7 cricketers from Warlingham C.C. & 3 friends

## AUCTION

*Management Strategy*
— None, like many in real life
*Managerial Accumen*
— Signed two ropey defenders, midfield never lived up to expectations but Messrs. Shearer & Flounders were acquired on the cheap ($15 & $4 respectively), so not all bad.
*Player* — Costliest: Tony Coton; Cost: $25; Worth it: No

## THE SEASON

*Best player & why*
— Duncan Shearer but Tony Coton is best keeper in the country playing behind the worst defence.
*League high & lows*
— From 9th to 2nd but still points adrift. Good transfer signings have been the reason.
*League Ambition(s)*
— To be higher than Turnbull's Trotters (next door neighbour) & Real Ale FC (my little brother)
*Transfers* – Roberts (Huddersfield), Wilkinson (Middlesbro'), Newman (Norwich) & Gleghorn (Birmingham) proved to be the best buys. Narbett & Babb failed to live up to expectations.
*Experience gained*
— Don't waste too much on defenders or midfielders, save your money for the strikers. Look out for players who may be categorised out of position.

## COMMENTS

The whole idea is brilliant! I have had to change my allegiance of undying loyalty to Crystal Palace by having to sample the occasional delights of Gillingham on a wet Wednesday.

I would like to see the retention of 10 transfer options with more transfers between teams within the League using the transfer funds available, say a prize for the team that ends the season with the most Dream League Dollars.

## Joint 79th National Dream League

# DREAM LEAGUE – CHAPTER 2

## SCREAMING ALICE F.C.

| | | |
|---|---|---|
| Andy Flounders<br>18/8/91<br>Rochdale | Iwan Roberts<br>4/11/91<br>Huddersfield Town | Duncan Shearer<br>17/8/91<br>Blackburn Rovers |
| Jason White<br>28/1/92<br>Scunthorpe United | | Paul Wilkinson<br>9/9/91<br>Middlesbrough |
| Ian Benjamin<br>17/9/91<br>Southend United | Sean Farrell<br>25/2/92<br>Fulham | Nigel Gleghorn<br>2/12/91<br>Birmingham City |
| Phil Babb<br>4/11/91<br>Bradford | | Rob Newman<br>9/9/92<br>Norwich City |
| | Nigel Spink<br>26/3/92<br>Aston Villa | |

**PLAYERS SOLD**
Andy Garner, Niall Quinn, John Taylor, Paul Dalton, David Gilbert, Jon Narbett, Tony Adams, Frank Gray, Tony Coton

## PIA ZADORA DREAM LEAGUE

| | Goals for this period | Goals against this period | Points this period | Points Season to date | |
|---|---|---|---|---|---|
| BORIS YELTSIN'S R&B ARMY | 7 | | 7 | 108 | 1 |
| SCREAMING ALICE | 2 | | 2 | 83 | 2 |
| PHILISTINES | 5 | | 5 | 80 | 3 |
| REAL ALE | 1 | 1 | | 69 | 4 |
| TURNBULL'S TROTTERS | 2 | 1 | 1 | 68 | 5 |
| THE GARGOYLES | 5 | 1 | 4 | 61 | 7 |
| DYNAMO CHICKEN | 4 | 3 | 1 | 59 | 6 |
| SUMORIANS | 9 | 7 | 2 | 50 | 8 |
| RUSS'S ROVERS | 1 | | 1 | 47 | 9 |
| LAGER TOPS | 8 | | 8 | 46 | 10 |

# REVIEWS

League Name      - Highfield St. James Dream League
Team Name        - Real Newcassel
Team Owner(s)    - Ross Williams
Team Motto       - Drink Beer, Often
Team Colours     - Shirts: Black & White Stripes
                 - Shorts: Black
                 - Socks: Black & White
                 - Eyes: A Red Mist
Team Logo        - The Bridge supported by Ale Bottles
Description League – Friends and Business Associates and patrons of local pub.

## AUCTION
*Management Strategy*
— Watch your players play in real life
*Managerial Acumen*
— Aldridge and Peacock had a great partnership, dubious goalkeeper aquisitions.
*Player* — Costliest: John Aldridge; Cost: $40; Worth It: Top Scorer – Enough said.

## THE SEASON
*Best Player and Why*
— John Aldridge, his Friday night scoring regularly set me up for good weekends. Brett Angell, good consistent scoring all season, kept morale high when half my side were missing through suspension.
*League Highs & Lows*
— Top albeit briefly for one month. Best goaiscoring team and first to 100 goals in our League but also saddled myself with the worst defence.
*League Ambition*
— Beat anybody, only winners at Real Newcassel unlike the real thing who get satisfied with mediocrity.
*Transfers* – Bolstered front line with prompt purchase of Wayne Biggins and Steve White. Re-bolstered front line with prompt sale of Steve White after eight weeks and no goals.
*Experience Gained*
— Look for proven goalscorers in all positions who remain with an unchanged side in the same division. Otherwise concentrate on a good defensive unit, a keeper NOT from Birmingham City.

## COMMENTS
Watching for 'Live' Dream League goals at the same time following sides around the country. Real Newcassel would not have won the Dream League Fair Play award with the sending off record we amassed. Other than a Newcastle win, nothing better than to see one of your 'own' players score in real life.

## Joint 106th National Dream League

## REAL NEWCASSEL F.C.

| | | |
|---|---|---|
| John Aldridge<br>9/9/91<br>Tranmere Rovers | Brett Angell<br>9/9/91<br>Southend United | Wayne Biggins<br>7/10/91<br>Stoke City |
| Alex Rae<br>9/9/91<br>Millwall | | David Speedie<br>9/9/91<br>Blackburn Rovers |
| Gavin Peacock<br>9/9/91<br>Newcastle United | Ian Rodgerson<br>9/9/91<br>Birmingham City | Gary Speed<br>25/2/92<br>Leeds United |
| Colin Calderwood<br>25/2/92<br>Swindon Town | | Eric Young<br>28/1/92<br>Crystal Palace |
| | Tim Clark<br>24/3/92<br>Huddersfield Town | |

**PLAYERS SOLD**
Nigel Clough, John Taylor, Steve White, Tony Adams, Brian Tinnion, Tony Coton, Thomas Martin

## HIGHFIELD ST. JAMES DREAM LEAGUE

| | Goals for this period | Goals against this period | Points this period | Points Season to date | |
|---|---|---|---|---|---|
| MELCHESTER | 4 | 1 | 3 | 85 | 1 |
| REAL NEWCASSEL | 9 | 4 | 5 | 81 | 2 |
| BARNHAM | 7 | | 7 | 74 | 3 |
| BOUGHTON NORTH END | 2 | | 2 | 52 | 4 |
| OAKLEY 'OPEFULS | 6 | 1 | 5 | 38 | 5 |
| PROXY | 2 | | 2 | 34 | 6 |
| TRENT ENDERS | 3 | 1 | 2 | 23 | 7 |
| METAL WORKERS | 1 | | 1 | 21 | 8 |
| DISTONS DISASTERS | 3 | 1 | 2 | 13 | 9 |
| WIGLEYS WINGLESS WONDERS | 1 | 3 | −2 | 10 | 10 |

# REVIEWS

League Name       - Tower Three Dream League
Team Name         - Fortuna Strongbowler
*Team Owner(s)*   - Alan Armstrong
*Team Motto*      - Our Cider Stronger
*Team Colours*    - Shirts: Apple; Shorts: Apple Socks : Short
*Team Logo*       - Ball, Bow and Arrow

**FORTUNA STRONGBOWLER**

*Description of League:*
A group of Manchester University Old Boys, all who lived in House 3 of a tower block, thus the name with relations and friends including the only female, my fiance.

## AUCTION
*Management Strategy* – Fairly shambolic
*Managerial Acumen*
- Only conscious decision was to buy a cheap keeper (Crossley) and exchange him for Schmeichel. Well happy to get Deane, Gabbiadini and Peacock for DL$6 but I made the mistake of having dollars at the end of the auction

*Player* – Costliest: Teddy Sheringham; Cost: $17; Worth it : Not exactly

## THE SEASON
*Best player & why*
- Gavin Peacock (Newcastle Utd), who nearly outscored my best striker

*League highs & lows*
- 6 weeks into the season I was eighth and getting considerable grief from the girlfriend, who was hovering between 2nd and 3rd. Since then I created the best midfield in the country (Gleghorn, Baker and Peacock) that has taken me to the top

*League Ambition(s)*
- To finish on top of my girlfriend, owner of the Three Legged Raiders, or I will never live it down. Winning our league would be quite good as well

*Transfers* – Adding Baker and Gleghorn to the team gave me the goals to rise up the table, with Schmeichel the best possible replacement at the back.

*Experience Gained*
- We all felt sorry for one of our colleagues, who sold Bamber "because Blackpool scored 5 and he didn't get any, so he must be crap", and replaced him with Durie! How wrong can you be.

## COMMENTS
We all live in various parts of the UK. I am in Belfast and the other team owners are in Blackpool, Manchester, Basingstoke and the Midlands. It has been a great way of keeping in touch. Our 92/93 Auction date is already set, a serious reunion no doubt.

## Joint 110th National Dream League

# DREAM LEAGUE – CHAPTER 2

## FORTUNA STRONBOWLER FC

Clive Allen
28/1/92
West Ham United

Kevin Gallacher
4/11/92
Coventry City

Teddy Sheringham
1/9/91
Nottingham Forest

David White
25/2/92
Manchester City

Paul Wilkinson
4/11/91
Middlesbrough

Paul Baker
1/9/91
Hartlepool United

Nigel Gleghorn
4/11/91
Birmingham City

Gavin Peacock
1/9/91
Newcastle United

Phil Babb
7/10/91
Bradford

Gary Gill
1/9/91
Cardiff City

Peter Schmeichel
9/9/91
Manchester United

**PLAYERS SOLD**
Steve Butler, Brian Deane, Marco Gabbiadini, Ian Marshall, Mike Newell, Mick Quinn, Simon Milton, Jon Narbett, Mark Crossley

## TOWER III DREAM LEAGUE

|  | Goals for this period | Goals against this period | Points this period | Points Season to date | |
|---|---|---|---|---|---|
| SAFE HANDS FCS | 4 |  | 4 | 83 | 1 |
| FORTUNA STRONGBOWLER | 6 | 1 | 5 | 80 | 3 |
| SURGICAL STRIKERS | 5 |  | 5 | 79 | 4 |
| DAVE'S DYNAMIC DEVILS | 3 | 1 | 2 | 78 | 2 |
| CD PLAYERS | 6 | 4 | 2 | 74 | 5 |
| THE DRILLERS | 7 | 1 | 6 | 59 | 6 |
| THREE LEGGED RAIDERS | 6 | 7 | −1 | 34 | 7 |
| INTER BEER | 1 |  | 1 | 28 | 8 |
| GAZZA TEARS | 1 | 2 | −1 | 17 | 9 |
| NO NAME FC | 1 | 1 |  | 12 | 10 |

League Name    –   One 'D' in Dream League
Team Name      –   Golden Wonders
*Team Owner*   –   Mike Parsons
*Team Motto*   –   OOH Bully Bully
*Team Colours* –   Shirts: Gold; Shorts: Gold; Socks: Gold
*Team Logo*    –   A Golden Wonder heading the ball
*Description of League* – Friends and Workmates

## AUCTION

*Management Strategy*
– To get Steve Bull at all costs and let the rest take care of themselves

*Management Acumen*
– Bullish

*Players* – Costliest: Steve Bull; Cost: $41; Worth It?: Yes..just.

## THE SEASON

*Best player and why?*
– Brian Tinnion, a goalscoring defender. Gary Bull in the first round of transfers.

*League Highs & Lows*
– Mid table mediocrity. Highs were being first place in October and taking the Armitage Shanks Bowl Final to a replay and being first to 100 goals. The lows were losing in the first round of the National Dream League Challenge Cup and conceding far too many goals.

*League Ambition*
– Overtake Athletico Nelson...."They think it's all over..."

*Transfers*
– Achieved a high scoring team but lousy goals against record. The worst deal was selling Andy Flounders just before he started scoring, replacing him with Steve White as he stopped scoring.

*Experience Gained*
– Make a bigger investment in my keeper and take more care when bidding tactically to push player prices up.

## COMMENTS

An increased level of interest in football on a broader scale. Going to matches to see "my boys" perform. A greater knowledge of all four divisions and realising just how useful Ceefax can be.

## Joint 153rd National Dream League

# DREAM LEAGUE – CHAPTER 2

## GOLDEN WONDERS FC

Gary Bull
19/8/91
Barnet

Steve Bull
19/8/91
Wolverhampton W.

Rod McDonald
9/9/91
Walsall

Phil Stant
30/12/91
Mansfield Town

Steve White
4/11/91
Swindon Town

Paul Cook
9/9/91
Wolverhampton W.

Nigel Gleghorn
4/11/91
Birmingham City

Jon Narbett
9/9/91
Hereford

Rob Newman
9/9/91
Norwich City

Brian Tinnion
29/8/91
Bradford

Martin Thomas
4/11/91
Birmingham City

**PLAYERS SOLD**
Steve Butler, Andy Flounders, Paul Merson, David Puckett, Paul Williams, John Deary, Dave Lee, Sterling Worrell, Richard Dryden, Mark Crossley, Nigel Spink.

## THERE'S ONLY ONE 'D' IN DREAM LEAGUE

|  | Goals for this period | Goals against this period | Points this period | Points Season to date | |
|---|---|---|---|---|---|
| ATHLETICO NELSON | 5 |  | 5 | 90 | 1 |
| GRIFFOS GYPO'S | 4 | 1 | 3 | 78 | 2 |
| THE TOFFEES | 10 | 4 | 6 | 78 | 3 |
| LEFT FOOTERS | 6 |  | 6 | 67 | 4 |
| GOLDEN WONDERS | 2 | 5 | –3 | 66 | 5 |
| THE ADAMS FAMILY | 7 | 1 | 6 | 65 | 6 |
| FC MADCHESTER | 7 | 1 | 6 | 65 | 6 |
| LEGIA WALSALL | 2 |  | 2 | 47 | 8 |
| SCUMERVILLA | 2 | 7 | –5 | 36 | 9 |
| INTER THE FOURTH | 4 | 2 | 2 | 31 | 10 |

# REVIEWS

League Name     – The Original Dream League
Team Name       – MET-WRØ
*Team Owner*    – Peter Wroe
*Team Motto*    – Charm. Leverage. Money.
*Team Colours*  – Shirts: Navy
                – Shorts: Blonde
                – Socks: Black
*Team Logo*     – New York Skyline (where it all began) and Ball with Viking name

*Description of League:*
Contempories of the Class of '74 at British Airways and regulars at The Railway in South London. The first Dream League.

## AUCTION

*Management Strategy*
– Set a budget for each position

*Managerial Acumen*
– Try to avoiding knee jerk transfer activity

*Player* – Costliest: Dalien Atkinson; Cost: $20; Worth It?: Not at all.

## THE SEASON

*Best Player & Why*
– David White for consistency and Andy Flounders for persistence

*League Highs & Lows*
– Never really got going, injuries denting my ambitions. Had a good National Dream Team Cup run, goals coming from all positions on the right days.

*League Ambition*
– When you create something as original as Dream League one should be better than fifth but that's football and there is always next season and the Cups.

*Transfers*
– Clive Baker of Barnsley conveniently transferred to Coventry and I subsequently picked up Steve Ogrizovic. Unfortunately Terry Butcher left and Don Howe took over.

*Experience Gained*
– Try not to let your prejudices against rival clubs effect your buying. For example the United fan who would not buy a City player for anything.

## COMMENTS

You are holding the future that is called Fantasy Sports, in your hands.

## Joint 443rd National Dream League

DREAM LEAGUE - CHAPTER 2

## MET-WRØ FC

| Mark Bright | Andy Flounders | Mike Small |
| 28/7/91 | 28/7/91 | 4/11/91 |
| Crystal Palace | Rochdale | West Ham United |

David White
28/1/92
Manchester City

Jason White
28/1/92
Scunthorpe United

| Ian Benjamin | Nigel Gleghorn | Paul Groves |
| 28/7/91 | 2/12/91 | 28/7/91 |
| Southend United | Bimingham City | Blackpool |

Steve Bruce
28/7/91
Manchester United

Robert Ullathorne
28/7/91
Norwich City

Steve Ogrizovic
4/11/91
Coventry City

**PLAYERS SOLD**

Dalien Atkinson, Steve Butler, Gordon Durie, Martin Foyle, Niall Quinn, Mark Ward, George Parris, Brian Tinnion, Clive Baker

## ORIGINAL DREAM LEAGUE

|  | Goals for this period | Goals against this period | Points this period | Points Season to date |   |
| --- | --- | --- | --- | --- | --- |
| NOT VERY ATHLETIC FC | 6 |  | 6 | 119 | 1 |
| THREE G'S | 3 |  | 3 | 72 | 2 |
| LIBERO PARTY | 1 | 1 |  | 67 | 3 |
| SCOOBY & SHAGGY UNITED | 2 |  | 2 | 64 | 4 |
| MET-WRØ | 4 | 2 | 2 | 46 | 5 |
| WARREN WIZARDS | 5 | 2 | 3 | 45 | 6 |
| GAY BLADES | 5 | 1 | 4 | 34 | 7 |
| RED HOT PEPPERS | 2 | 1 | 1 | 32 | 8 |
| IN THE NET FC | 2 |  | 2 | 28 | 9 |
| NEW KENTONIA FC | 2 |  | 2 | 22 | 10 |

# REVIEWS

League Name       –   Acme Dream League
Team Name         –   Macca's Muckers
*Team Owner(s)*   –   Alasdair McNabb
*Team Motto*      –   Go For It, Whatever They Look Like
*Team Colours*    –   Shirts: Red & Green tartan
                  –   Shorts: Red
                  –   Socks: Green
*Team Logo*       –   Scottish Highlander with right leg on the ball

*Description of League:*
10 employees and friends of major advertising agency.

## AUCTION
*Management Strategy*
– Buy the best
*Managerial Accumen*
– Keeper let in too many, good defence, strong midfield and non-existent strike force, apart from Dion Dublin, all in all not too good
*Player* – Costliest: Stuart Pearce; Cost: $25; Worth it: No

## THE SEASON
*Best Player & why*
– Steve Castle always seemed to score when the strikers had one of their off days. Good, reliable midfielder
*League highs & lows*
– Managed 8th place at one stage but as my keepers continued their bad form, I did have Chris Woods, and my strikers kept missing, I soon took over 10th place.
*League Ambition(s)*
– To finish 9th
*Transfers*
– Achieved nothing. My three keepers have performed consistently badly and every time I bought a striker he stopped scoring like Kerry Dixon & Gordon Durie
*Experience gained*
– Go for proven players rather than ones with potential and definitely do not buy any of England's keepers (Woods, Seaman or Martyn)

## COMMENTS
Stockport vs. Leyton Orient on a Friday night suddenly becomes an integral part of your weekend entertainment.

## Joint 517th National Dream League

# DREAM LEAGUE - CHAPTER 2

## MACCA'S MUCKERS FC

John Barnes
30/12/91
Liverpool

Dion Dublin
18/8/91
Cambridge United

Maurice Johnston
2/12/91
Everton

Chris Kiwomya
25/2/92
Ipswich Town

Paul Wilkinson
7/10/91
Middlesbrough

Steve Castle
18/8/91
Leyton Orient

Mike Hazard
18/8/91
Swindon Town

Gordon Strachan
18/8/91
Leeds United

Stuart Pearce
18/8/91
Nottingham Forest

Neil Thompson
9/9/91
Ipswich Town

Chris Woods
7/10/91
Sheffield Wednesday

**PLAYERS SOLD**
Darren Beckford, Luther Blisset, Kerry Dixon, Gordon Durie, Jimmy Quinn, Stuart Rimmer, Keith Jones, Leigh Palin, Paul Holmes, Tony Coton.

## ORIGINAL DREAM LEAGUE

|  | Goals for this period | Goals against this period | Points this period | Points Season to date |  |
|---|---|---|---|---|---|
| SPENCE UNITED | 1 | 1 |  | 98 | 1 |
| REAL MADRAS | 3 | 1 | 2 | 76 | 2 |
| BIFFO'S BRUISERS | 7 | 1 | 6 | 69 | 3 |
| THAMESFORD UNITED | 5 |  | 5 | 68 | 4 |
| ZULU WARRIORS | 5 | 5 |  | 57 | 5 |
| MANCHESTER CITY | 10 | 4 | 6 | 52 | 6 |
| DONALDS DUCKS FC | 4 |  | 4 | 50 | 7 |
| LUNCHTIME FC | 5 | 7 | -2 | 43 | 8 |
| MACCA'S MUCKERS | 3 |  | 3 | 41 | 9 |
| JUDAS WANDERERS | 2 |  | 2 | 28 | 10 |

| | | |
|---|---|---|
| League Name | – | War No Cup Dream League |
| Team Name | – | 58 Memories |
| Team Owner(s) | – | Tony La Fave |
| Team Motto | – | Pride For Ever More |
| Team Colours | – | Shirts: Red |
| | – | Shorts: Black |
| | – | Socks : Red |
| Team Logo | – | "58" and ball |
| Description of League | – | National Dream Team League |

**58 memories**
Pride For Ever More

## AUCTION

*Management Strategy*
– Concentrate on 2nd, 3rd and 4th division players

*Managerial Acumen*
– Sound defence that has not changed all season, strong midfield with Baker (Hartlepool) joining Hignett (Crewe) and the outstanding Philliskirk getting strong support from Beardsley up front

*Player* – Costliest: Schmeichel; Cost: $37; Worth it: Definitely

## THE SEASON

*Best player & why*
– Schmeichel, for obvious reasons

*League highs & lows*
– Stayed top most of the way, concerned when Bruce and Parker suffered long term injuries and Schmeichel took some heat

*League Ambitions*
– To stay exactly where I am and go for more cup glory!

*Transfers*
– After careful study of my existing team, widespread changes were made. Having gone to Blackpool and seen/heard first hand what their fans thought of Taylor's goalscoring ability, he had to go, as did 4 others. Unfortunately, apart from Baker and Schmeichel, the others were not much better.

*Experience gained*
– Definately select proven goalscorers in every position and hope your keeper proves himself.

## COMMENTS

The Cup competitions give added excitement to the Dream League Championships, even to the extent when you hope your keeper concedes a few against one of your strikers in case of the GKF.

# DREAM LEAGUE – CHAPTER 2

## 58 MEMORIES FC

Peter Beardsley
17/8/91
Everton

Kevin Gallacher
17/8/91
Coventry City

Tony Philliskirk
2/12/91
Bolton Wanderers

Stuart Rimmer
2/12/91
Chester City

Guy Whittingham
2/12/91
Portsmouth

Paul Baker
7/10/91
Hartlepool United

Craig Hignett
17/8/91
Crew Alexandra

Darren Rowbotham
7/10/91
Birmingham City

Stuart Pearce
17/8/91
Nottingham Forest

Neil Thompson
17/8/91
Ipswich Town

Peter Schmeichel
17/8/91
Manchester United

**PLAYERS SOLD**
David Howells, Liam Robinson, Keith Jones, Mark Taylor, Brian Parkin

## Excerpt from National Dream Team League

|  | Points | Position |
|---|---|---|
| FC LIQUIDATORS | 87 | 64 |
| PAPERBACK CITY | 87 | 64 |
| MONDAY NIGHT FOOTBALL | 86 | 66 |
| 58 MEMORIES | 86 | 66 |
| FAMOUS WEMBLY TURF | 86 | 66 |
| IT IS ALL OVER | 86 | 66 |
| DINOS ROVERS | 86 | 66 |
| ASTRA AGGRO | 86 | 66 |
| LA EXILES | 86 | 66 |
| THE CARDINAL | 85 | 73 |

# Dream League™ NATIONAL CUP TOURNAMENTS 91/92

— 3 —

## THE NATIONAL DREAM LEAGUE CHALLENGE CUP

When we set out in August 1991 we did not realise that the final would be contested in such a great spirit with so much attention. To select a team from each League added a lot of debate to many Transfer Auctions and put plenty of pressure on the selected teams. Once a team was selected and entered it was 'frozen' so that any transfers the team owner might make only applied to his League side not the Cup team.

The qualifying rounds sorted out a first round proper and from there on the rounds were scheduled to coincide with the FA Cup weekends, although all goals scored in Cup or League matches counted for the Dream League cup competitions. Due to the TV scheduling or more appropriately the uncertainty of TV scheduling Dream League games were played over Saturday and Sunday, except the final which was to cover all eventualities being played from Friday through to Monday if required.

In the 1992/93 season Cup matches will probably be played over a weekend as more games are being played on Fridays and Mondays.

The FA Cup is probably the finest knock-out football tournament in the world. Add the extra pressure of those cup performances effecting your team's (and League's) progress, things can get very interesting in front of the live

# DREAM LEAGUE - CHAPTER 3

game on a Sunday afternoon. We call it TV Agony as one will usually end up willing Lukic to concede at least two or Neville Southall to keep a clean sheet against Arsenal.

The First Round proper coincided with the real Third Round, Wrexham shook up a few Dream Team safe bets and more than a little disappointment was expressed on account that the Leeds/Manchester affair (part two) did not contribute to the results. I thought they knew a thing or two about weather in Yorkshire.

Match of the round was surely in South London where BRIDGET'S BEAUTIES of The Railway Bell showed the way by popping four into the net only to be outgunned by the five BORUSSIA MOSSELYGLADBACH recorded representing the Tameside Blundersliega near Manchester.

There was drama from the merseyside team HIGHBOD ATHLETIC (Elm Tree Dream League) with four to thwart three from PEMBURY PIRATES of the Gilbert & Sullivan Dream League, Covent Garden. The quote from Pirates owner Andy Goodsell, "Gutted", certainly eschewed verbosity and the chorus simply broke down in tears.

A North/South clash saw CLUB 81 (Arsenal Dream League) go through AND win with David Seaman in goal, Duncan Shearer maintained the balance, leaving MOSELEY CELTIC (Cumberland Dream League) displeased with another couple of surprises past Tony Coton at Ayresome Park.

Only two teams failed to record a sausage, cut a record, catch a rabbit or report a goal of type, style or significance. It was to be a replay otherwise known as Elvis Presley Hound Dog Karaoke time. If they cannot score a goal then maybe they should sing for some laughs. Giant Killing Factor only kicks in when there is something on the board from both sides. BOCA OLD BOYS from The Pear Tree in Cheshire had to face-off once more with PRESTON DEEP END from the Tetley's Dream League of Leeds for another cross pennine encounter.

The Blundersliega Dream Liega, Edgbaston (not to be confused with the aforementioned Tameside) put forward the delightfully named BOLTON WEDDING TACKLE. The draw paired Wedding Tackle with FC SLIGHTLY TUBBY representing the Drink 'Til It Hurts Dream League of Harrow.

This was a game for everyone to enjoy as two different schools of thought went into it. It started off damp and it got worse and by the end of the afternoon when it was very wet, FC Slightly Tubby were on top. Two goals no less by Tony Philliskirk of none other than Bolton Wanderers, doing the dirty on 'Tackle'. Tackle came back on Sunday through a Mark Carter goal for Barnet, but it wasn't enough. If only it hadn't rained in Leeds, the honeymoon could've been very very different.

Highbury proved to be the shock venue for Dream League in the second round. Goals against Seaman and Schmeichel dramtically affecting the shape of 'The Big One' as the National Dream League Challenge Cup became known.

The advert buying whizz-kid owners at The Acme Dream League have a tense Sunday afternoon of TV Agony with Neville, will he or won't he? He

## THE NATIONAL CUP TOURNAMENTS

didn't and SPENCE UNITED saw off the illustrious SICK AS A BRIGHTLY COLOURED TROPICAL BIRD FC from Fat Harry's Super League.

Big guns in Oxfordshire at The Crown South Moreton, RICHARD'S ROVERS blazing three and derailing LOKOMOTIV SPOTTER in the process. The pub match of the round saw The Packhorse (GORTON RANGERS) ease past The Halfway House (WANDSWORTH WANDERERS) with three goals and David Seaman between the posts. Gorton's reward was a tie against National League leaders, TWO LEFT FEET FC.

FC Slightly Tubby, heroes of the first round, got turned over by a team from The B&Q DIY Dream League. PSV HANGOVER with Gobbelaar to boot, dance and parry scored three, Neil Thompson's 49th minute effort securing victory.

The Elvis Presley Hound Dog Karaoke award went to RED ROCK UNITED at The Ram's Head in Langley Park, near Durham and BEXLEY UNITED at the Don-Alan Litho Dream League. It is not as easy as it looks, scoring week in week out.

The Third Round proper and 800 teams are now reduced to sixteen, things are getting tight as GKF separates Red Rock United (27) and Richard's Rovers (14) and PSV Hangover sink Preston Deep End on the more goals by strikers rule. Alan Smiths' one (of the magnificent seven that afternoon) being the one that did it.

Paul Baker of Hartlepool gave Spence United the win over BARNHAM from Rugby. Highbod Athletic were the high scorers with three over SAFE HANDS FC from Belfast and the Tower Three Dream League, the goals coming in from Paul Groves, Mark Carter and Guy Whittingham.

Paul Groves again, this time with Stuart Pearce and Teddy Sheringham had THE A TEAM, the Lonsdale Dream League side from Newcastle, seeing off FLEETING ANTELOPES. Gary Blissett, destined to become a Dream League legend, scores for AC TORNADO and The Swan Dream League remove RED STAR NORMANTON of The Groin Strain League from the competition.

A big upset in the quarter finals. Two Left Feet going very strong in the National League, tripped out of the cup on giant killing factor to Spence United who had a larger proportion of lower division players. The double is no longer a possibility but two from Peter Beardsley and one from Steve Bull sealed the fate of The A Team on behalf of PSV Hangover. Dog fighting in West London enables AC Tornado to shoot down Borussia Mossleygladbach with accurate firing from John Magilton and Iwan Roberts. The other semi final place was claimed by Red Rock United on giant killing factor 27 to 24.

High flying John Aldridge secured a Cup Final place for AC Tornado with two goals and Iwan Roberts added a third, Schmeichel let one go by to peg the scoring at 2. At Red Rock, Dave Bamber recorded a brace and Dean Holdsworth netted the third only for Middlesbrough to concede two against Watford reducing their points to only 1. In the other semi final PSV Hangover were on course for the shakes. A heady cocktail of a spirited Pompey attack at Highbury and a Grobbelaar punch made for shaky times and TV agony. Neil Thompson had already secured an advantage by scoring at Southend in the

Ipswich victory. Spence United self inflicted further damage with Palace getting two goals at Goodison. Spence were in deep from the start missing two of their match winners. Saunders elbowed himself out of contention and Molby got lost when he strayed from the centre circle. It was PSV's day, summed up when one of their defenders, Steve Nicol, headed off the line from Colin Clarke.

## THE FINAL

It was certainly a colourful affair with both teams sporting brightly designed strips, without sponsors names and as yet, unavailable to parents of replicants.

The spotlight fell on the two team owners, Robin Lorimor and Russ Allan. Robin, a former Air Traffic Controller with the Royal Air Force and Russ, a Careers Officer at Sheffield County Council.

It was a great final, heroes and villains and no referees. AC Tornado got off to a flying start with goals from John Aldridge and Gary Blissett.

But the hero for PSV Hangover was undoubtedly Craig Hignett of Crewe popping in two early goals in the 13th and 19th minutes away to Walsall. Gary Blisset pulled one back for the Tornados but Peter Beardsley in the 33rd minute made it 3-1 at half time. John Aldridge stepped onto the scene in the 60th minute with yet another goal at Prenton Park to make it 3-2 but Alan Smith in the 85th minute at Highbury tipped the wings of AC Tornado to put the match virtually out of reach. And Grobbelaar/Hooper kept a clean sheet unlike the villain, Peter Schmeichel of AC Tornado who waved at Gary Lineker's farewell performance. In the crowd that day, being a season ticket holder, was Russ Allan watching the game through the fingers of the hands holding his head.

Russ stated "Obligingly up stepped Gary to supply a goal that might scupper AC Tornado, even more obligingly the United fans concealed my surpressed pleasure by sportingly chanting the lad's name"

Final Score: PSV Hangover 4 AC Tornado 1

## NATIONAL DREAM LEAGUE CHALLENGE CUP WINNERS 91/92
# PSV HANGOVER
### B&Q DIY DREAM LEAGUE
### SHEFFIELD

## THE NATIONAL CUP TOURNAMENTS

### NATIONAL DREAM LEAGUE CHALLENGE CUP

Official Programme
Weekend 1st May - 3rd May

## AC Tornado  The Swan Dream League

*AC Tornado*

Owner: Robin Lorimor - Air Traffic Controller, West Drayton, Middlesex
Strip: Grey Shirts and Shorts with Red, White and Blue Roundels.

Peter Schmeichel

Rob Newman          Graeme Le Saux

Andy Payton     John Magilton     Nigel Gleghorn

Iwan Roberts     Jimmy Gilligan

Steve White          John Aldridge          Gary Blissett

---

Alan Smith          Steve Bull          Duncan Shearer

Brett Angell     Peter Beardsley

Craig Hignett     Simon Milton     Steve Nicol

Neil Thompson          Mitchell Thomas

Bruce Grobbelaar

## PSV Hangover  The B&Q DIY Dream League

Team Owner: Russ Allen - Careers Officer, Sheffield CC, Sheffield.
Strip: Bloodshot Shirts and Shorts, Lager coloured socks with white tops.

Dream League Football a fantasy based on reality and out of this world

# DREAM LEAGUE – CHAPTER 3

## THE DREAM TEAM CHALLENGE CUP

The regional preliminary rounds in February established the teams with a goal difference of two or more. Scorecheck, our faithful computer support, then examined the teams with plus one, one team had scored three goals and two others with giant killing factors as low as 16 secured their places in the tournament proper.

On the weekend of February 15th and 16th the tournament proper kicked into action. Some great named teams were gone, but some interesting ties were coming up. RED STAR FOXES of Leicester against RELEGATE STROLLERS of the Midlands with Teddy Sheringham getting the winner with a 77th minute penalty.

Michelle McKenzie's ALBERTVILLE were paired with AILSA CRAIG FC from Scotland and needed a giant killing factor (19 to 15) to go though with both owners agonising over the goals conceded by Ludo Miklosko and Steven Pears. The picaresque BLUE IN TOPAZ from Berkshire drew a blank with a Martin Foyle goal at Leicester being cancelled out by Eric the Viking letting Palace slip one in at White Hart Lane. DOUBLE DAVID FC from Essex then secured victory with a Mike Loram goal in the 58th minute at Brentford.

Susan Bale's MAGIC DRAGONS drew the German Bundesliga inspired CHISWICK 04 on Schalke ground and despite Steven Pears conceding one (again) Ian Wright and Mike Small carried the Welsh team to victory. WILBEFORZA quashed the debate of ARGUMENTATIVE LEIPZIG with first half goals from Stuart Rimmer at Chester (4 minutes) and Alex Rae on the half hour at the Den against Grimsby.

The founders' team MET-WRO had a blinder scoring six with four of the five strikers scoring and Ogrizovic conceding nothing to blow FORTUNA HOLMFIRTH away despite efforts from Stuart Pearce and Paul Groves. One the Swedish owned Dream Teams SVEGS 1K got hoofed out of the competition by the GUERNSEY DONKEYS on the more goals scored rule. Michael Edward's CHELVER ATHLETIC raised a toast to Steve Lovell's hat trick at Gillingham and David White's brace at Maine Road as he sent INVERNESS UNITED on the low road home 5-4.

BAYERN SELL made it through with another of the magnificent seven, in this case Paul Merson's effort to see off RED ISSUE DREAMERS of Warrington. That afternoon Chris Woods was also representing EXPRESS FORMATION who inevitably shot out of the event by seven goals. Neil English's YE OLDE TEAM not having to do much at all with such self inflicted injury. CAISTOR WEDNESDAY added to Dream Team folklore with a goal by Stuart Pearce at Bristol City. Combining that with David Speedie's hat trick at Newcastle they eliminated STUART PEARCE'S LEFT FOOT FC from Loughborough 4-1.

TOM KEETLEY ORIENT FC and ATLETICO BOOTHAM both fielded David Speedie and a penalty by Mike Conroy in the 46th minute at Scunthorpe won the match as Atletico conceded the Sheffield Wednesday goal at Highbury through their represenative, David Seaman.

# THE NATIONAL CUP TOURNAMENTS

## THE SECOND ROUND

The round reinforced the claim of CHICKEN KIEV 82. Having demolished the STINKY RABBITS in the first round 4-1, they were now firing from all over the Gorky with Roy Keane, Mike Conroy and David White seeing off RACING CLUB WAYSIDE from Cheshire.

APEX ATHLETIC from Lancashire got off to a good start when Ian Benjamin scored at Brighton in the third minute and Mark Bright added two against Norwich. The in form David White rounded off the day and BAYERN SELL were history, unable to muster any reply whatsoever despite fielding the likes of Bull, Merson and Shearer.

The big match of the round was between DYNAMO DONNY of South Yorkshire and UTD CIVIL SERVICE, Steve Gilbert's team from Essex. Both teams lined up with John Lukic between the sticks so it was set for a goalscoring bonanza. And it was, with six different players scoring. Nial Quinn put the DYNAMOS ahead after only 3 minutes, Steve Norris pulled one back for UTD just before Jeremy Goss added another, Norwich's fourth at Palace, on the stroke of half time. In the second half Don Page opened up the gap with a goal for Rotherham at Scarboro and Stuart Rimmer sealed the fate of UTD in the 85th minute equalising for Chester at Darlington. Roy Keane pulled one back on the Sunday at White Hart Lane with a great header from a corner in The Rumbelows Cup semi-final but it wasn't enough for UTD Civil Service who went out 4-2.

TOM KEETLEY ORIENT saw off the founder's team MET-WRO on the more goals rule, Toms' 3/1 beating the Mets 2/0. The four goals at Selhurst Park ended the dreams of DOUBLE DAVID who had put their faith in Nigel Martyn. EAST GIDEA enjoyed the Roy Keane goal to rub salt into the wounds. ALBERTVILLE also benefitted from the goalscoring feats of Norwich and continued to impress. Could a team owned by a female make it to the final? Michelle was the only one left as The MAGIC DRAGONS were beaten by a Chris Kiwomya goal playing for the Jersey based team, THE THROSTLES. 58 MEMORIES scrapped through on the more goals by strikers rule, THE REPORTERS needing either Roy Keane or Stuart Pearce to add another for victory.

The third round saw the emergence of the 90/91 National Dream League Champions, THE LIBERO PARTY. John Magilton and John Fashanu combined to out run RED STAR FOXES for a place in the quarter finals.

TOM KEETLEY ORIENT rode out the GUERNSEY DONKEYS with a Lormor/Magilton/Nugent treble. CHELVER ATHLETIC went at the boots of EAST GIDEA. Steve Bull unable to make up the deficit caused by Bobby Mimms picking three out of the net at Twerton Park. CHICKEN KIEV 82 keep a clean sheet and benefit from CAISTOR WEDNESDAY's John Lukic conceding Paul Allen's 48th minute strike at White Hart Lane.

ALBERTVILLE get on top of DYNAMO DONNY, Andy Flounders getting the winner in the 58th minute at Rotherham.

Ceefax now has a really useful purpose, clocking the goals on Saturday evenings. All we need is for them to have all four divisions results like they present the third and fourth, the score, name of scorer and the time.

There were a few gifts in the quarter finals. 58 MEMORIES accepted Peter Beardsley's goal at Norwich with relish to defeat the LIBEROS with the only goal of their game. Tim Brown's WILBE-FORZA got the better of TOM KEETLEY with two goals by Dean Saunders. EAST GIDEA also needed Dean Saunders to help them past YE OLDE TEAM who were let down at the back with Tim Clarke of Huddersfield not having a good day at St. Andrews.

CHICKEN KIEV 82 had a marvellous encounter with ALBERTVILLE. Wayne Biggins netted the first for KIEV after 16 minutes and Mike Conroy put Burnley ahead and KIEV two up just before half time. But after numerous episodes of The Manager, Michele McKenzie's team fought back, David Hirst then Andy Flounders to level the match in the eighty third minute, exciting stuff in Dream League. Then up pops the mustard man, Roy Keane, to score the winner for KIEV and Forest in the 88th minute at the City Ground.

Into the semis and QPR provided the shake up putting four past Lukic representing two of the semi finalists. CHICKEN KIEV 82 made things slightly one sided adding a brace from John Aldridge and yet another brace from Mark Carter. 58 MEMORIES moved into the final with the cushion of the QPR attack and a Neil Thompson goal for Ipswich, yet another.

## THE FINAL

A great game, twelve goals, both teams with Schmeichel so it had to be he who scores the most. The spotlight was on, Craig Treanor owner of Chicken Kiev 82 started his football career as a gate attendant at Accrington Stanley FC. It wasn't a job advertised at the Jobcentre as his granny was a Director of the club at the time. A real life Burnley supporter, starting out at Turf Moor aged five with Dad, double pleasure to be enjoyed with Mike Conroy scoring for Chicken and 'The Clarets'.

In the other corner Tony La Fave, mastermind of 58 Memories, a United fan since 1983 told us he "climaxed at Rotterdam last year singing his heart out". Tony has been on a number of scouting missions, when unable to see United play, to check on players for his Dream Team and puts his success down to "being able to score from all positions".

And in the final, goals came from almost everywhere. 58 Memories opened up with the salvo from Craig Hignett to go two up after 19 minutes. David White pulled one back in the 31st minute, then Conroy levelled the scoring in 32 minutes only for Beardsley to make it 3-2 one minute later! Half-time MEMORIES a goal up and a chance to catch one's breath. The restart, Aldridge for KIEV and then White again, 4-3 KIEV. Sixty seven minutes Guy

## THE NATIONAL CUP TOURNAMENTS

Whittingham levels at 4-4. Sixty eight minutes and David White gets his hat-trick and the lead for the Chickens. MEMORIES are reeling, it was a body blow more so because it was a City player doing it. They couldn't get back, KIEV raised the oven temperature and browned off with two more goals, both from Mark Carter for Barnet at York. A mighty 7-4 reduced to 6-3 as the Lineker goal sailed into the net at Old Trafford in the 86th minute.

## CHICKEN KIEV 82
Strip: Golden Shirts, Red Shorts, Oven Baked Socks

```
                    Schmeichel
         Darby                     Curle
  Thompson S.       Payton         Keane
         Conroy                    Biggins
         Carter     Aldridge       White
```

---

```
     Beardsley    Gallacher    Philliskirk
          Rimmer              Whittingham
       Baker       Hignett     Rowbotham
          Pearce              Thompson N.
                  Schmeichel
```

## 58 MEMORIES
Strip: Red Shirts, Black Shorts, Red Socks

NATIONAL DREAM TEAM
CHALLENGE CUP

WINNERS 91/92
### CHICKEN KIEV 82

# Dream League™
# NATIONAL DREAM LEAGUE 91/92
## — 4 —

Whatever happened to AUSSIE'S KOALAS, RED ROCK UNITED, SPORTING VLADIVAR and FC SLIGHTLY TUBBY? These were the teams blazing the trail in September of 1991 at the top of the National Dream League.

Dynamo Dirtbag and Critchley Crunchers very much in contention through the autumn fell away as the true nature of Dream League football emerged as winter lowered the temperature.

Saint & Greavsie and The Match provided the ideal window for Dream Team owners to see 'their' players in action and the round up of real League goals was the equivalent of many scouting missions, BBC of course providing the FA Cup goals.

The Transfer Market was very active, goalscorers were making their name in the lower divisions and early rounds of the FA Cup and Rumbelows Cup. Wednesday nights were taking on new meaning as the unknowns became heroes and questions were asked about 'proven talent' like Durie and Flounders.

By October Lineker had 12 League goals compared to Aldridge with 5 League and 6 in the Rumbelows. Dean Holdsworth only had 7 in the League but 5 in the Rumbelows and behind him in the charts was Wayne Biggins potting all of his 10 in the Third Division. Baker of Hartlepool was making a mark and Iwan Roberts was being noticed at Huddersfield. Duncan Shearer grabbed the headlines with four goals against Plymouth. Carl Dale and Kevin Francis both models of consistency as they hit four goals in as many games.

"Knee Jerk" was the oft quoted phrase for some of the Transfers that took place. David Seaman being the most expensive goalkeeper and by Christmas the most transferred.

By November the average tally of goals per game was 2.71. Dion Dublin reached the top goalscorers list and Gleghorn in Midfield gets to double

# DREAM LEAGUE - CHAPTER 4

### National Dream League Top Ten – February

| | | | |
|---|---|---|---|
| 1. | Two Left Feet | – | 106 |
| 2. | Dodgy Dealers | – | 92 |
| 3. | Pride of all Europe | – | 91 |
| 4. | Pembury Pirates | – | 90 |
| 5. | Robert Burns | – | 89 |
| 5. | Bolton Wedding Tackle | – | 89 |
| 7. | Spence United | – | 86 |
| 7. | Not Very Athletic FC | – | 86 |
| 9. | Dynamo Dirtbag | – | 85 |
| 10. | Kingswood Knights | – | 83 |
| 10. | Wandsworth Wanderers | – | 83 |

figures, Peacock also in midfield is on 9. Andrei Kanchelskis although popular with team owners only scored his first goal in the win over Sheffield United. Steven Pears and Tim Clarke are almost invincible at home but the away form is dubious. While Schmeichel and Lukic maintain the best records overall. To own a scoring Goalkeeper, especially a non penalty taker, is Dream League at its' highest level and Maidstone's Iain Hesford pops one in at home to Hereford.

The National League is lead by Two Left Feet over Dynamo Dirtbag by only one point 58 to 57. Bright Sparks make a showing at joint fourth. Pembury Pirates at 48th, Bolton Wedding Tackle at 38th. The top six teams are from leagues registered at public houses. Two Left Feet (The Victory), Dynamo Dirtbag (Rifle Brigade), Wandsworth Wanderers (Halfway House), Critchley Crunchers (Sutton Arms), Bright Sparks (The Musketeer), Sporting Vladivar (The Cricket)

It was also a pub team at the very bottom, Red Star Timperley on minus 8!

By December Bernie Slaven was in the limelight as Middlesbrough chased Cambridge in Division Two. John Williams at Swansea make it five goals in three games and Mike Conroy scored five in four for Burnley. Phil Stant at Mansfield is sought after by owners with an impressive 12 in League games only. The Birmingham and West Brom defences are looking solid enough for a number of investments. Ian Wright continued to get on the end of everything and Brett Angell industriously took his total to 14 scoring his ninth goal in seven games and equalling a 70 year old club record at Southend.

The Dodgy Dealers ever present in the Transfer Market make a move and overhaul Dirtbag for second spot. Wedding Tackle tookover fourth and a new top ten emerged. Two Left Feet had yet to sell or buy a player since the start of the season.

The new year and the FA Cup. Maurice Johnston and Clive Allen feature high on a lot of shopping lists. Jacki Dziekanowski is snapped up by a few teams and rewards them with an FA Cup goal at Leicester. Blackburn's home record increases the value of Bobby Mimms and McIlhargey at Blackpool starts to create transfer activity as Blackpool push for a promotion spot. The

### National Dream League Top Ten – March

| | | | |
|---|---|---|---|
| 1. | Two Left Feet | – | 113 |
| 2. | Dodgy Dealers | – | 105 |
| 3. | Bolton Wedding Tackle | – | 104 |
| 4. | Not Very Athletic FC | – | 102 |
| 5. | Spence United | – | 100 |
| 6. | Pembury Pirates | – | 99 |
| 7. | Wandsworth Wanderers | – | 96 |
| 8. | Pride of all Europe | – | 95 |
| 9. | Athletico Bootham | – | 93 |
| 10. | Kingswood Knights | – | 92 |
| 10. | Queens College Rovers | – | 92 |

# THE NATIONAL DREAM LEAGUE 1991/92

### National Dream League Top Ten – April

| | | |
|---|---|---|
| 1. Two Left Feet | – | 138 |
| 2. Bolton Wedding Tackle | – | 120 |
| 3. Dodgy Dealers | – | 118 |
| 4. Not Very Athletic FC | – | 113 |
| 5. Pembury Pirates | – | 111 |
| 6. Athletico Bootham | – | 108 |
| 7. Pride of all Europe | – | 104 |
| 8. Tottering Despots | – | 103 |
| 8. Goals United | – | 103 |

removal of many First Division clubs from the FA Cup reduce the scoring potential for the Dream Teams their players represent and replays start to pose problems for defences. Aldridge still scoring.

A player's strike looms on the horizon and Ron Atkinson urges all his players to strike and after 513 minutes of goalless football Cyrille Regis obliges. Injuries to Barnes, Rush, Tinnion start to alter the performances of high flying teams. Suspensions also create adverse effects. Andy Watson becomes a Dream League find playing out of position according to the Player Guide for 91/92 and scores four in four games for Carlisle. David Kelly at Newcastle has a purple patch potting four goals in only three games.

Norwich put three past Liverpool and owners with Grobbelaar show concern although not heart failure. Robert Fleck enjoying himself and providing two of them. Mark Hughes scores two before being suspended to keep in contact with top goalscorer Brian McClair. Stoke tighten up at the back with only 29 goals against

Two Left Feet started to consolidate their position at the top of the National Dream League in March taking a size fourteen advantage over Dodgy Dealers.

### National Dream League Final Placings 91/92

| | | |
|---|---|---|
| 1. Two Left Feet | – | 143 |
| 2. Bolton Wedding Tackle | – | 125 |
| 3. Dodgy Dealers | – | 123 |
| 4. Not Very Athletic FC | – | 119 |
| 5. Pembury Pirates | – | 119 |
| 6. Athletico Bootham | – | 117 |
| 7. Goals United | – | 112 |
| 8. Tottering Despots | – | 110 |
| 9. Kingswood Knights | – | 109 |
| 10. Faldos Boyos | – | 108 |
| Boris Yeltsin's R&B Army | – | 108 |

The top ten teams all have very different line ups with Dave Bamber being the most popular player representing five of them. Rearranged matches from the Winter freeze kept a number of teams in contention, the Sutton Arms Dream League no longer boasting two teams in the top five.

Dodgy Dealers closed the gap mainly aided by QPR and Manchester City both netting four past Lukic. Leeds damaged Not Very Athletic putting five past Hans Segers. But Manchester United's ever worsening defensive record weakened the Dodgy Dealers' campaign. Dodgy having used all their transfer options were soley reliant on their first eleven. Meanwhile Two Left Feet picked up Gleghorn, Peacock and Gannon at the transfer deadline to add the punch to open an 18 point lead going into the last score period.

**DREAM LEAGUE - CHAPTER 4**

## TWO LEFT FEET
### The Victory Dream League
Owner: John Knight

Dave Bamber
4/9/91 – Blackpool

Steve Bull
4/9/91 – Wolverhampton W.

Dean Holdsworth
4/9/91 – Brentford

Ian Rush
26/3/91 – Liverpool

Duncan Shearer
4/9/91 – Blackburn Rovers

Nigel Gleghorn
26/3/92 – Birmingham City

Paul Groves
4/9/91 – Blackpool

Gavin Peacock
26/3/92 – Newcastle United

Jim Gannon
26/3/92 – Stockport County

Andy Watson
26/3/92 – Carlisle United

John Lukic
4/9/91 – Leeds United

**PLAYERS SOLD** – Don Goodman, Mike Hazard, Andy Payton, Craig Shakespeare, Steve Staunton

## BOLTON WEDDING TACKLE
### Blundersliega Dream League
Owner: Steve Ackerman

Tony Adcock
25/2/92
Peterborough United

Dave Bamber
1/9/91
Blackpool

Mark Carter
1/9/91
Barnet

David Hirst
2/12/91
Sheffield Wednesday

Alan Shearer
1/9/91
Southampton

John Beresford
7/10/91
Portsmouth

Gavin Peacock
1/9/91
Newcastle United

Paul Williams
25/2/92
Derby County

Stuart Pearce
1/9/91 – Nottingham Forest

Andy Watson
25/2/92 – Carlisle United

John Lukic
1/9/91 – Leeds United

**PLAYERS SOLD** – Gordon Durie, Dean Holdsworth, Ian Marshall, Teddy Sheringham, Warren Joyce, Neil Webb, Earl Barrett, Paul Elliott

## DODGY DEALERS
### Sutton Arms Dream League
Owner: Brad Collins

John Aldridge
18/8/91 – Tranmere R

Andy Flounders
18/8/91 – Rochdale

Tony Philliskirk
18/8/91 – Bolton W.

Paul Wilkinson
4/11/91 – Middlesbrough

Ian Wright
18/8/91 – Arsenal

Paul Baker
18/8/91 – Hartlepool Utd

RobertCodner
18/8/91– Brighton & Hove A.

Nigel Gleghorn
4/11/91 – Birmingham C

Roger Eli
9/9/91 – Burnley

Brian Tinnion
9/9/91 – Bradford

Peter Schmeichel
9/9/91 – Manchester United

**PLAYERS SOLD**
Darren Beckford, David Puckett, Ian Rush, David Speedie, David Gilbert, John Magilton, Darren Rowbotham, Richard Dryden, Mel Sterland, Nigel Martyn.

## NOT VERY ATHLETIC FC
### Original Dream League
Owner: Jules Rastelli

John Aldridge
28/7/91 – Tranmere R

Darren Beckford
28/7/91 – Norwich City

Paul Merson
28/7/91 – Arsenal

Duncan Shearer
28/7/91 – Blackburn Rovers

Ian Wright
28/7/91 – Arsenal

Roy Keane
28/7/91 – Nottingham Forest

Andy Payton
8/7/91 – Middlesbrough

Gavin Peacock
28/7/91 – Newcastle Utd

Lee Dixon
28/7/91 – Arsenal

Roger Eli
28/7/91 – Burnley

Hans Segers
28/7/91 – Wimbledon

**PLAYERS SOLD**
None!

**DREAM LEAGUE – CHAPTER 4**

# NATIONAL DREAM LEAGUE 91/92
## (FINAL PLACINGS – TOP 100)

| TEAM | Pts | Pos | TEAM | Pts | Pos |
|---|---|---|---|---|---|
| TWO LEFT FEET | 143 | 1 | RED STAR NORMANTON | 98 | 29 |
| BOLTON WEDDING TACKLE | 125 | 2 | BORUSSIA MOSSLEYGLADBACH | 98 | 29 |
| DODGY DEALERS | 123 | 3 | RACING CLUB DE SEVEN KINGS | 97 | 36 |
| NOT VERY ATHLETIC FC | 119 | 4 | CHOLSEY DYNAMOS | 97 | 36 |
| PEMBURY PIRATES | 119 | 4 | BOCA OLD BOYS | 97 | 36 |
| ATLETICO BOOTHAM | 117 | 6 | ASHBOURNE LINFIELD | 96 | 39 |
| GOALS UNITED | 112 | 7 | RED STRIPE BELGRADE | 96 | 39 |
| TOTTERING DESPOTS | 110 | 8 | MOYS MARVELS | 96 | 39 |
| KINGSWOOD KNIGHTS | 109 | 9 | CHICKEN KIEV 82 | 95 | 42 |
| FALDO'S BOYOS | 108 | 10 | PUKEY MUCAS | 95 | 42 |
| BORIS YELTSIN'S R&B ARMY | 108 | 10 | REAL MORDEN | 95 | 42 |
| RED STAR PARCELS | 106 | 12 | JAY SEAS XI | 94 | 45 |
| DER SLIVED FC | 105 | 13 | PIGS TROTTERS | 94 | 45 |
| COSMOS | 104 | 14 | SPARIGIES | 93 | 47 |
| QUEENS COLLEGE ROVERS | 104 | 14 | ENDEAVOURERS FC | 92 | 48 |
| GRIMTHORPE CITY | 104 | 14 | NORTHDOWN RAIDERS | 92 | 48 |
| O.S.G. GHOSTS | 102 | 17 | TORPEDO TOTLEY | 92 | 48 |
| DYNAMO DIRTBAG | 102 | 17 | BOCA GERIATRICS | 92 | 48 |
| GREENLEES UNITED | 101 | 19 | FRUEN FLYERS | 91 | 52 |
| WANDSWORTH WANDERERS | 101 | 19 | REDSTAR KEYNSHAM | 91 | 52 |
| RUSTING ROVERS | 101 | 19 | RACING WREXHAM | 91 | 52 |
| PRIDE OF ALL EUROPE | 101 | 19 | CLUB 81 | 91 | 52 |
| MOULTONS END ACADEMICALS | 101 | 19 | ROBERT BURNS | 90 | 56 |
| SICK AS A BRIGHTLY COLOURED TR | 99 | 24 | INTER EVERYTHING | 90 | 56 |
| HALIFAX TOWN | 99 | 24 | ATHLETICO NELSON | 90 | 56 |
| BRIGHT SPARKS | 99 | 24 | AFC SWINDLE | 89 | 59 |
| TOMMY'S LANKEY LEGS | 99 | 24 | GOONERS | 89 | 59 |
| JOHN MCCARTHY'S LIBRARY FINES | 99 | 24 | ELITE | 89 | 59 |
| UNIVERSIADE | 98 | 29 | CRITCHLEY CRUNCHERS | 88 | 62 |
| MIKES MARVELS | 98 | 29 | FLEETING ANTELOPES | 88 | 62 |
| WEST WICKHAM WANDERERS | 98 | 29 | ALBION ALLSTARS | 87 | 64 |
| SPENCE UNITED | 98 | 29 | THROUGH THE GREEN | 87 | 64 |
| BEXLEY UNITED | 98 | 29 | RICHMOND VIKINGS | 86 | 66 |

## THE NATIONAL DREAM LEAGUE 1991/92

| TEAM | Pts | Pos | TEAM | Pts | Pos |
| --- | --- | --- | --- | --- | --- |
| PADGATE HEELERS | 86 | 66 | EAST GIDEA | 82 | 85 |
| BEIGHTON & HOVE ALBION | 86 | 66 | BARKING PARIAH | 82 | 85 |
| CHESTER DRAWS | 86 | 66 | ATHLETIC PATHETICO | 82 | 85 |
| FC PLODDERS | 86 | 66 | SHOVELLERS | 82 | 85 |
| FC SLIGHTLY TUBBY | 86 | 66 | FULCHESTER UNITED | 82 | 85 |
| VERA'S ARROWS | 86 | 66 | HAMMERTON ACADEMICALS | 82 | 85 |
| FC HAMMER | 85 | 73 | DEATHS HEAD WHIPPETS | 81 | 94 |
| REAL ENTERTAINERS | 85 | 73 | WYLDE GREEN GRASSHOPPERS | 81 | 94 |
| PSV HANGOVER | 85 | 73 | REAL SOCKEM | 81 | 94 |
| MELCHESTER | 85 | 73 | WARE WANDERERS | 81 | 94 |
| ROGERUM UNITED | 84 | 77 | REAL NEWCASSEL | 81 | 94 |
| SPORTING VLADIVAR | 84 | 77 | EXTREMELY UNATHLETICAL | 81 | 94 |
| MICKS GUNNERS | 83 | 79 | RELDAS | 80 | 100 |
| SAFE HANDS FCS | 83 | 79 | FULKIRK | 80 | 100 |
| BUTLIN BOYS | 83 | 79 | F.C.B. | 80 | 100 |
| DREAD STAR | 83 | 79 | FORTUNA STRONGBOWLER | 80 | 100 |
| RED ROCK UNITED | 83 | 79 | FALLING STANDARD | 80 | 100 |
| SCREAMING ALICE | 83 | 79 | BRIDGET'S BEAUTIES | 80 | 100 |
| FAT BUDDHA'S FIRST XI | 82 | 85 | PHILISTINES | 80 | 100 |
| KNYPERSLEY KICKERS | 82 | 85 | THE EAGLETS | 80 | 100 |
| WHITES WONDERS | 82 | 85 | AC TORNADO | 80 | 100 |

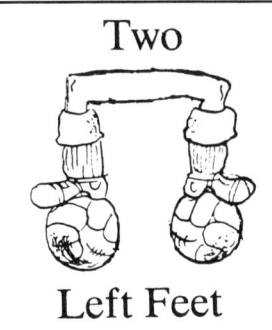

Two

Left Feet

### JOHN KNIGHT'S
### TWO LEFT FEET FC
of the Victory Dream League
in Leicester, are the
### NATIONAL DREAM LEAGUE
### CHAMPIONS 1991/92

**DREAM LEAGUE**

# Dream League™
# HOW TO PLAY DREAM TEAM
## — 5 —

You can start anytime of the season. This is your opportunity to pick the team of your dreams. It can be yours and yours alone, or ownership could be shared with a friend for the Clough/Taylor or Atkinson/Gray or Curbishley/Gritt approach, or with the family.

You can offer dad the Managers' role in return for the registration fee and for you to run the team. If you sign up mum as physio you've got it made. The Tommy Docherty Rule. Of course, if I am addressing dad right now. You could be building a family owned team to be proud of at the office, pub and on the playground.

Observe, indicate and manoeuvre, how many times have you thought how easy it would be to run a football team, as easy as driving a car? With a family owned team you have three or more points of view all of which could be valuable when selecting the team. But if the wife wants John Barnes in the team because of his legs you might have problems.

Then, true love, sharing Dream Team ownership with your one and only. I warm to the story in Dream League seasons past, where girl purchased a Dream Team for boy. Boy falls in love with Team. Girl, hacked off but not to be outdone, secretly purchases her own team. The two teams incredibly achieve similar positions in the National League alternating one above the other. Girl drops subtle hints to no avail, in a moment of weakness when she's on top, she let's it slip, she own's the rival team. He's impressed, they merge, ground sharing becomes a reality and he gets the honeymoon in

# DREAM LEAGUE – CHAPTER 5

Sweden and two season tickets out the joint budget account before a new three piece suite.

If only Mrs Maxwell had tried the same, big Bob might not have taken a dive in a water logged Spanish area. Then we could've had the first eleven from the Bank of England to sort it all out and save a few pension funds and football clubs.

So, ownership is sorted out for your team. If a few friends want a team as well, that's fine, but take care to differentiate between Dream Team and Dream League.

"Dream Team is where you simply pick your team and compete nationally against all other Dream Team Owners. For Dream League you need at least ten team owners to form a league and have an auction".

## How to Pick Your Team

Carefully select your team in the 2-3-5 formation. Read the Auction Guide for tips on what to look for in a player and refer to the Player Guide to satisfy yourself that your decision is in keeping with the style of your team. Style is important in Fantasy Football. Only you can imagine the pass from Gordon Strachan to Dean Saunders who hits the bar for Gary Bull to snap up the rebound. Only style will give you a motto and a strip for your team, very important, if you get it right, you might be lining up your Dream Team in that very strip with success in the National Dream Team Competitions.

Is your Dream Team a mass of all stars or are you part of the new emerging football culture that is familiar with football outside of the Premier League? Have you spotted the next Darren Anderton and is he related to anyone we know? Bear in mind the Giant Killing Factor for Cup Competitions. A higher proportion of lower division players may see you getting your way through the tough cup competitions.

Once you have registered for Dream Team you will receive confirmation your team is in "Scorecheck" and details of your Transfer Options during the course of the season.

You will automatically be entered into the National Dream Team League and the National Dream Team Challenge Cup. We also envisage local Vase and Trophy Events where we will set competitions for Dream Teams where owners live in specific regions.

Transfers are a key to your pursuit of success and not unlike real team owners and managers you will be under pressure to shape your team with goalscorers, they in turn will have to deliver the goods. In this book are many tails of 'He dried up, I sold him, he started scoring' or 'He was scoring regularly, I bought him, he dried up'.

Dream League Football is not necessarily fair but a great deal of enjoyment for the whole season, and each month we will send you details of your League position.

# DREAM TEAM REGISTRATION FORM

Photocopy this form or cut it out and send it to
**Dream League HQ, PO Box 235, Egham, Surrey TW20 9HT**

I would like to register my Dream Team for all competitions, Scorecheck and Transfer Service for the 1992/93 season.

Team Owners Name ..................................................................................

Address ......................................................................................................

..................................................................................................................

................................................................ Post Code ..........................

Telephone Numbers ..................................................................................

My Dream Team is called ................................................................... FC.
Refer to Player Guide for Codes and Correct name spellings

| CODE | Players Name |
|---|---|
| Goalie .................................... | .................................................... |
| Defender ................................ | .................................................... |
| Defender ................................ | .................................................... |
| Midfield ................................. | .................................................... |
| Midfield ................................. | .................................................... |
| Midfield ................................. | .................................................... |
| Striker ................................... | .................................................... |
| Striker ................................... | .................................................... |
| Striker ................................... | .................................................... |
| Striker ................................... | .................................................... |
| Striker ................................... | .................................................... |

I understand that the fee is £12.00 including VAT and post and packing. I enclose a cheque/postal order for £12.00 to register my Dream Team for the 1992/93 season. Or please debit my credit card number

Visa/Mastercard .................................................... Expiry ..........................

Name on Card ..........................................................................................

Signature ..................................................................................................

# DREAM LEAGUE

# HOW TO PLAY DREAM LEAGUE

## — 6 —

This is what it is really all about. Buying a team at Auction facing the sternest of competition from your nine rival team owners and making a goal scoring machine that fits neatly in top slot of your local Dream League. You could rely on luck or you could rely on skill or even divine intervention. It can all just happen, so don't forget that Fantasy element in football.

Free market forces are different wherever you go and influenced by many factors, history, religion, primary local resources, climate, politics and cashflow.

Take Italy, a footballing nation with more than a little passion. A cluttered history, virtually one party religion, natural resources splendidly at one with the climate (the food and the wine), politics are extreme (52 governments since the war) and cash rules. Trust me on the last one I worked very hard for eighteen months bringing the world of credit cards and football together in Italy. All will be revealed but that's another book.

Market forces dictate there must be success at any price. Hence nowadays AC Milan, Juventus, Roma swan around with open cheque books and buy African villages to secure budding talent. The Milanese learn a little geography, the owners get more support for their tax right-offs and small countries benefit by a new Mercedes Benz franchise, owned by the budding players' parents.

The fantasy is this. Liverpool, Tottenham, Manchester United and the other big seven, your choice not mine, are restricted by a budget.

Martin Edwards, Terry Venables and David Moores etc to make the game more interesting are only allowed to spend £10,000,000 to create a team from

# DREAM LEAGUE - CHAPTER 6

scratch to compete against each other.

Off you go, do it. And at the start of the season we will give you another ten million in case some one catches a cold. Bless you.

Free market forces will determine everything because there is a very different catalogue of history, religion, local resources, climate and politics at each club.

I leave out cashflow because that is between companies house, the shareholders and the clubs' accountants, basically the oil of the machine, mostly created by attendance money. The fantasy immitates reality, your Team, your Dream is purchased for DL $100 and you've got nine others to compete with, so how good are you?

If you read this book you will be half way there and certainly have an advantage of somebody who hasn`t read this book and thinks they have grasped the basics.

First and foremost, who do you want to be in your Dream League?

Workmates, friends, regulars at your local pub or club?

A team can be owned by more than one person (see Dream Team) and we have some great examples of different Dream Leagues already operating;

**In pubs:** Some with up to four owners per team with Monthly competitions raising funds for prizewinings or charity

**In offices:** The sales department with one team and production department another. Some where each person in the department or on the factory floor has a team.

**In schools:** Visionary teachers are using Dream League to entertain and educate at the same time

The majority are ten football followers who fancy their chances at hoovering up whatever might be in the pot in May and enjoy ten months of hassle free entertainment based on their favourite sport.

When you form a Dream League you need an HQ, an address to which all correspondence will be sent. Somewhere all team owners will see the updated league tables pinned on the notice board. If your group of ten are far flung (ex workmates, ex college palls) then be prepared to do a little bit of photocopying and shelling out for phone and mail costs. Dream League can of course do that for you, but we are strictly a soft sell operation and fun comes first.

You've got ten budding team owners, you now need to set a date for the Auction and you will need our Auction Pack of course. Ideally each of your team owners will have a copy of this book because:

a) The Auction Guide and Player Guide is indispensable.
b) They can keep their own scorecheck and follow their teams' progress and identify weakness in their line up during the season.
c) It costs the same money to photocopy it as to buy the original.

## HOW TO PLAY DREAM LEAGUE

Auction Pack Includes:
> 10 x DL $100
> 1 Master Auction sheet/Registration/Data Form
> 10 Team Owner Auction cards
> 1 HQ addressed envelope
> Automatic entry into National Dream League & National Dream League Challenge Cup Competitions & Regional Vase Competitions
> A monthly League Table from our "Scorecheck System"
> Regular copies of 'doing Dream League' our irreverent naming names newsletter.

Auction date/Auction pack. You are all set. Two basics:

a) If your auction is in a pub, try to get the publican/manager/landlord to have a team.
b) If your auction is at the office, or place of work, switch the phones off, this is serious.

It is possible to run an auction by telephone, but you would be missing one of the great social dividends Dream League offers unless you either work for or own real shares in British Telecom.

An Auction will never start on time. Big shots will be plying the timid with whatever to reduce their bidding capability and the quiet ones will be asking subtle but incisive questions in an attempt to learn of others goalscoring objects of desire.

Golden Rule. The Auctioneer needs to be somebody not prone to lip-slippage after four pints or keen to immitate a 1950's tobacco salesman. The Auctioneer can own a team, but he/she needs to remember to bid.

Start the bidding with Goalkeepers, and only one team owner can own the Blackpool goalkeeper, you cannot buy a reserve goalkeeper. If for some reason a player is not in the Player Guide, he must be announced prior to the bidding in his positional category, eg., If Van Basten signs for Leeds in the summer, then he needs to be added to the Auction List as a Striker prior to bidding on that category.

Fill in the team names on the Master Auction card and during the course of the Auction try to substitute the chosen team names for their letter, eg., John Lukic $10 MET-WRO, $11 The Wizards, $15 for the Liberos, sounds a lot better than A $10, B $11 and F $15. Some are apt to dither.

Going once, going twice, gone?. Goalkeepers first etc., ensure that after each category you cash up. This has a psychological effect of parting with real cash and for those who are over spending early it will wake them up about the category of players. It is also a good time to sum up the various strategies.

49

# DREAM LEAGUE – CHAPTER 6

An auction will take two to three hours and is invariably great fun, and a major part of the game although you have many more transfer auctions to look forward too during the course of the season.

The auctioneer will be filling in the Master Record as players get sold and each team owner will be making his own Auction card for his own record.

When serious bidding has finished in any category say nine owners have their goalkeeper, then the Auctioneer should ask who the tenth owner wants to buy for $1. Keeps it simple.

It is sometimes handy to have an auctioneers' assistant to keep an eye on the cash tallies and what each team has left to spend but the Master Record has all the calculations built in for 'at a glance' reckoning. It is easier than 501 on the dart board that's for sure.

After the end of the Auction the Auctioneer should check each individuals Auction card so that the teams match those on the Master Record, when all confirmed send to Dream League in the envelope provided with the Registration details and name and address of each team owner.

Re-distribute the cash so that each team owner is replenished to the tune of DL$100 for transfers during the course of the season. We do the rest, simply fill in the form opposite and send with your registration fee. We suggest you split the Registration/Auction Pack Fee between the 10 team owners.

## The Rick Parry Rule

A successful auction is making sure the bidding goes sky high when you do not have to dish out the money.

# DREAM LEAGUE REGISTRATION FORM

Photcopy this form or cut it out and send it with your payment to:
**Dream League HQ, PO BOX 235, Egham, Surrey TW20 9HT**

I would like to register my Dream League for Scorecheck and all National Competitions and Transfer Service for the 1992/93 Season.

League Secretary, Name ................................................................................

League Name: The.......................................................................Dream League

Address (To which all correspondence should be sent) ........................................

................................................................................................................

................................................................................................................

............................................................................ Post Code ...................

Telephone No.'s:Home ..........................................Office....................................

I understand that in addition to our Registration I will be sent an Auction Pack for 10 teams (£9 per team) as described for our Auction Night. I understand that the cost is £90 including VAT and post and packing. I enclose cheque/postal order for £90 or please debit my credit card number

Visa/Mastercard .......................................... Expiry .......................

Name on Card ................................................................................

Signature ................................................................................

# DREAM LEAGUE

# Dream League™

# THE RULES

— 7 —

## IT IS ALL ABOUT GOALS

## Objective

To put together a football team that can outgun all the others, consistently, to be top of a Dream League (10 Teams) or reach the dizzy heights of being National Dream League Champion and winning the New Spirit of Football Trophy as seen on the front cover.

To create a goalscoring machine that can battle through against all the imponderables of Cup Football to take the Dream League Vase (10 Teams) on regular occasions or to go all the way and play at Head Stadium in Imagination Park for the National Dream League Challenge Cup.

## Dream Leagues (Dream Teams)

Ten teams constitute a Dream League, less is not so interesting. If you are unable to get ten team owners together register for Dream Team.

### The Graeme Souness Rule

When a Dream Team owner gets the opportunity for open heart surgery, ensure reins are handed to a co-owner as results later that month will help you out of the anaesthetic.

**DREAM LEAGUE - CHAPTER 7**

More than ten teams is not recommended (we worked it out) but group ownership is. More than one person owning a team is good news, it raises the value of a team in a League. It has even been known that teams in some leagues have changed hands for real money when an owner has left town or gone overseas. And, unlike Aldershot FC a Dream Team owner simply cannot pass on debts to a prospective buyer.

Ten teams can keep 40-50 footie fans very interested.

## Team Line Up

A Team is made up of eleven players, in the following format:

| | |
|---|---|
| 1 | Goalkeeper |
| 2 | Defender Defender |
| 3 | Midfield Midfield Midfield |
| 5 | Striker Striker Striker Striker Striker |

A player's position is that according to the Player Guide in this book.

## How to Score

**Goals For**
Goals scored in the Premier League, Football League, the Rumbelows Cup and the FA Cup all count in Dream League Football and also goals scored by English teams in the European Cup, European Cup Winners Cup and UEFA Cup. And the Welsh entrant into European competition if competing in the Football League.

### The Scott Barrett Rule

You have ten players scoring for you, eleven if you choose a rather adventurous goalkeeper. Once you have secured a player (see Auction) he plays for your team.

### The Clive Allen Rule

If he transfers from his club in real life, you automatically follow him and continue to pick up his goal scoring record for the new club. Don Goodman, WBA/Sunderland, Marco Gabbiadini Sunderland/Palace/Derby, Ian Wright Palace/Arsenal, Ian Ormondroyd Villa/Derby/Leicester, and Clive Allen, where do we start?

# THE RULES

It is a fact that the football authorities have little interest in who scored in a match as their concern rests on the results and did the game start on time. It is usually down to the club to iron out any goal scoring discrepancies that are contradicted by various football reporters.

You know the scene, old Brian is lurking in the penalty area, bonuses and pride at stake. Old Gary is defending resolutely but not getting the run of the ball of late. The ball springs round the six yard box like a pinball and yes, tilt, its an own goal.

You pick up the paper. Brian scored? The real story was probably ....Well he was getting close to his new record at the club, old Gary shouldn't be blamed etc! It ultimately rests with the club. And how often do the newspapers report on a different game to the one you have witnessed with your very own pork pies?

Own goals do not count against the player popping them in, they will only count against the goalkeeper/goalkeeper's team that concedes the goal.

> ## The Gary Mabbutt Rule
>
> Imagine that Stuart Pearce has got sixteen in the oppositions' net and then flips one under his own crossbar. He is not back to fifteen.

**Goals Against**
Goals conceded in the Premier League, Football League, the Rumbelows Cup and the FA Cup all count in Dream League Football and also goals conceded by English teams in the European Cup, European Cup Winners Cup and UEFA Cup. And the Welsh of course, that is if anybody signs the keeper of the Druid attempt for European glory.

> ## The Les Sealey Rule
>
> If your goalkeeper is dropped, censured, injured, fined, smacked or caught planting carrots, you inherit the new boy or reserve.
>
> If your goalkeeper is transferred to another club you still inherit the new boy. You have acquired the defensive record of the club and unless you enter into any transfer activity you stay with that club, whoever is between the posts.
>
> Imagine this: Team A, Neil Madrid, in your Dream League, has signed Grobbelaar at the auction. Team B, Andylecht, has secured Bobby Mimms. Graeme does a deal with Kenny and Mimms ends up at Anfield, Andylecht's defensive record continues to be Blackburn's. He also cannot buy the Liverpool defence/goalkepper because Neil Madrid are rejoicing at the big and very attractive picture. At the next Transfer Auction Andylecht can either stick with the Mimms replacement or get into the market for a new defence. See Constitutional Team.

**DREAM LEAGUE – CHAPTER 7**

**Points**
Dream League Points are the difference between Goals For and Goals Against, eg.,

Your Team Scores 6 and concedes 3          6 minus 3 = 3 points

At the end of the season the top 5 of your table might be:
| | |
|---|---|
| Lumpy Jumpers | GF 156 GA 42 Pts 114 |
| FC Slightly Tubby | GF 146 GA 32 Pts 114 |
| Andylecht | GF 150 GA 37 Pts 113 |
| Neil Madrid | GF 152 GA 42 PTS 110 |

If two teams are equal on points the team scoring the higher number of goals is placed higher.

## Auction

Each team must have eleven players purchased at auction (or selected through a Dream Team entry) for no more than DL $100. No team may bid for a player it cannot afford. After the initial auction a further DL $100 is made available to each team for transfer auctions throughout the season.

## Constitutional Team

If a player is transferred overseas or even to Scotland he must be replaced at the next transfer auction to maintain a properly constituted team. No real life player can be owned by more than one Dream Team in the same Dream League of 10 teams created at auction, nor by transfer activity during the course of the season.

### The Paul Williams Rule

There are five Paul Williams playing in the League at various positions and levels, no prizes for signing all five although consideration would be given for the best assembled BALD XI or FAT/SHORT XI or as expressed by the Galloping GGs FC all players with surnames beginning with the same letter. Indulgence is encouraged like a LEFT FOOTED XI, it is your football fantasy in the good old 2-3-5

# THE RULES

## Season

The Dream League Season runs from 15 August to the play off finals in May. The Season is broken down into ten Scorecheck periods:

| No. Period | First Day of Period | Last Day of Period (Last Monday in month) |
|---|---|---|
| 1 August | August 15th | August 31st |
| 2 September | September 1st | September 28th |
| 3 October | September 29th | October 26th |
| 4 November | October 27th | November 30th |
| 5 December | December 1st | December 28th |
| 6 January | December 29th | January 25th |
| 7 February | January 26th | February 22nd |
| 8 March | February 23rd | March 29th |
| 9 April | March 30th | April 26th |
| 10 May | April 27th | May 31st |

You can start your League at any time during the season and Leagues starting in July and August will enjoy most value and more experience for the national competitions.

## Transfers

During the course of the season each team is allowed to acquire new players to replace those they wish to transfer out of their team.

### The Jack Walker Rule

All Dream Team owners have the same amount of money to use as they see fit during the course of the season, no sugar-daddies on the horizon in this game.

Transfers must be like for like. Defender for defender, midfield player to replace midfield player etc to maintain a properly constituted team.

A maximum of two goalkeepers can be sold and acquired during the course of the season.

New players should be acquired at a Transfer Auction with the team owners using their DL $100 transfer fund. Transfer details must be submitted to HQ by the last Friday of each month. Full information is supplied in the Auction Pack when you register for Dream League or Dream Team.

# DREAM LEAGUE – CHAPTER 7

## The Steve Moran/Andy Flounders Rule

Don't be too disappointed when the player you sell goes and scores a hat-trick when he is no longer wearing your colours.

## The Chris Woods Rule

Your Dream Team goalkeeper has a series of tough away matches with the centre back injured and right back suspended. You offload and then read about his heroics keeping them all to nil-nil draws while your new man, an international and World Cup prospect lets seven and four go by in the winter sunshine.

## The Gordon Taylor Rule

Protecting your players. For those who have been playing Dream League over the last two years or for those of you who wish to adopt a long term view of team building. You can adopt a protection system that will keep your key players scoring for you in the future seasons. Watch the percentages, a long term contract could cripple your spending power just like at Swansea City, Bristol City and Wolves.

The protection system works by using the price for which you buy a player, as being their salary. For example if you have paid DL$18 for Dave Bamber in 91/92 and you wish to keep him for the 92/93 season you will have to pay 150% of his original auction price ie: DL$27. This is equivalent to a pay rise expected by a successful player. Of course if you put the player back into auction you might get him for less (or have to pay more, or make somebody else pay more.) There is a minimum of DL$15 for a protected player. If you got Darren Anderton for a DL$8 last season, to keep him will cost you DL$15 not DL$12.

Another example Gary Bull, DL $24 at auction in 92/93. To keep him you have to pay DL $36 in 93/94 or he goes up for grabs as a free agent.

## The George Eastham Rule

Freedom of Contract means the above rule can be vetoed by your Dream League committee and every player goes into the auction at the start of each season come what may.

## THE RULES

# Competitions

### National Dream League
Each Dream League team acquired at auction and registered for Scorecheck is automatically entered into the National League, the National Dream League Competition for big prizes in football travel and the New Spirit of Football Trophy.

You may be 5th in your own Dream League but one extra goal could move you from 500th to 469th in the National League! One goal against could see you plummet thousands of places. Pride here when you meet other Dream Team owners, which you will of course, outside of your League and around the country. Dream League owners have ways of recognising each other, but it's a secret. Mind you buying a lapel pin helps, added status when catching your very own players in action on a wet Wednesday for Maidstone versus Crewe, swelling the crowd to 1051.

### National Dream League Challenge Cup
All registered Leagues have the opportunity to submit a Team to represent them in the the NDLCC. This is when it is League versus League which could mean office versus office or pub versus pub etc. The prizes reflect that and the team entered will be representing all of that Leagues' team owners. See The Vase Competition below as an ideal way of selecting your League's side.

Prizes for the 91/92 season were trips to Sweden for the European Championships. Each year the prizes will increase in number. At the end of 92/93 season, winners can expect to be at the FA Cup Final, European Cup Final and the European Cup Winners Cup Final, or the opportunity to visit foreign countries to watch international or local club matches. Whatever it is, you'll like it, we enjoy travel and sports in a very stylish manner and are sure you will enjoy whatever we put together. Trips to Belle Vue to watch Doncaster taking on the might of Carlisle can be arranged if you prefer a chip supper to some of the places we know in Milan or Barcelona.

The 1993/94 Season prizes will all be extended trips to the World Cup Finals in America. So experience of playing Dream League in 92/93 will be of great value.

### Local Competition
It has been known that when a team is destined for mediocrity, it's position in Dream League will reflect just that. Starting out 10th and getting to 4th is

## The Peter Shreeves Rule
Starting out top in September and sliding to 9th by May will not get you many accolades from the Dream Team owners we know.

# DREAM LEAGUE - CHAPTER 7

good. Starting out 5th and staying 5th is not exactly thrills and spills.

To alleviate any beleagured or becalmed team owners we have three monthly competitions that apply to your league only.

i) The Manager of the Month
ii) Shooting Star Award

and for the organised amongst you
iii) The Monthly Vase

It is important to note you do not have to bet money in Dream League, but it certainly gives it an edge. Principle money, we call it. No different from spending 4 hours on a golf course playing 18 holes for a pound even though it cost hundreds to buy the clubs, get the membership to a club and cost you more than your winnings getting the drinks in at the bar.

Dream League is as harmless as the office sweep on the Grand National and with Dream League there is more skill than sticking in a pin and is less painful for the horse.

---

## The Fines and Charity Rule

You may like to add a little spice by inflicting fines on team owners to raise the kitty or create a fund for charity donations. If a player is sent off, the team owner has to pay a £1, an Own Goal could be another £1 and one we really enjoy, when a player gets a hat-trick being as the team owner is so jubilant he can cough up another £1. Especially when he's Scottish and has been holding onto Gordon Durie for six months for patriotic reasons. They all add up for prize-winnings or charity donations.

---

If in doubt, use marbles, Mars bars and DL $'s of course.
i) Manager of the Month
Awarded to the team with the highest goal difference in a scorecheck period
ii) Shooting Star
Awarded to the team that scores the most goals in a scorecheck period or second most if Manager of the Month's performance scoops both prizes.

You will be surprised to see that the same teams will not win every month. In the Armstrong Gun Dream League in Surrey where Fruen's Flyers started slowly moved into the top three around Christmas, were vying for the top spot for the remainder of the season Terry Fruen never won a Manager of the Month, on the other hand Sheffield Steel FC won four Manager of the Month awards but ended up in 8th (Chris Woods in goal..ouch!).

## THE RULES

iii) Monthly vase
Knockout competition for teams in the your Dream League.

With ten teams you need a preliminary round. At your league meeting draw 4 teams out of the hat for the two preliminary matches. Place names on the preliminary squares for the draw of the first round proper (see diagram). Each week move to the next round and in four weeks you will have a Vase Winner. (aka The Armitage Shanks Bowl in The Only One 'D' in Dream League of Islington, London). Play each round on consecutive weekends.

**Figure 1**                      First       Semi       The
                                  Round       Final      Final
                           ___
Preliminary Round                  ___
                           ___                ___
                                   ___
                           ___                           ___
Preliminary Round                  ___
                           ___                ___
                                   ___
                                                         ___
                                   ___
                                                ___
                                   ___


## Elimination in the Cup

You decide the winner of a knockout by comparing the two teams' records over any given period. Saturday only is popular but with the advent of more Friday and Sunday games, especially as big guns like John Aldridge and Wayne Biggins regularly get Saturday off we suggest 'the Weekend Series'. Then at least, unless one of your players is suspended or injured, everybody gets to field a full side all with a chance of scoring.

The winner of a tie is:
1. The team with the largest goal difference (3/0 beats 2/0)

If undecided
2. The team which has scored the most goals (5/2 beats 3/0)

If undecided
3. The team which has scored the most goals using strikers

**DREAM LEAGUE - CHAPTER 7**

For example: Real Newcassel score 4 concede 2 for 2 pts. Met-Wro score and concede the same for a 2-2 draw. Real Newcassel scored three through Mick Quinn a striker, Met-Wro using two midfield goals and two striker goals go out.

If either team has neither scored a goal nor conceded one (you can win a Cup game 0 to -1 of course) then you require a replay, otherwise....GKF - far better than penalty shoot-outs.

The GKF is the GIANT KILLING FACTOR

---

### The Graham Kelly Rule

Allocate each of your players a number of 1 to 4 according to which division they are playing in. The Premier is considered 1, the Third Division 4. Add the numbers for all eleven players and you have your giant killing factor. If you have a higher proportion of lower division players, your high GKF will win the day when tied with teams of more Premier Division players.

---

NB: GKF will be used in all National and Regional Cup Competitions. Examples are:

**LOKOMOTIV SPOTTER**
(91/92 Line Up) The Phuktifino Dream League
Owner: Ian Rudkins – GKF 16

| | | |
|---|---|---|
| Steve Pears | – | Middlesbrough 2 |
| George Parris | – | West Ham 1 |
| Dean Austin | – | Southend 2 |
| Nick Henry | – | Oldham 1 |
| Robert Codner | – | Brighton 2 |
| Steve Castle | – | Leyton Orient 3 |
| David White | – | Manchester City 1 |
| Mike Small | – | West Ham 1 |
| Teddy Sheringham | – | Notts Forest 1 |
| Frank McAvennie | – | West Ham 1 |
| Matthew Le Tissier | – | Southampton 1 |

**THE STINKY RABBITS**
(91/92 Line Up) The Villa Dream League
Owner; Ian Cox – GKF 23

| | | |
|---|---|---|
| Neville Southall | – | Everton 1 |
| Brian Tinnion | – | Bradford 2 |
| Lawrence Osborne | – | Gillingham 4 |
| Nigel Gleghorn | – | Birmingham 3 |

# THE RULES

| Robert Codner | – | Brighton 2 |
| Paul Baker | – | Hartlepool 3 |
| Mathew Le Tissier | – | Southampton 1 |
| David Hirst | – | Sheffield Wednesday 1 |
| Don Goodman | – | Sunderland 2 |
| Kevin Gallacher | – | Coventry City 1 |
| Steve Bull | – | Wolverhampton 2 |

Two examples of Giant Killing Factor, keep an eye on players in the lower divisions.

## Governing Body

Nice when you can get your hands on one and there is only one!
It is your league and barring the appointment of a real club chairman to your Dream League, then it is made up of ten votes on all matters. A secretaries' job is an easy one (unless he is lumbered with checking all the scores because your Dream League does not wish to enter the National Competitions) but the best Leagues get through the season when it is all democratic..ish.

## The Ken Bates Rule

If your Dream League secretary is making too many one-off decisions without due and proper consultation, sack him, depose him or chain him to the electrified perimeter fence.

Ideal way of sorting out anything is to put it to vote, and we do recommend that everybody be in attendance at the Dream League meetings, usually the Transfer Auction Night or else face another fine for not turning up. And in your absence you may be voted in as organiser of the Missed Penalty Competition.

## Computer Aides

Running a Dream League on a computer is easy, we can even provide a 3.5" floppy with all the data on it, to make it even easier. What was a little tricky was creating a system to run 10,000 plus Dream Leagues, which is why we took two years to get it tested and right for the maximum amount of enjoyment. The other thing to remember is, should you take a holiday, forget a midweek game, not lock your macros or cross check all transfer activity you can be in very serious trouble by November both real-life and imaginary.

Save yourself any hassle from other Team Owners and sign up with Dream League HQ for Scorecheck and and the National Competitions. Have fun and watch how Dream League changes your view on football.

**DREAM LEAGUE**

> # The Alan Sugar Rule
> You can win your Dream League, take the riches, and thoroughly enjoy yourself for a whole season, all with a limited interest in football

# Dream League™ AUCTION GUIDE — 8 —

## Goalkeepers

You already know from the rules that you are inheriting the defensive record of your goalkeeper's real life club. If your goalkeeper gets injured you either take the consequence with his understudy or you are back into decision-making mode, do you transfer him? If he goes to another club, you have to decide whether to stay with the club or buy another goalkeeper at another club.

So, what do you look for in a goalkeeper? Certainly a man that communicates with his back four. You know that David Seaman was the highest priced goalkeeper in Dream League History, but the new season bought a certain lack of communication between the Arsenal midfield and back four. As suspected by more than a few, the England goalie was a little prone (or not experienced) to the curving ball and full frontal stabs from twelve yards and regular televised episodes of 'David and the Onion Bag' resulted in the most transferred Dream League goalkeeper by December 1991.

Take into account that if a goalkeeper is with a successful team he is likely to encounter long cup runs and replays thus conceding more goals than you would first expect. Your goalkeeper may be in Europe which is very sexy when faced with Icelandic partimers of no worthy attributes but not so pretty when picking three out of the net on a hot night in Lisbon the following spring.

If the rival team owners in your Dream League have a particular goalkeeper in mind, ie they support Leeds and they want John Lukic no matter what it

# DREAM LEAGUE - CHAPTER 8

costs, now is the time to get them spending to deplete their war chest for purchasing strikers. If you end up with Lukic, not a bad deal, they are a youngish team with at least another two seasons together barring Gordon 'Bananas' Strachan the wonderman who may well influence the proceedings from the touchlines in years to come.

Professional teams recently promoted may show their goalkeepers up when it comes to higher division play. Ludo Miklosko is a perfect example. West Ham smothered all before them in Division II only to be fighting a relegation battle from August last year. Watch Bill Mercer at Rotherham this season. It might even be a good idea to go for a goalkeeper on a team that was unluckily relegated or that just missed out on promotion in the play-offs. Tim Clarke at Huddersfield a likley candidate along with Stuart Naylor at West Bromwich.

Dream League Goalkeepers are an investment. If you've bagged one and the papers start saying "strongest line up in years", or they say "he (your goalkeeper) could be in line for major role in the 1994 World Cup" you might have troubles ahead, it might even be worth selling him at a profit in the first transfer period. Newspapers add pressure, putting the microscope on their acclaimed 'stars'.

Dream League of course, allows you to dig deep into the wealth of our footballing talent and test your English football town geography. It is a bit like enjoying a musician, you heard him accidently on a trip or on some obscure radio station. You buy the record and enjoy that feeling that this is your discovery. It all goes out the window though when Rod Stewart does a cover version of no particular value (other than to him and his fans) and your discovery is popularised and everybody is on the bandwagon, and it's your wagon! The opposite occurs in Dream League, you select an obscure goalkeeper with a good defence in front of him and from the shadows of the big names and by Christmas everybody is lauding his ability but unlike the records of a favourite artist your rivals cannot buy him, because you already have him.

When Butcher left Coventry there was a sharp intake of breath, Butcher knows quite a bit about defending and a little Italian. When Don Howe got on board SS Coventry, the stage was set for Orgisovic to put on music, light the lights and become a Dream League "star". Who wouldn't be with 8 or 9 guys keeping you company in your own box all programmed with they "shall not score". It lasted for five or six weeks until Gordon Durie woke up and then they bought Les Sealey as cover! The lights went out.

When buying a goalkeeper dig deep into the player guide, look for a cheapie, check out possible division III and IV Championship contenders. McIlhargey was a sensation last season. Take the by-pass around Barnet, go back there when you are looking for goals to be scored for you.

A good plan is, if you're going into the big time, like a Lukic and a Schmeichel, buy cheap, keep very quiet about any interest and come into their bidding as late as possible. If not push bidding up to get the advantage later on. Take care at this stage, you may get lumbered with a Segers or a Martyn.

Watch for transfers in the Summer. A good stopper in the back four is transferred to another club, your goalkeeper may be vulnerable, exposed or just plain frightenend. If all else fails look at the pictures buy a tall one, he may just tip one over the bar for you and win the Big Match. And who had heard of Peter Schmeichel last August and now he is the number one in the League.

## Defenders

These guys are valuable. "Worth their weight in goals". Your five players upfront may or may not be firing on all cylinders but in any crunch game, last day of the scoring period to decide the Manager of the Month, the Shooting Star or a Cup Match when just one goal is needed to upset the balance, it will be a defender that scores. Heroes like Pearce, Eli, Gannon & Mabbutt. Europe has its influence at all positions and if you fancy a player that will see European action the price may just be pushed up at the auction.

### The Steve Bruce Rule

Penalty Takers. There were about 348 penalties scored last season. If you select a defender who plays with a springboard artist up front and you reap the reward you are truly playing Dream League at it's highest level.

Division Three accrued more goals through penalties than any other division with 104, 9 in FA Cup matches and 9 in the Rumbelows Cup. First Division teams scored the most in the Rumbelows (10) but only 3 in the FA Cup. The First Division teams scored a total 82 goals by penalty kicks. The Second Division was 75 and the fourth 87. Interesting facts from Dream League for you to use to your advantage.

Spot the newcommer. Take a lad who wants a footballing career in the limelight and the right back position is the only opening. He gets in the team, and yes you've spotted it, before Christmas he is wearing number '9' but the player guide says defender. You're in Dream League Heaven. Look at Ian Marshall, Brian Tinnion and Andy Watson. Your aim is 150 goals minimum. Ten from a defender is good, very good. But are they worth spending all your Dream League dollars on?

And then there is the traditional British-type defender or 'Basketball Player' as one top european coach remarked. We are talking Terry Evans (6'5" at Brentford) Gary Pallister 6'4" and Andy Pearce also at 6'4". The Dead Ball Kings. The corner comes over and they are on the end of it. One nil down and two minutes left, your man ends the match as the emergency centre forward.

# DREAM LEAGUE - CHAPTER 8

## Midfield

The dynamos that turn the strikers' lights on. They can hit and run 30 yards plus they can smell a goalkeeper off his line and play the through ball.

Consensus makes a great midfield player. Hoddle, Robson, Strachan, Peacock all fabulous players who could and can also score goals. Dream League is all about goals, don't forget this is fantasy, based on reality. Your selection of a player could benefit from an insight of a teams' traditional style of play or more cynically the managers' level of security.

Teams that enjoy the reputation of "a good footballing side" let's say Norwich, will probably have four or five guys who pop in eight a piece with a star up front, Robert Fleck, who hoovers up the rebounds and benefits from the woodwork or defensive errors especially those delicious half-baked back passes that formed a trend on boggy pitches last season. At Swindon last season Duncan Shearer had Hoddle and Hazard splitting open defences, Dunc hoovered them up although Hazard was still getting the odd goal.

However if the manager of a team is excruciatingly crippled by the prospect of "the full backing of the board" then you can guess that any 4:4:2 or a 5:3:2 is going to be good for the goalie but not much use for the libero talent that you had in mind.

Look for midfielders who were once out and out strikers. When the going is good they will naturally move up field for a poke to take the dressing room sweep money. The theory follows that the other 4:4:2 to be wary of is when the boss dictates that it is only Harry and Eric upfront who should be scoring. Therefore your midfield players are really deep wingers (half-backs) and if the manager dictates an ariel bombardment of the twin towers of Harry and Eric then save your money.

Midfield players often save the day Captain Fantastic, Bryan Robson (take out injury insurance), or Gordon Strachan (free transport to the ground) or even make your day like Paul Gascoinge PC (pre-cruciate) when they are scoring goals. But they're not much good flat out on the treatment table.

Dig around for experience players enjoying late Summers or Autumns in the lower division Clubs. They're usually called upon to hit the match deciding penalty or pushed up when a junior all-star losses his bottle up front after some particularly nasty digs from the opposition hit-man.

When assembling your midfield ensure that they are scoring on the field as well as off it. Beware of the high priced darlings of the press - you will not win your Dream League with players that always take the corners. Look at the goals scored column.

You will not win prizes in Dream League for a Jan Molby diagonal pass centre circle to corner flag nor for a creative Neil Webb stab halfway line to the 18 yard box.

On a Saturday night, the last thing you should be doing is looking down at what you've scored and saying "where's the midfield?"

AUCTION GUIDE

## The Paul Stewart Rule

A regular potter of goals upfront for Blackpool and Manchester City and each one was expected because he was a striker. Terry Venables asked him to do another job and thereafter each goal seemed like a bonus, a miracle even. Numbers on the shirt mean nothing in Dream League, your bible for the position of players is the Player Guide at the back of this book. A possibly contentious issue this but as we mentioned with Defenders, if you sign a player who is registered as a Midfield player and spends the season with an 11 on his shirt getting lots of hugs and kisses for his striking ability, good job.

## Strikers

The glory boys, those that wack it, tap it and nod it from some inconceivable angles into goal. We rejoice, we sing, we thank our lucky stars and extol the virtues of football boots with white flaps or green stripes or whatever they like.

But how many Dream League Dollars will it take to get the five you want or more to the point, you need. You have by now read about the auctions in the 91/92 review. "Bully at any price", "Aldo for me, open cheque".

Four goals on a wintry night in Austria against a team of professionals (gas fitters, postmen, printers) is all very well but Maltese half backs rarely take prisoners and your boy could be out for a month after a mistimed turn on a lumpy continental pitch. Further agony is suffered as you will be able to see it all on TV. Be careful of your Euro players potential with regards to their nationality. Rush, McClair, Saunders, Hughes, Giggs could all sit it out for the goal bonanza if the managers are juggling with excessive 'foreigners' in their squads.

The real question is how much money (DL$) have you got left and what has everybody else got? It is part of the game that, at the auction, it is announced who has what left in DL$ prior to auctioning defender, midfield and striker. This ploy is also designed to help those who experience or are prone to mathematical difficulties or ensure everyone has paid up for their team so far. Make sure your banker can be trusted at the auction. If he signs 5 x $20 strikers you know you've got problems.

You need five. Five of footballs' finest to don your strip and be able to, well, just do it, on a regular basis for ten months no questions asked. Easy? You've got nine other team owners around you and who have probably read this chapter too. Those that haven't read this book eliminate from your master plan and sell them options on your players when you decide to transfer them. You are now entering the zone where, if you have done your homework (reading

**DREAM LEAGUE - CHAPTER 8**

this book) you may qualify as one of the big five in your Dream League where at least five team owners will have to talk upto you purely on the basis of your success and sheer brilliance at acquiring a goalscoring machine to match the best.

You may or may not have made a note of who has bought who and for what in the Goalkeeper, Defender and Midfield categories. Either way NOW is the time, more than any to record who spends what and deduct it from their Strikers' war chest as you proceed. If you have a fan of a particular Club in your league, you can guess that he will be looking for that heartwarming joy, double deluxe style, when a player you own also scores for the club you support. You may want him yourself, the service he will get next season looks good. The manager drives a new car (fully paid for) has a fixed interest mortgage from the 70's, so it could be a good bet. And when your signing Lee Chapman blasts three past your goalkeeper Nigel Martyn AND you're a Palace fan, you don't know wether to laugh or cry.

How do you value a Dream League Striker? How do they do it in real life come to that? It certainly isn't just the goals.

The formula is

$$\frac{90}{14} \quad \frac{\text{Scored}}{\text{Season}} \quad \frac{92}{11} \quad \times 100 \quad \frac{\text{Ab sq}}{18 \text{ yds}} \quad - \text{Vag 2} = \text{DL \$16 ish}$$

---

### The Niall Quin Rule

You watch your man score a hat-trick during the previous season and you add him to your list of probables. His name comes up at auction, in you go and he costs DL$18. As the season goes on you come to realise that the hat-trick was a mere blip in his score-chart, as missed chances, headers off the line and troublesome ankle injuries proliferate. He goes.

---

Watch transfers in the Summer, we accept that a players' club may change but positionally the Players Guide is law in Dream League football. Take notice of players that step down a rung or two. Think what Dalien Atkinson could have done for Tranmere compared to what Aldridge might have achieved at Villa. Steve Norris, a darling at Halifax but dry until Christmas. Andy Flounders took three months to settle into a scoring pattern. A player's club is important. If you look deeper than TV coverage you will find that statistically a top Premier League club will play as many matches as Bury or Carlisle.

# AUCTION GUIDE

How come? The Cup games at the beginning of the season, those Wednesday night thrashes that produce instant top goal scoring heroes before Christmas. Then there are FA Cup 1st and 2nd rounds plus the replays. Everything to play for - money basically and a dream of a Premier League side away from home in the 3rd round, stone walling it for a replay.

A team that regularly gets through half a dozen cup games before Christmas usually does so with an abundance goals. "He was scoring, I bought him, he dried " that was probably due to the fact that his team were unceremoniously dumped out of one or both cups and by which time, with the media in assistance, all the stoppers in his division knew his inside leg measurement.

Do not be misled by goals scored in competitions not sanctioned by Dream League. Many sources show Kevin Francis of Stockport scoring 24 or more goals but in Dream League he is only 17 as we do not count goals scored in The Autoglass or ZDS competitions.

Try it the other way round, buy a player in August to do a job for you until Christmas. If he stays the course and makes the later rounds when the big 22 step in you can crow with pride what a great job he has done for you, just before you sell him for the YTS you read about in the Manchester Evening news who is cooking up a storm at Walsall.

There are absolutely no prizes for good house keeping, you buy a team with DL $80 fine, DL $100 fine, in Dream League football the game is a fantasy and nobody at the auction can go over the budget or make profits by selling 16 year old supporters a shirt that advertises 18 year old beer.

It's not how much money, its what you do with it that matters, in a cerebral sort of way. If you have twenty dollars left and one player to get and your opposite numbers do not know it's your last player, enjoy yourself make others spend money on players they are not really sure about, try to control it. Believe me its fun at an Auction.

Having experienced more than most I can offer these broad insights.
a) Auctions never start on time.
b) 50% of team owners will feign serious interest when all they want is out and out victory.
c) At least one Herbert will try to buy the Reserve goalkeeper of Liverpool, Manchester United, Arsenal etc. Fine Him!
d) The quickest Auction I've seen is 2 hours. The longest (and most entertaining) was three and a half hours. If you are at the pub (good place, beer breaks scheduled prior to defenders, midfielders, strikers) then you have to allow three hours.
e) The team you buy will never be exactly what you envisaged prior to the Auction.

Good Luck and ensure you register for Scorecheck and the National Competitions. We have some very interesting developments on the back burner that will put you at the forefront of Fantasy Sports in the UK.

**DREAM LEAGUE – CHAPTER 8**

> ## WARNING
> If you plan to go it alone without support wear a tin helmet, double check all scores and scorers, check the initials of the players you are recording, ensure you're covered for the telephone calls, postage and photocopying, in time and in money.

# Dream League™

## SCORECHECK

## — 9 —

This is where you can indulge your very personal analysis of your Fantasy Football Team. This series of extremely detailed Scorecheck tables will enable you to keep tabs on your performance for everyday of the season. You could also join in Scorecheck and be with thousands of other Team Owners in National Competitions, you could even do both. For those with the 91/92 Portfolios, photocopy theses pages and they fit the pocket on the right inside cover.

All examples relate to the start of a season.

### 1. KEY

| | | |
|---|---|---|
| A | = | Goalkeeper  D = Defender  M = Midfield  S = Striker |
| – | = | Did not play (Injured or Dropped) |
| 0 | = | Played without scoring |
| 1 | = | Played and scored one goal or 2 etc. |
| 2 | = | Your guess |

For Scorecheck periods refer to Chapter 7 – Rules, page 53

### 2. HOW TO COMPLETE SCORECHECK

a) You have selected your Team (either by Auction in Dream League or by personal selection in Dream Team) and entered as shown in **Fig A** overleaf. Unfortunately one of your selections David Platt, has departed for sunnier climes. Simply write – against each of the days you wanted him to play since you cannot make a replacement for the first six weeks of the season.

b) If Dave Bamber scores 2 goals on the first day of the season put two under that date under his name. If David Seaman concedes two on the first Saturday you annotate the same as a minus figure in the goalkeeper box. Easy so far.

c) Continuing to mark the Scorecheck period as suggested until the end of the first two periods, now it is time for Transfer action!
   i) David Platt has to go, Steve Castle is the man you acquire.
   ii) John Barnes is injured and you need a replacement, let's say you pick up Iwan Roberts
   iii) David Seaman is letting too many go past him and through him so you need a replacement at the back. Try to avoid England keeper's in future. Let's say you acquire Steve McIlhargey.

d) After putting the names of your players departing (players sold), onto the Transfer List, **Fig B.** overleaf shows how you can fill in the next part of Scorecheck.
   i) The likes of a David Platt wouldn't have scored so the Transfer Factor is not affected.
   ii) John Barnes scores one for you before damaging a toe kicking cans at TV sets. Therefore his goal goes into the Transfer Factor box.
   iii) David Seaman concedes fourteen so that number needs to go into the Goalkeeper's Transfer Factor box.
   iv) As none of the new players have either scored or conceded goals for you their carry-over figure is zero.
   v) The totals are calculated as follows;

| | | |
|---|---|---|
| GOALS FOR | = | Carry Over + Transfer Factor |
| GOALS AGAINST | = | Goalkeeper Carry Over + Transfer Factor |
| POINTS | = | Goals For – Goals Against |

e) **Fig C** overleaf is an example of a completed Scorecheck period. This is the fun part that will keep you searching for your goalscorers in the daily papers every day. If your score looks like this at the end of October 1992, you will be heading for the big time.

f) Easy. But to be part of the National League and having automatic entry into the National Challenge Cup competitions you need to be Registered with Dream League HQ. Then you can compete against other teams from all over the country, receive our informative newsletter and above all receive a monthly table detailing your scores and progress and transfer activities.

**SCORECHECK**

# FIGURE A

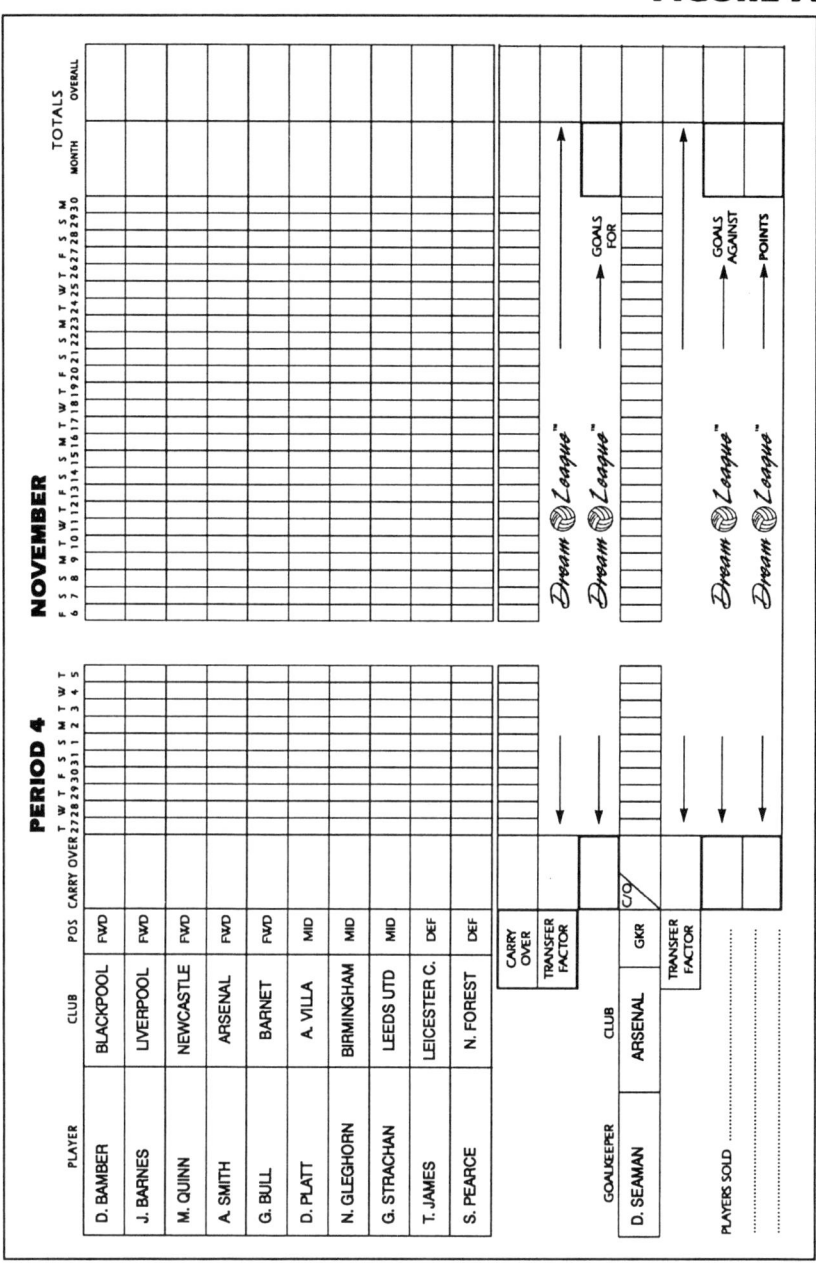

# DREAM LEAGUE – CHAPTER 9

## FIGURE B

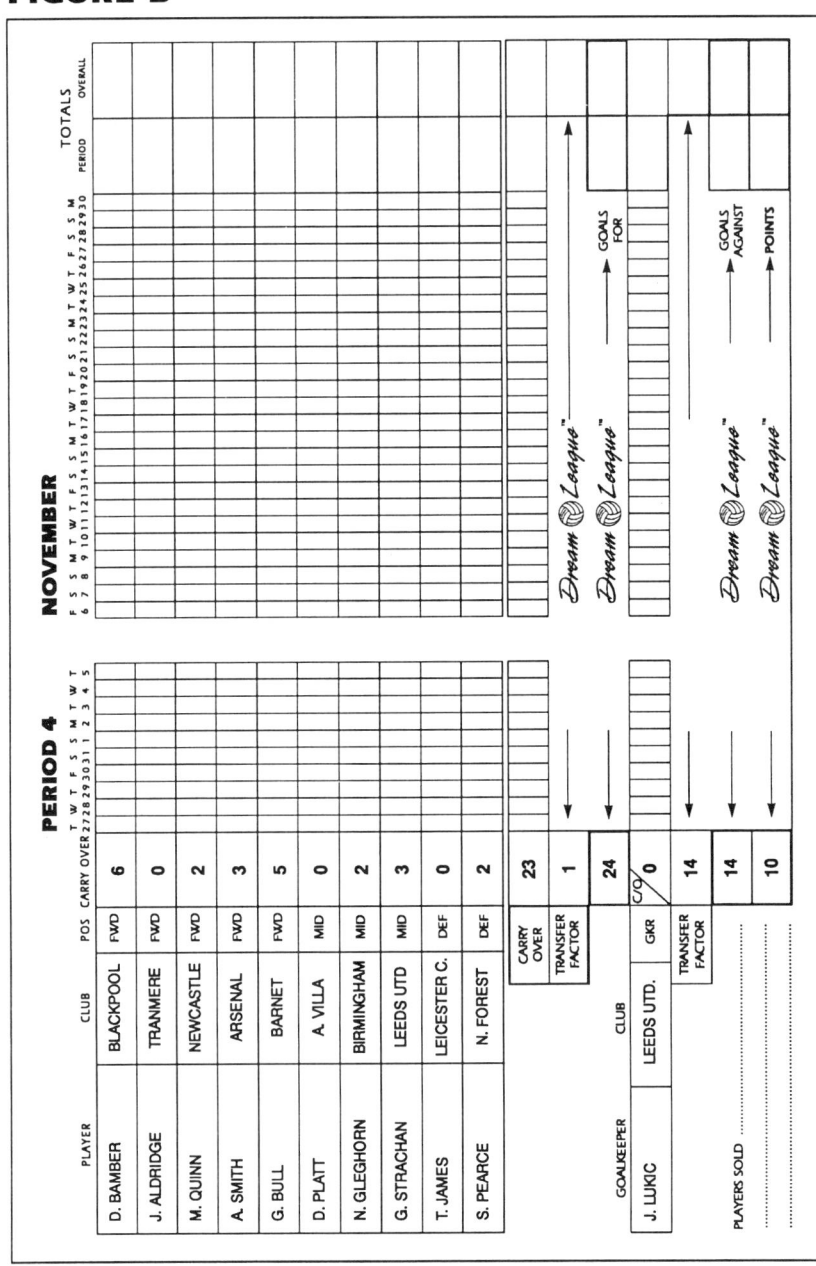

### PERIOD 4 / NOVEMBER

| PLAYER | CLUB | POS | CARRY OVER |
|---|---|---|---|
| D. BAMBER | BLACKPOOL | FWD | 6 |
| J. ALDRIDGE | TRANMERE | FWD | 0 |
| M. QUINN | NEWCASTLE | FWD | 2 |
| A. SMITH | ARSENAL | FWD | 3 |
| G. BULL | BARNET | FWD | 5 |
| D. PLATT | A. VILLA | MID | 0 |
| N. GLEGHORN | BIRMINGHAM | MID | 2 |
| G. STRACHAN | LEEDS UTD | MID | 3 |
| T. JAMES | LEICESTER C. | DEF | 0 |
| S. PEARCE | N. FOREST | DEF | 2 |

CARRY OVER: 23
TRANSFER FACTOR: 1

| GOALKEEPER | CLUB | | |
|---|---|---|---|
| J. LUKIC | LEEDS UTD. | GKR | 0 |

TRANSFER FACTOR: 24

Goals For: 14
Goals Against: 14
Points: 10

PLAYERS SOLD ........

*Dream League™* (×3)

# SCORECHECK

## FIGURE C

### PERIOD 4

| PLAYER | CLUB | POS | CARRY OVER | 27 28 29 30 31 1 2 3 4 5 |
|---|---|---|---|---|
| D. BAMBER | BLACKPOOL | FWD | 6 | - - - - - 0 - - - 0 |
| J. ALDRIDGE | TRANMERE | FWD | 0 | - 1 - - 2 - - - - 1 |
| M. QUINN | NEWCASTLE | FWD | 2 | - - - - 0 - - - - - |
| A. SMITH | ARSENAL | FWD | 3 | - - 0 - 0 - - - - 0 |
| G. BULL | BARNET | FWD | 5 | - - 3 - 0 - - - - - |
| D. PLATT | A. VILLA | MID | 0 | - - 0 - 0 - - - - - |
| N. GLEGHORN | BIRMINGHAM | MID | 2 | - - 0 - 0 - - - - 0 |
| G. STRACHAN | LEEDS UTD | MID | 3 | - - 0 - 0 - - - - 0 |
| T. JAMES | LEICESTER C. | DEF | 0 | - - - - - - - - - - |
| S. PEARCE | N. FOREST | DEF | 2 | - - 0 - 0 - - - - - |

CARRY OVER: 23  
TRANSFER FACTOR: 1  
— — 4 — 2 0 0 — — 1

| GOALKEEPER | CLUB | | | |
|---|---|---|---|---|
| S. MC'ILHARGEY | BLACKPOOL | GKR | 0 C/O | - - 0 - 0 - - - - - |

TRANSFER FACTOR: 14  
14  
10

PLAYERS SOLD .............................

### NOVEMBER

F S S M T W T F S S M T W T F S S M T W T F S S M T W T F S S M
6 7 8 9 10 11 12 13 14 15 16 17 18 19 20 21 22 23 24 25 26 27 28 29 30

| | | | TOTALS |
|---|---|---|---|
| | | PERIOD | OVERALL |
| - 1 - - 0 - - 1 - - 2 - - 0 - - 0 - - 0 - - 1 - | 6 | 12 |
| - 0 - - 1 - - 1 - - 0 - - 0 - - 2 - - 0 - - 0 - | 6 | 6 |
| - 2 - - 0 - - 1 - - 0 - - 0 - - 0 - - 0 - - 0 - | 4 | 6 |
| - 1 - - 0 - - 0 - - 0 - - 0 - - 0 - - 0 - - 0 - | 1 | 4 |
| - 0 - - 2 - - 2 - - 0 - - 0 - - 1 - - 0 - - 1 - | 7 | 12 |
| - 0 - - 0 - - 0 - - 0 - - 0 - - 0 - - 0 - - 0 - | 0 | 0 |
| - 2 - - 1 - - 0 - - 0 - - 0 - - 0 - - 0 - - 1 - | 4 | 6 |
| - 0 - - 1 - - 0 - - 0 - - 0 - - 0 - - 0 - - 0 - | 1 | 4 |
| - 0 - - 0 - - 0 - - 0 - - 0 - - 0 - - 0 - - 0 - | 0 | 0 |
| - 0 - - 1 - - 0 - - 0 - - 0 - - 0 - - 0 - - 0 - | 1 | 3 |
| - 6 - - 4 - - 2 1 - 0 2 - - 0 0 - 2 2 - - 3 1 - | 30 | 53 |

*Dream League™* → 1

| - - - - - - - - - - - - - - - - - - - - - - - - | 30 | 54 |
|---|---|---|
*Dream League™* → GOALS FOR

| - 2 - - 1 - - 1 - - 0 - - 0 - - 1 - - 1 0 - 0 - | 4 | 4 |

*Dream League™* → GOALS AGAINST  
*Dream League™* → POINTS

| | 14 | 14 |
| | 4 | 18 |
| | 26 | 36 |

77

**DREAM LEAGUE – CHAPTER 9**

# PERIOD 1

| PLAYER | CLUB | POS | CARRY OVER | T W T F S S M T W T |
|---|---|---|---|---|
|  |  | FWD |  |  |
|  |  | FWD |  |  |
|  |  | FWD |  |  |
|  |  | FWD |  |  |
|  |  | FWD |  |  |
|  |  | MID |  |  |
|  |  | MID |  |  |
|  |  | MID |  |  |
|  |  | DEF |  |  |
|  |  | DEF |  |  |

| | | CARRY OVER | |
|---|---|---|---|
| | | TRANSFER FACTOR | ← |
| | | | ← |

| GOALKEEPER | CLUB | | | |
|---|---|---|---|---|
|  |  | GKR | C/O |  |
|  |  | TRANSFER FACTOR |  | ← |

PLAYERS SOLD ......................................................
............................................................................
............................................................................

← 
←

**SCORECHECK**

# AUGUST

F S S M T W T F S S M T W T F S S M T W T F S S M T W T F S S M
15 16 17 18 19 20 21 22 23 24 25 26 27 28 29 30 31

TOTALS
MONTH  OVERALL

*Dream League*™ →

*Dream League*™ → GOALS FOR

*Dream League*™ → GOALS AGAINST

*Dream League*™ → POINTS

**DREAM LEAGUE – CHAPTER 9**

# PERIOD 2

| PLAYER | CLUB | POS | CARRY OVER | T 1 | W 2 | T 3 | F 4 | S 5 | S 6 | M 7 | T 8 | W 9 | T 10 |
|---|---|---|---|---|---|---|---|---|---|---|---|---|---|
|  |  | FWD |  |  |  |  |  |  |  |  |  |  |  |
|  |  | FWD |  |  |  |  |  |  |  |  |  |  |  |
|  |  | FWD |  |  |  |  |  |  |  |  |  |  |  |
|  |  | FWD |  |  |  |  |  |  |  |  |  |  |  |
|  |  | FWD |  |  |  |  |  |  |  |  |  |  |  |
|  |  | MID |  |  |  |  |  |  |  |  |  |  |  |
|  |  | MID |  |  |  |  |  |  |  |  |  |  |  |
|  |  | MID |  |  |  |  |  |  |  |  |  |  |  |
|  |  | DEF |  |  |  |  |  |  |  |  |  |  |  |
|  |  | DEF |  |  |  |  |  |  |  |  |  |  |  |

| | CARRY OVER | |
|---|---|---|
| | TRANSFER FACTOR | ← |
| | | ← |

| GOALKEEPER | CLUB | GKR | C/O | | | | | | | | | | |
|---|---|---|---|---|---|---|---|---|---|---|---|---|---|

| | TRANSFER FACTOR | ← |
|---|---|---|

PLAYERS SOLD ……………………………………………

………………………………………………………………

………………………………………………………………

| | ← |
|---|---|
| | ← |

**SCORECHECK**

# SEPTEMBER

F S S M T W T F S S M T W T F S S M T W T F S S
1 11 2 13 14 15 16 17 18 19 20 21 22 23 24 25 26 27 28

TOTALS
MONTH    OVERALL

*Dream League*™

*Dream League*™ → GOALS FOR

*Dream League*™ → GOALS AGAINST

*Dream League*™ → POINTS

**DREAM LEAGUE – CHAPTER 9**

# PERIOD 3

| PLAYER | CLUB | POS | CARRY OVER | T 29 | W 30 | T 1 | F 2 | S 3 | S 4 | M 5 | T 6 | W 7 | T 8 |
|---|---|---|---|---|---|---|---|---|---|---|---|---|---|
| | | FWD | | | | | | | | | | | |
| | | FWD | | | | | | | | | | | |
| | | FWD | | | | | | | | | | | |
| | | FWD | | | | | | | | | | | |
| | | FWD | | | | | | | | | | | |
| | | MID | | | | | | | | | | | |
| | | MID | | | | | | | | | | | |
| | | MID | | | | | | | | | | | |
| | | DEF | | | | | | | | | | | |
| | | DEF | | | | | | | | | | | |

|  |  |
|---|---|
| CARRY OVER | |
| TRANSFER FACTOR | ← |

| GOALKEEPER | CLUB | GKR | C/O | |
|---|---|---|---|---|

| TRANSFER FACTOR | ← |
|---|---|

PLAYERS SOLD ..........................................
..........................................................
..........................................................

**SCORECHECK**

# OCTOBER

| F | S | S | M | T | W | T | F | S | S | M | T | W | T | F | S | S | M | T | W | T | F | S | S | TOTALS |
|---|---|---|---|---|---|---|---|---|---|---|---|---|---|---|---|---|---|---|---|---|---|---|---|---|
| 9 | 10 | 11 | 12 | 13 | 14 | 15 | 16 | 17 | 18 | 19 | 20 | 21 | 22 | 23 | 24 | 25 | 26 | | | | | | | MONTH / OVERALL |

*Dream League*™

*Dream League*™ → GOALS FOR

*Dream League*™ → GOALS AGAINST

*Dream League*™ → POINTS

**DREAM LEAGUE – CHAPTER 9**

# PERIOD 4

| PLAYER | CLUB | POS | CARRY OVER | T 27 | W 28 | T 29 | F 30 | S 31 | S 1 | M 2 | T 3 | W 4 | T 5 |
|---|---|---|---|---|---|---|---|---|---|---|---|---|---|
| | | FWD | | | | | | | | | | | |
| | | FWD | | | | | | | | | | | |
| | | FWD | | | | | | | | | | | |
| | | FWD | | | | | | | | | | | |
| | | FWD | | | | | | | | | | | |
| | | MID | | | | | | | | | | | |
| | | MID | | | | | | | | | | | |
| | | MID | | | | | | | | | | | |
| | | DEF | | | | | | | | | | | |
| | | DEF | | | | | | | | | | | |

| | | |
|---|---|---|
| CARRY OVER | | |
| TRANSFER FACTOR | | ← |
| | | ← |

| GOALKEEPER | CLUB | | | |
|---|---|---|---|---|
| | | GKR | C/O | |

| TRANSFER FACTOR | | ← |
|---|---|---|

PLAYERS SOLD ..................................... ← 

................................................................ ←

**SCORECHECK**

# NOVEMBER

| S | S | M | T | W | T | F | S | S | M | T | W | T | F | S | S | M | T | W | T | F | S | S | M |
|---|---|---|---|---|---|---|---|---|---|---|---|---|---|---|---|---|---|---|---|---|---|---|---|
| 7 | 8 | 9 | 10 | 11 | 12 | 13 | 14 | 15 | 16 | 17 | 18 | 19 | 20 | 21 | 22 | 23 | 24 | 25 | 26 | 27 | 28 | 29 | 30 |

**TOTALS**
MONTH    OVERALL

*Dream League*™

*Dream League*™ → GOALS FOR

*Dream League*™ → GOALS AGAINST

*Dream League*™ → POINTS

**DREAM LEAGUE – CHAPTER 9**

# PERIOD 5

| PLAYER | CLUB | POS | CARRY OVER | T 1 | W 2 | T 3 | F 4 | S 5 | S 6 | M 7 | T 8 | W 9 | T 10 |
|--------|------|-----|------------|---|---|---|---|---|---|---|---|---|----|
|  |  | FWD |  |  |  |  |  |  |  |  |  |  |  |
|  |  | FWD |  |  |  |  |  |  |  |  |  |  |  |
|  |  | FWD |  |  |  |  |  |  |  |  |  |  |  |
|  |  | FWD |  |  |  |  |  |  |  |  |  |  |  |
|  |  | FWD |  |  |  |  |  |  |  |  |  |  |  |
|  |  | MID |  |  |  |  |  |  |  |  |  |  |  |
|  |  | MID |  |  |  |  |  |  |  |  |  |  |  |
|  |  | MID |  |  |  |  |  |  |  |  |  |  |  |
|  |  | DEF |  |  |  |  |  |  |  |  |  |  |  |
|  |  | DEF |  |  |  |  |  |  |  |  |  |  |  |

| | CARRY OVER | |
|---|---|---|
| | TRANSFER FACTOR | ← |
| | | ← |

| GOALKEEPER | CLUB | GKR | C/O | | | | | | | | | | |
|---|---|---|---|---|---|---|---|---|---|---|---|---|---|
|  |  |  |  |  |  |  |  |  |  |  |  |  |  |

| | TRANSFER FACTOR | ← |
|---|---|---|

PLAYERS SOLD ..........................................
..........................................................
..........................................................

← 
←

**SCORECHECK**

# DECEMBER

| F | S | S | M | T | W | T | F | S | S | M | T | W | T | F | S | S | M | T | W | T | F | S | S | | TOTALS | |
|---|---|---|---|---|---|---|---|---|---|---|---|---|---|---|---|---|---|---|---|---|---|---|---|---|---|---|
| 1 | 2 | 3 | 4 | 5 | 6 | 7 | 8 | 9 | 10 | 11 | 12 | 13 | 14 | 15 | 16 | 17 | 18 | 19 | 20 | 21 | 22 | 23 | 24 | 25 | 26 | 27 | 28 | | MONTH | OVERALL |

*Dream League*™ ⟶

*Dream League*™ ⟶ GOALS FOR

*Dream League*™ ⟶ GOALS AGAINST

*Dream League*™ ⟶ POINTS

**DREAM LEAGUE – CHAPTER 9**

# PERIOD 6

| PLAYER | CLUB | POS | CARRY OVER | T 29 | W 30 | T 31 | F 1 | S 2 | S 3 | M 4 | T 5 | W 6 | T 7 |
|---|---|---|---|---|---|---|---|---|---|---|---|---|---|
|  |  | FWD |  |  |  |  |  |  |  |  |  |  |  |
|  |  | FWD |  |  |  |  |  |  |  |  |  |  |  |
|  |  | FWD |  |  |  |  |  |  |  |  |  |  |  |
|  |  | FWD |  |  |  |  |  |  |  |  |  |  |  |
|  |  | FWD |  |  |  |  |  |  |  |  |  |  |  |
|  |  | MID |  |  |  |  |  |  |  |  |  |  |  |
|  |  | MID |  |  |  |  |  |  |  |  |  |  |  |
|  |  | MID |  |  |  |  |  |  |  |  |  |  |  |
|  |  | DEF |  |  |  |  |  |  |  |  |  |  |  |
|  |  | DEF |  |  |  |  |  |  |  |  |  |  |  |

CARRY OVER

TRANSFER FACTOR ←

←

| GOALKEEPER | CLUB | | | |
|---|---|---|---|---|
|  |  | GKR | C/O |  |

TRANSFER FACTOR ←

PLAYERS SOLD ..................................................... ←

................................................................................

................................................................................ ←

**SCORECHECK**

# JANUARY

| F S S M T W T F S S M T W T F S S M T W T F S S | TOTALS |
|---|---|
| 8 9 10 11 12 13 14 15 16 17 18 19 20 21 22 23 24 25 | MONTH  OVERALL |

*Dream League*™ ⟶

*Dream League*™ ⟶ GOALS FOR

*Dream League*™ ⟶ GOALS AGAINST

*Dream League*™ ⟶ POINTS

**DREAM LEAGUE – CHAPTER 9**

# PERIOD 7

| PLAYER | CLUB | POS | CARRY OVER | T 26 | W 27 | T 28 | F 29 | S 30 | S 31 | M 1 | T 2 | W 3 | T 4 |
|---|---|---|---|---|---|---|---|---|---|---|---|---|---|
|  |  | FWD |  |  |  |  |  |  |  |  |  |  |  |
|  |  | FWD |  |  |  |  |  |  |  |  |  |  |  |
|  |  | FWD |  |  |  |  |  |  |  |  |  |  |  |
|  |  | FWD |  |  |  |  |  |  |  |  |  |  |  |
|  |  | FWD |  |  |  |  |  |  |  |  |  |  |  |
|  |  | MID |  |  |  |  |  |  |  |  |  |  |  |
|  |  | MID |  |  |  |  |  |  |  |  |  |  |  |
|  |  | MID |  |  |  |  |  |  |  |  |  |  |  |
|  |  | DEF |  |  |  |  |  |  |  |  |  |  |  |
|  |  | DEF |  |  |  |  |  |  |  |  |  |  |  |

| | CARRY OVER | |
|---|---|---|
| | TRANSFER FACTOR | ← |
| | | ← |

| GOALKEEPER | CLUB | GKR | C/O | | | | | | | | | | |
|---|---|---|---|---|---|---|---|---|---|---|---|---|---|
|  |  |  |  |  |  |  |  |  |  |  |  |  |  |

| | TRANSFER FACTOR | ← |
|---|---|---|

PLAYERS SOLD ..................................................  ←
..................................................
..................................................  ←

**SCORECHECK**

# FEBRUARY

| F | S | S | M | T | W | T | F | S | S | M | T | W | T | F | S | S | M | T | W | W | T | F | S | S | TOTALS |  |
|---|---|---|---|---|---|---|---|---|---|---|---|---|---|---|---|---|---|---|---|---|---|---|---|---|---|---|
| 5 | 6 | 7 | 8 | 9 | 10 | 11 | 12 | 13 | 14 | 15 | 16 | 17 | 18 | 19 | 20 | 21 | 22 | | | | | | | | MONTH | OVERALL |

*Dream League*™ ⟶

*Dream League*™ ⟶ GOALS FOR

*Dream League*™ ⟶ GOALS AGAINST

*Dream League*™ ⟶ POINTS

**DREAM LEAGUE – CHAPTER 9**

# PERIOD 8

| PLAYER | CLUB | POS | CARRY OVER | T 23 | W 24 | T 25 | F 26 | S 27 | S 28 | M 1 | T 2 | W 3 | T 4 |
|---|---|---|---|---|---|---|---|---|---|---|---|---|---|
|  |  | FWD |  |  |  |  |  |  |  |  |  |  |  |
|  |  | FWD |  |  |  |  |  |  |  |  |  |  |  |
|  |  | FWD |  |  |  |  |  |  |  |  |  |  |  |
|  |  | FWD |  |  |  |  |  |  |  |  |  |  |  |
|  |  | FWD |  |  |  |  |  |  |  |  |  |  |  |
|  |  | MID |  |  |  |  |  |  |  |  |  |  |  |
|  |  | MID |  |  |  |  |  |  |  |  |  |  |  |
|  |  | MID |  |  |  |  |  |  |  |  |  |  |  |
|  |  | DEF |  |  |  |  |  |  |  |  |  |  |  |
|  |  | DEF |  |  |  |  |  |  |  |  |  |  |  |

|  | CARRY OVER |  |
|---|---|---|
|  | TRANSFER FACTOR |  |

| GOALKEEPER | CLUB | GKR | C/O |
|---|---|---|---|
|  |  |  |  |

|  | TRANSFER FACTOR |  |
|---|---|---|

PLAYERS SOLD ............................................................
........................................................................................
........................................................................................

**SCORECHECK**

# MARCH

| F | S | S | M | T | W | T | F | S | S | M | T | W | T | F | S | S | M | T | W | T | F | S | S | M | T | W | W | T | F | S | S |
|---|---|---|---|---|---|---|---|---|---|---|---|---|---|---|---|---|---|---|---|---|---|---|---|---|---|---|---|---|---|---|---|
| 5 | 6 | 7 | 8 | 9 | 10 | 11 | 12 | 13 | 14 | 15 | 16 | 17 | 18 | 19 | 20 | 21 | 22 | 23 | 24 | 25 | 26 | 27 | 28 | 29 |

**TOTALS**
MONTH    OVERALL

*Dream League*™ ⟶

*Dream League*™ ⟶ GOALS FOR

*Dream League*™ ⟶ GOALS AGAINST

*Dream League*™ ⟶ POINTS

**DREAM LEAGUE – CHAPTER 9**

# PERIOD 9

| PLAYER | CLUB | POS | CARRY OVER | T 30 | W 31 | T 1 | F 2 | S 3 | S 4 | M 5 | T 6 | W 7 | T 8 |
|---|---|---|---|---|---|---|---|---|---|---|---|---|---|
| | | FWD | | | | | | | | | | | |
| | | FWD | | | | | | | | | | | |
| | | FWD | | | | | | | | | | | |
| | | FWD | | | | | | | | | | | |
| | | FWD | | | | | | | | | | | |
| | | MID | | | | | | | | | | | |
| | | MID | | | | | | | | | | | |
| | | MID | | | | | | | | | | | |
| | | DEF | | | | | | | | | | | |
| | | DEF | | | | | | | | | | | |

| | | |
|---|---|---|
| | CARRY OVER | |
| | TRANSFER FACTOR | |

| GOALKEEPER | CLUB | | | |
|---|---|---|---|---|
| | | GKR | C/O | |

| | TRANSFER FACTOR | |
|---|---|---|

PLAYERS SOLD ......................................................
................................................................................
................................................................................

**SCORECHECK**

# APRIL

| F | S | S | M | T | W | T | F | S | S | M | T | W | T | F | S | S | M | T | W | T | F | S | S | TOTALS | |
|---|---|---|---|---|---|---|---|---|---|---|---|---|---|---|---|---|---|---|---|---|---|---|---|---|---|
| 9 | 10 | 11 | 12 | 13 | 14 | 15 | 16 | 17 | 18 | 19 | 20 | 21 | 22 | 23 | 24 | 25 | 26 | | | | | | | MONTH | OVERALL |

*Dream League*™ ⟶

*Dream League*™ ⟶ GOALS FOR

*Dream League*™ ⟶ GOALS AGAINST

*Dream League*™ ⟶ POINTS

**DREAM LEAGUE – CHAPTER 9**

# PERIOD 10

| PLAYER | CLUB | POS | CARRY OVER | T 27 | W 28 | T 29 | F 30 | S 1 | S 2 | M 3 | T 4 | W 5 | T 6 |
|--------|------|-----|------------|------|------|------|------|-----|-----|-----|-----|-----|-----|
|  |  | FWD |  |  |  |  |  |  |  |  |  |  |  |
|  |  | FWD |  |  |  |  |  |  |  |  |  |  |  |
|  |  | FWD |  |  |  |  |  |  |  |  |  |  |  |
|  |  | FWD |  |  |  |  |  |  |  |  |  |  |  |
|  |  | FWD |  |  |  |  |  |  |  |  |  |  |  |
|  |  | MID |  |  |  |  |  |  |  |  |  |  |  |
|  |  | MID |  |  |  |  |  |  |  |  |  |  |  |
|  |  | MID |  |  |  |  |  |  |  |  |  |  |  |
|  |  | DEF |  |  |  |  |  |  |  |  |  |  |  |
|  |  | DEF |  |  |  |  |  |  |  |  |  |  |  |

| | CARRY OVER | |
|---|---|---|
| | TRANSFER FACTOR | ← |
| | | ← |

| GOALKEEPER | CLUB | GKR | C/O | | | | | | | | | | |
|------------|------|-----|-----|---|---|---|---|---|---|---|---|---|---|
|  |  |  |  |  |  |  |  |  |  |  |  |  |  |

| | TRANSFER FACTOR | ← |
|---|---|---|

PLAYERS SOLD ......................................................... ← 

......................................................................... ←

.........................................................................

**SCORECHECK**

# MAY

| F | S | S | M | T | W | T | F | S | S | M | T | W | T | F | S | S | M | T | F | T | F | S | S | M | TOTALS MONTH | OVERALL |
|---|---|---|---|---|---|---|---|---|---|---|---|---|---|---|---|---|---|---|---|---|---|---|---|---|---|---|
| 7 | 8 | 9 | 10 | 11 | 12 | 13 | 14 | 15 | 16 | 17 | 18 | 19 | 20 | 21 | 22 | 23 | 24 | 25 | 26 | 27 | 28 | 29 | 30 | 31 | | |

*Dream League*™

*Dream League*™ → GOALS FOR

*Dream League*™ → GOALS AGAINST

*Dream League*™ → POINTS

# DREAM LEAGUE

# Dream League™
# PLAYER & GOALIE GUIDE
— 10 —

This guide will give you all the facts you need to create your Dream Team ready for Dream League competitions, local and national. It is also an interesting record of how some players have peaked and troughed, sometimes under the heavy burden of exhorbitant transfer fees.

The positions we have allocated will be used for the 1992/93 Dream League season and be the reference for transfers and the properly constituted team rule.

The goal records are for the seasons 1989/90, 1990/91 and the season just past, 1991/92. The goals recorded are those a player has scored in the Football League, FA Cup and Rumbelows Cup competitions in that particular season. For goalkeepers it is the number of goals his team conceded. **SEE QUICK REFERENCE ON PAGE 221 FOR 1991/92 GOALS.**

Obviously a number of players will change clubs as deals are struck between the real life managers and chairmen during the summer and into the season. You can of course keep a record of the transfers by making notes by the appropriate players. Blank entries are provided for you to complete when new players join the League, e.g. non-league teams, youth trainees, foreign imports.

You may also like to fill in the cost of each player at your auction to give you a record of your Dream League's buying style. Loan is where a player is possibly on the move, not sure about his future, in limbo or being used as a stopgap.

The comments have been supplied by fans of the football clubs themselves. Fanzine Editors, Supporters Club Secretaries, Ripened Season Ticket Holders and those that have a view on Saturday afternoons whatever the weather and despite the shambles on the pitch.

If you think you have a better view and would like to submit alternative pen pictures for your Premier League or Football League team, please send them to:

**Dream League Publishing, PO Box 235, Egham, Surrey TW20 9HT**

DREAM LEAGUE – CHAPTER 10      90 91 92

# PLAYER GUIDE

**ABBO – Abbott Greg**   Halifax Town      **Midfield**   4   1   1   DL$........
Born: Coventry – 14/12/1963
Comments: Needs a Costello in Midfield

**ABEL – Abel Graham**   Chester City      **Defender**   8   6   9   DL$........
Born: Runcorn – 17/09/1960
Comments: Consistent and reliable defender who can cane the opposition

**ABLE – Ablett Gary**   Everton      **Defender**   0   0   1   DL$........
Born: Liverpool – 19/11/1965
Comments: Double take at derby games

**ABRA – Abraham Gareth**   Cardiff City      **Defender**   1   0   0   DL$........
Born: Merthyr Tydfil – 13/02/1969
Comments: Product of its youth scheme at Ninian Park

**ACHA – Achampong Kenny**   Leyton Orient      **Striker**   0   4   2   DL$........
Born: London – 26/06/1966
Comments: Kenny's coming back to form?

**ADMI – Adams Mick**   Southampton      **Defender**   0   0   3   DL$........
Born: Sheffield – 08/11/1961
Comments: Micky can either play left-back or left side of midfield

**ADNE – Adams Neil**   Oldham Athletic      **Striker**   5   7   5   DL$........
Born: Stoke – 23/11/1965
Comments: Doesn't need the judo

**ADST – Adams Steve**   Doncaster Rovers      **Striker**   1   1   0   DL$........
Born: Sheffield – 07/05/1959
Comments: Steve's lost what touch he had

**ADAM – Adams Tony**   Arsenal      **Defender**   6   4   2   DL$........
Born: London – 10/10/1966
Comments: Twice winner of the Supporter's Player of the year

**ADCT – Adcock Tony**   Peterborough United   **Striker**   6   3   15   DL$........
Born: Bethnal Green – 27/02/1963
Comments: Another prolific striker from Northampton

**AGAN – Agana Tony**   Leeds United      **Striker**   12   3   5   DL$........
Born: London – 02/10/1963
Comments: Loan

**AGNP – Agnew Paul**   Grimsby Town      **Defender**   2   0   0   DL$........
Born: Lisburn – 15/08/1965
Comments:  Paul's another defender whose lost his touch

---

## Dream League Trivia

*Which goalkeeper did not concede a goal in 1,142 minutes of international play?*

Answer: Dino Zoff

# PLAYER GUIDE                                         90 91 92

**AGNE – Agnew Steve**  Blackburn Rovers   **Midfield**   8   8   0   DL$........
Born: Shipley – 09/11/1965
Comments: Used to be a prolific scorer

**AIZL – Aizlewood Mark**  Bristol City   **Midfield**   1   2   1   DL$........
Born: Newport – 01/10/1959
Comments: Age and vision in midfield

**ALBI – Albiston Arthur**  Chester City   **Defender**   0   1   0   DL$........
Born: Edinburgh – 14/07/1957
Comments: Arthur's experience should help at Moss Rose

**ALDR – Aldridge John**  Tranmere Rovers   **Striker**   1   0   33   DL$........
Born: Liverpool – 18/09/1958
Comments: Aldo's close to breaking the club goal record

**ALEX – Alexander Graham**  Scunthorpe Utd   **Defender**   0   0   6   DL$........
Born: Coventry – 10/10/1971
Comments: Baby Face, good shot but has a bad Gazza haircut

**ALEI – Alexander Ian**  Bristol Rovers   **Midfield**   1   2   2   DL$........
Born: Glasgow – 26/01/1963
Comments: "Jock", is a popular all action player

**ALEK – Alexander Keith**  Lincoln City   **Striker**   13   3   1   DL$........
Born: Nottingham – 14/11/1958
Comments: Tall, powerful striker

**ALLB – Allen Bradley**  Queens Park Rangers   **Striker**   0   2   5   DL$........
Born: Harold Wood – 13/09/1971
Comments: Another of the famous Allen clan

**ALCH – Allen Chris**  Oxford   **Striker**   0   0   1   DL$........
Born: Oxford – 18/11/1972
Comments: Product of the Youth team

**ALLC – Allen Clive**  West Ham United   **Striker**   11   7   13   DL$........
Born: London – 20/05/1961
Comments: Probably the most travelled £1m. player in the country

**ALLE – Allen Malcolm**  Millwall   **Striker**   2   7   6   DL$........
Born: Dioniolen – 21/03/1967
Comments: A member of the Welsh squad that can actually speak welsh

**ALLM – Allen Martin**  West Ham United   **Midfield**   11   5   2   DL$........
Born: Reading – 14/08/1965
Comments: Skilful midfielder

**ALLP – Allen Paul**  Tottenham Hotspur   **Midfield**   8   3   5   DL$........
Born: Aveley – 28/08/1962
Comments: Member of the second most famous family in football

**ALLW – Allison Wayne**  Bristol City   **Striker**   0   7   11   DL$........
Born: Huddersfield – 16/10/1968
Comments: Prolific scorer for the Robin's

**ALLO – Allon Joe**  Port Vale   **Striker**   18   33   2   DL$........
Born: Gateshead – 12/11/1966
Comments: Loan

**AMPA – Ampadu Kwame**  W.B.A.   **Striker**   0   2   3   DL$........
Born: Bradford – 20/12/1970
Comments: Albion always have one person with a silly name

> # Dream League Trivia
>
> *How many goals did Dixie Dean score in
> 1927/28 for Everton?*
>
> Answer: 60

**ANDC – Anderson Colin** Walsall  **Midfield**  0  2  3  DL$........
Born: Newcastle – 26/04/1962
Comments: Midfielder who likes to press forward

**ANDE – Anderson Viv** Sheffield Wednesday  **Defender**  0  3  4  DL$........
Born: Nottingham – 29/08/1956
Comments: Experience and occasionally a goal from the back

**ANDD – Anderton Darren** Tottenham  **Striker**  0  0  13  DL$........
Born: Southampton – 03/03/1972
Comments: Brilliant youngster, now coached by Venables

**ANGE – Angell Brett** Southend United  **Striker**  24  19  22  DL$........
Born: Marlborough – 20/08/1968
Comments: Natural goalscorer

**ANGU – Angus Terry** Northampton Town  **Defender**  0  2  2  DL$........
Born: Coventry – 14/01/1966
Comments: Commanding central defender

**ANSA – Ansah Andy** Southend United  **Striker**  1  9  9  DL$........
Born: Lewisham – 19/03/1969
Comments: Another of the Shrimpers prolific strikers

**ANTH – Anthrobus Steve** Wimbledon  **Striker**  4  0  0  DL$........
Born: Lewisham – 10/11/1968
Comments: Steve's lost his scoring touch

**ARCH – Archdeacon Owen** Barnsley  **Striker**  4  2  6  DL$........
Born: Greenock – 04/03/1966
Comments: Owen's rapidly becoming the Tykes arch goal scorer

**ARCS – Archibald Steve** Reading  **Striker**  2  0  0  DL$........
Born: Glasgow – 27/09/1956
Comments: Steves getting a bit long in the tooth

**ARMS – Armstrong Chris** Millwall  **Striker**  3  10  5  DL$........
Born: Newcastle – 19/06/1971
Comments: Skilful youngster

**ARMG – Armstrong Gordon** Sunderland  **Midfield**  12  6  11  DL$........
Born: Newcastle – 15/07/1969
Comments: Brilliant youngster from YTS

**ARNS – Arnott Sandy** Gillingham  **Striker**  0  0  3  DL$........
Born: Chatham – 18/10/1973
Comments: Product of the Gills Youth Team

**ASHB – Ashby Barry** Watford  **Defender**  1  0  0  DL$........
Born: London – 21/11/1970
Comments: Central defender who reads the game well

# PLAYER GUIDE

## 90 91 92

**ASHC – Ashcroft Lee** Preston North End   **Striker**   0   1   5   DL$........
Born: Preston – 07/09/1972
Comments: Lee's an exciting young winger

**ASHD – Ashdjian John** Scarborough   **Midfield**   0   0   10   DL$........
Born: London – 13/09/1972
Comments: Prolific and skilful

**ASHK – Ashley Kevin** Wolverhampton W.   **Defender**   1   0   1   DL$........
Born: Birmingham – 31/12/1968
Comments: Regular goalscorer, 1 a season, a bad year '91

**ASHU – Ashurst Jack** Doncaster Rovers   **Defender**   0   1   0   DL$........
Born: Coatbridge – 12/10/1954
Comments: Jack's experience in defence is useful to the Rovers

**ASPI – Aspin Neil** Port Vale   **Defender**   0   1   0   DL$........
Born: Gateshead – 12/04/1965
Comments: Vale Park's popular central defender

**ASPW – Aspinall Warren** Portsmouth   **Striker**   0   6   6   DL$........
Born: Wigan – 13/09/1967
Comments: Warren can't score more than six

**ATKP – Atkin Paul** York City   **Defender**   1   0   1   DL$........
Born: Nottingham – 03/09/1969
Comments: "Hoof 2". Competes in the highest, longest ball competition

**ATKB – Atkins Bob** Preston North End   **Defender**   1   0   0   DL$........
Born: Leicester – 16/10/1962
Comments: Career has suffered through injury

**ATKM – Atkins Mark** Blackburn Rovers   **Defender**   9   4   6   DL$........
Born: Doncaster – 14/08/1968
Comments: A first team regular from apprentices

**ATBR – Atkinson Brian** Sunderland   **Midfield**   0   0   4   DL$........
Born: Darlington – 19/01/1971
Comments: Another of the promising youngsters at Roker Park

**ATKI – Atkinson Dalien** Aston Villa   **Striker**   14   0   1   DL$........
Born: Shrewsbury – 21/03/1968
Comments: Getting used to English football after a season in Spain

**ATGR – Atkinson Graeme** Hull City   **Midfield**   1   0   8   DL$........
Born: Hull – 11/11/1971
Comments: Product of the Tigers Youth Scheme

**ATTE – Atteveld Ray** Bristol City   **Midfield**   1   0   2   DL$........
Born: Amsterdam – 08/09/1966
Comments: Newly arrived from Goodison

**AUSD – Austin Dean** Tottenham Hotspur   **Defender**   0   1   2   DL$........
Born: Hemel Hempstead – 26/04/1970
Comments: Deans no mini in defence

**AYLO – Aylott Trevor** Oxford   **Striker**   2   1   6   DL$........
Born: London – 26/11/1957
Comments: Useful striker at the Manor Ground

**BABB – Babb Phil** Bradford   **Defender**   0   10   4   DL$........
Born: Lambeth – 30/11/1970
Comments: Popular with the fans at Valley Parade when up front

# DREAM LEAGUE – CHAPTER 10

**90 91 92**

BAID – **Bailey Danny**   Reading   **Midfield**   2   2   0   DL$........
Born: Leyton – 21/05/1964
Comments: Strong midfield player often likened to Terry Hurlock

BAIL – **Bailey Dennis**   Queens Park Rangers   **Striker**   19   6   11   DL$........
Born: Lambeth – 13/11/1965
Comments: Well travelled favourite with the Ranger's faithful

BAIJ – **Bailey John**   Bristol City   **Defender**   1   0   0   DL$........
Born: Liverpool – 01/04/1957
Comments: Another old-timer at Ashton gate

BAIC – **Bailie Colin**   Cambridge United   **Defender**   0   2   0   DL$........
Born: Belfast – 31/03/1964
Comments: Colins lost sight of goal

BAKG – **Baker Graham**   Fulham   **Midfield**   2   1   0   DL$........
Born: Southampton – 03/12/1958
Comments: Lord Lucan has been seen more often

BAKP – **Baker Paul**   Hartlepool United   **Striker**   17   13   16   DL$........
Born: Newcastle – 05/01/1963
Comments: Score's more than a baker's dozen

BALL – **Ball Kevin**   Sunderland   **Defender**   2   4   1   DL$........
Born: Hastings – 12/01/1964
Comments: Skilful back player

BAMB – **Bamber Dave**   Blackpool   **Striker**   3   17   33   DL$........
Born: St. Helens – 01/02/1959
Comments: Mr Goalscorer

BANG – **Banger Nicky**   Southampton   **Striker**   0   3   0   DL$........
Born: Southampton – 25/02/1971
Comments: Nicky's lost his touch around the box, not a sausage last year

BANK – **Banks Ian**   Barnsley   **Midfield**   3   2   2   DL$........
Born: Mexborough – 09/01/1961
Comments: Skilful left sided player, also a keen cricketer

BANN – **Bannister Gary**   Oxford   **Striker**   2   14   5   DL$........
Born: Warrington – 22/07/1960
Comments: Erratic, can't handle the rough and tumble. On loan

BARA – **Baraclough Ian**   Grimsby Town   **Striker**   2   0   0   DL$........
Born: Leicester – 04/12/1970
Comments: Contract Player

BARP – **Barber Philip**   Millwall   **Striker**   2   1   4   DL$........
Born: Tring – 10/06/1965
Comments: In and out of the first team

---

## Dream League Trivia

*In 1962 Bobby Tambling had a hot streak. How many games did it take to score 23 goals?*

Answer: Thirteen (He scored in twelve)

*How many did he score in the next three months?*

Answer: Not a lot

---

104

| PLAYER GUIDE | | | 90 | 91 | 92 | |
|---|---|---|---|---|---|---|
| BARD – **Bardsley David**  Q.P.R. | Defender | 1 | 0 | 1 | DL$........ |
| Born: Manchester – 11/09/1964 | | | | | |
| Comments: Dave can play in most positions on the park | | | | | |
| BARH – **Barham Mark**  Brighton & Hove A. | Midfield | 3 | 6 | 2 | DL$........ |
| Born: Folkestone – 12/07/1962 | | | | | |
| Comments: Can also play on the wing | | | | | |
| BARS – **Barker Simon**  Queens Park Rangers | Midfield | 5 | 2 | 8 | DL$........ |
| Born: Farnworth – 04/11/1964 | | | | | |
| Comments: Midfielder who likes to get in the box | | | | | |
| BAEE – **Barkus Lee**  Reading | Striker | 0 | 0 | 1 | DL$........ |
| Born: Wokingham – 07/12/1974 | | | | | |
| Comments: Product of the Youth Scheme, strange hairdo | | | | | |
| BARL – **Barlow Andy**  Oldham Athletic | Defender | 1 | 0 | 2 | DL$........ |
| Born: Oldham – 24/11/1965 | | | | | |
| Comments: Long time Latic, who came from the youth team | | | | | |
| BARM – **Barlow Martin**  Plymouth Argyle | Midfield | 0 | 1 | 4 | DL$........ |
| Born: Barnstable – 25/06/1971 | | | | | |
| Comments: Right winger, promising product of the YTS | | | | | |
| BARB – **Barnes Bobby**  Peterborough United | Striker | 19 | 16 | 13 | DL$........ |
| Born: Kingston – 17/12/1962 | | | | | |
| Comments: Prolific scorer | | | | | |
| BADA – **Barnes David**  Sheffield United | Defender | 0 | 1 | 0 | DL$........ |
| Born: London – 16/11/1961 | | | | | |
| Comments: Well travelled and experienced defender | | | | | |
| BARN – **Barnes John**  Liverpool | Striker | 28 | 17 | 4 | DL$........ |
| Born: Jamaica – 07/11/1963 | | | | | |
| Comments: England's enigma, now on the comeback after injury kicking tin cans | | | | | |
| BAPA – **Barnes Paul**  Stoke City | Striker | 0 | 0 | 3 | DL$........ |
| Born: Leicester – 16/11/1967 | | | | | |
| Comments: Back to top form after injury | | | | | |
| BONY – **Barness Antony**  Newcastle United | Defender | 0 | 0 | 1 | DL$........ |
| Born: London – 25/03/1972 | | | | | |
| Comments: Promising youngster | | | | | |
| BAGA – **Barnett Gary**  Huddersfield Town | Striker | 1 | 1 | 5 | DL$........ |
| Born: Stratford – 11/03/1963 | | | | | |
| Comments: Gary's making a strong comeback after injury | | | | | |
| BAAN – **Barnsley Andy**  Carlisle United | Defender | 3 | 0 | 7 | DL$........ |
| Born: Sheffield – 09/06/1962 | | | | | |
| Comments: Goal scoring defender, could be a kiss of life | | | | | |
| BARR – **Barr Billy**  Halifax Town | Defender | 2 | 1 | 5 | DL$........ |
| Born: Halifax – 21/01/1969 | | | | | |
| Comments: Sounds like a Western hero | | | | | |
| BATO – **Barras Tony**  Stockport County | Striker | 0 | 0 | 5 | DL$........ |
| Born: Teeside – 29/03/1971 | | | | | |
| Comments: Maybe next season | | | | | |
| BTON – **Barratt Tony**  York City | Defender | 4 | 1 | 3 | DL$........ |
| Born: Salford – 18/10/1965 | | | | | |
| Comments: Hmmmm...... | | | | | |

# Dream League Trivia

*Why was John Petrie unlucky playing for Arbroath in the 36-0 win over Bon Accord?*

Answer: He scored thirteen goals

**BARE – Barrett Earl**  Aston Villa  **Defender  4  3  2  DL$........**
Born: Rochdale – 28/04/1967
Comments: Skilful defender

**BADE – Barrick Dean**  Rotherham United  **Midfield  0  2  1  DL$........**
Born: Hemsworth – 30/09/1969
Comments: Combines good vision with excellent passing of the ball

**BAGR – Barrow Graham**  Chester City  **Midfield  1  0  4  DL$........**
Born: Chorley – 13/06/1954
Comments: Assistant manager back after injury

**BAWC – Bart-Williams Chris**  Sheffield Wed  **Midfield  0  2  1  DL$........**
Born: Freetown – 16/06/1974
Comments: Skilful midfielder

**BARK – Bartlett Kevin**  Notts County  **Striker  8  15  9  DL$........**
Born: Portsmouth – 12/10/1962
Comments: Another well travelled "Magpie"

**BART – Barton Warren**  Wimbledon  **Defender  0  3  1  DL$........**
Born: London – 19/03/1969
Comments: Warren was Wimbledon's Player of the Year 90/91

**BATE – Bates Jamie**  Brentford  **Defender  0  3  2  DL$........**
Born: London – 24/02/1968
Comments: Long serving Bee. Major honour :- Winning a TV from Rumblelows

**BATT – Batty David**  Leeds United  **Midfield  0  0  2  DL$........**
Born: Leeds – 02/12/1968
Comments: Another star from the youth side and Graham Taylor's key to 94?

**BAZE – Bazeley Darren**  Watford  **Striker  0  0  7  DL$........**
Born: Northampton – 05/10/1972
Comments: Skilful winger, product of the youth policy at Vicarage Road

**BEAD – Beadle Peter**  Tottenham  **Midfield  2  7  7  DL$........**
Born: London – 13/05/1972
Comments: Watch out Beadle's about

**BEAG – Beagrie Peter**  Everton  **Midfield  0  2  6  DL$........**
Born: Middlesbrough – 28/11/1965
Comments: Well travelled and experienced midfielder and back flipper

**BEAR – Beardsley Peter**  Everton  **Striker  15  13  19  DL$........**
Born: Newcastle – 18/01/1961
Comments: Never scored less than 12 goals a season, never got a 10

**BERU – Beardsmore Russell**  Blackburn R.  **Midfield  2  0  0  DL$........**
Born: Wigan – 28/09/1968
Comments: Loan

| PLAYER GUIDE | | 90 | 91 | 92 | |
|---|---|---|---|---|---|

**BEAC – Beauchamp Joey** Oxford  Striker  0  0  10  DL$........
Born: Oxford – 13/03/1971
Comments: Very skilful youngster enjoying the big time

**BECH – Beaumont Chris** Stockport County  Striker  5  15  3  DL$........
Born: Sheffield – 05/12/1965
Comments: Lost his edge this season

**BENI – Beaumont Nigel** Wrexham  Defender  3  1  0  DL$........
Born: Pontefract – 11/02/1967
Comments: Long time serving Robin

**BEAV – Beavon Stuart** Northampton Town  Midfield  5  11  3  DL$........
Born: Wolverhampton – 30/11/1958
Comments: Experience in midfield but can score

**BECK – Beckford Darren** Norwich City  Striker  21  24  10  DL$........
Born: Manchester – 12/05/1967
Comments: Club's record signing at £925,000 from Port Vale

**BECJ – Beckford Jason** Birmingham City  Striker  0  1  2  DL$........
Born: Manchester – 14/02/1970
Comments: Partly paid for by club member's

**BEES – Beesley Paul** Sheffield United  Defender  1  1  2  DL$........
Born: Wigan – 21/07/1965
Comments: Back to fitness after injury

**BEEC – Beeston Carl** Stoke City  Midfield  2  2  5  DL$........
Born: Stoke – 30/06/1967
Comments: Skilful midfielder who can also play in defence. Gets a good send off

**BELM – Bell Michael** Northampton Town  Midfield  0  0  4  DL$........
Born: Newcastle – 15/11/1971
Comments: Made it through the ranks

**BELG – Bellamy Gary** Cardiff City  Defender  3  3  0  DL$........
Born: Worksop – 04/07/1962
Comments: Loan

**BENB – Benbow Ian** Hereford  Midfield  1  0  0  DL$........
Born: Hereford – 09/01/1969
Comments: Ians lost it lately

**BENC – Benjamin Chris** Chesterfield  Striker  0  1  0  DL$........
Born: Sheffield – 05/12/1972
Comments: Product of the Spireites Youth Scheme

**BENJ – Benjamin Ian** Southend United  Midfield  5  13  9  DL$........
Born: Nottingham – 11/12/1961
Comments: Favourite with the crowd at Roots Hall

**BENG – Bennett Gary** Sunderland  Defender  7  2  3  DL$........
Born: Manchester – 04/12/1961
Comments: Tall, strong, solid defender

**BEGA – Bennett Gary** Chester City  Striker  1  4  13  DL$........
Born: Liverpool – 20/09/1963
Comments: Gary's on his second spell with the Blues

**BENM – Bennett Michael** Wimbledon  Midfield  1  0  1  DL$........
Born: London – 27/07/1969
Comments: Micky's coming back from injury

**DREAM LEAGUE - CHAPTER 10**   **90 91 92**

BENT – **Bennett Tom**   Wolverhampton W.   **Defender**   0   0   2   DL$........
Born: Falkirk – 12/12/1969
Comments: Canny Scot, but canny score?

BEIA – **Bennyworth Ian**   Hartlepool United   **Defender**   2   0   1   DL$........
Born: Hull – 15/01/1962
Comments: Finding the goal again

BEJU – **Bent Junior**   Stoke City   **Striker**   0   2   3   DL$........
Born: Huddersfield – 01/03/1970
Comments: Loan

BEJA – **Benton James**   Northampton Town   **Striker**   0   0   1   DL$........
Born: County Wexford – 19/04/1975
Comments: Young striker in need of wages

BERE – **Beresford John**   Portsmouth   **Midfield**   0   2   8   DL$........
Born: Sheffield – 04/09/1966
Comments: Popular player at Fratton Park? Anfield?

BERG – **Bergsson Gudni**   Tottenham Hotspur   **Defender**   0   1   1   DL$........
Born: Iceland – 21/07/1965
Comments: International defender, likes to go forward

BERN – **Bernard Paul**   Oldham Athletic   **Midfield**   0   1   5   DL$........
Born: Edinburgh – 30/12/1972
Comments: Good prospect from youth

BEGR – **Berry Greg**   Leyton Orient   **Striker**   1   7   11   DL$........
Born: Essex – 05/03/1971
Comments: Leading light in the club's sponsor a goal scheme

BERL – **Berry Les**   Maidstone United   **Defender**   0   2   0   DL$........
Born: Plumstead – 04/05/1956
Comments: Strong in defence, weak in attack

BERT – **Bertschin Keith**   Aldershot   **Striker**   11   1   3   DL$........
Born: Enfield – 25/08/1956
Comments: Who has picked him up?

BIGG – **Biggins Wayne**   Stoke City   **Striker**   10   12   24   DL$........
Born: Sheffield – 20/11/1961
Comments: Bertie's the Potter's number one hit man

BILL – **Billing Peter**   Coventry City   **Defender**   0   0   1   DL$........
Born: Liverpool – 24/10/1964
Comments: Skill and vision in defence

BICH – **Billy Chris**   Huddersfield Town   **Striker**   0   0   2   DL$........
Born: Huddersfield – 02/01/1973
Comments: Chris isn't silly around goal

---

## Dream League Trivia

*How many hat tricks did Bill Rawlings score in his career at Southampton?*

Answer: 10

| PLAYER GUIDE | | | 90 | 91 | 92 | |

BIRC – **Birch Paul**  Wolverhampton W.  **Midfield**  0  2  10  **DL$**........
Born: West Bromwich – 20/11/1962
Comments: More than six of the best from Paul

BIRT – **Birtles Garry**  Grimsby Town  **Striker**  1  1  1  **DL$**........
Born: Nottingham – 27/07/1956
Comments: The Mariners widely travelled striker, now in defence

BISC – **Bishop Charlie**  Barnsley  **Defender**  2  2  0  **DL$**........
Born: Nottingham – 16/02/1968
Comments: Steady, reliable defender

BISH – **Bishop Eddie**  Crewe Alexandra  **Midfield**  9  7  4  **DL$**........
Born: Liverpool – 28/11/1962
Comments: Loan

BISI – **Bishop Ian**  West Ham United  **Midfield**  3  6  1  **DL$**........
Born: Liverpool – 29/05/1965
Comments: Longest hair in the "Hammer's" squad

BISS – **Bissett Nicky**  Brighton & Hove A.  **Defender**  6  0  1  **DL$**........
Born: Fulham – 05/04/1964
Comments: Coming back from a broken leg

BLAC – **Black Kingsley**  Nottingham Forest  **Midfield**  11  9  6  **DL$**........
Born: Luton – 22/06/1968
Comments: Pressing strongly for a re-call to the first team our Cilla

BLCL – **Blackmore Clayton**  Manchester Utd  **Midfield**  3  6  4  **DL$**........
Born: Neath – 23/09/1964
Comments: Versatile, either in midfield or as a full-back

BLAI – **Blackstone Ian**  York City  **Striker**  0  6  11  **DL$**........
Born: Harrogate – 07/08/1964
Comments: "Grimace". Scares defenders witless by grinning at them

BLAD – **Blackwell Dean**  Wimbledon  **Defender**  0  0  1  **DL$**........
Born: London – 05/12/1969
Comments: Reliable defender

BLAM – **Blake Mark**  Shrewsbury Town  **Defender**  0  2  0  **DL$**........
Born: Portsmouth – 19/12/1967
Comments: Stylish defender who is a big favourite with the fan's

BLMA – **Blake Mark**  Aston Villa  **Midfield**  0  0  2  **DL$**........
Born: Nottingham – 16/12/1970
Comments: Product of Villa's youth policy

BLAK – **Blake Nathan**  Cardiff City  **Defender**  0  4  8  **DL$**........
Born: Cardiff – 27/01/1972
Comments: Skilful and prolific product from Youth Team

BLAN – **Blake Noel**  Stoke City  **Defender**  0  3  0  **DL$**........
Born: Jamaica – 12/01/1962
Comments: Mastermind. Specialist Subject:Football

BLIG – **Blissett Gary**  Brentford  **Striker**  12  12  18  **DL$**........
Born: Manchester – 29/06/1964
Comments: Basher Bliss, scorer of many goals and winner of many ko's

BLIS – **Blissett Luther**  Watford  **Striker**  18  21  12  **DL$**........
Born: W. Indies – 01/02/1958
Comments: 'Boomerang's' the Hornet's all time record scorer and favourite son

# DREAM LEAGUE – CHAPTER 10  90 91 92

> ## Dream League Trivia
>
> *Which team conceded the most and a record number of goals in Division One in 1930/31 over only 42 matches?*
>
> Answer: Blackpool 125

**BODI – Bodin Paul** Swindon Town     **Defender**   5   0   2   DL$........
Born: Cardiff – 13/09/1964
Comments: Finding the goal again even from the back

**BODL – Bodley Mick** Barnet     **Defender**   0   0   1   DL$........
Born: Hayes – 14/09/1967
Comments: Resolute defender who has an eye for goal

**BOGI – Bogie Ian** Millwall     **Midfield**   3   8   0   DL$........
Born: Newcastle – 06/12/1967
Comments: Goals have been Ian's bogie this year

**BOND – Bond Kevin** AFC Bournemouth     **Defender**   0   2   3   DL$........
Born: London – 22/06/1957
Comments: Old time still producing the goods

**BOOK – Booker Bob** Brentford     **Midfield**   8   3   2   DL$........
Born: Watford – 25/01/1958
Comments: Used to gracing the parks of the elite

**BORR – Borrows Brian** Coventry City     **Defender**   1   6   1   DL$........
Born: Liverpool – 20/12/1960
Comments: Skilful right back

**BORT – Borthwick John** Darlington     **Striker**   2   11   4   DL$........
Born: Hartlepool – 24/03/1964
Comments: Only played for two teams in ten years

**BOUL – Bould Steve** Arsenal     **Defender**   0   0   1   DL$........
Born: Stoke – 16/11/1962
Comments: Ever present in the Championship winning team

**BOWD – Bowden Jon** Rochdale     **Midfield**   1   5   9   DL$........
Born: Stockport – 21/01/1963
Comments: Sharp shooter for the Dale

**BOWE – Bowen Mark** Norwich City     **Defender**   7   1   4   DL$........
Born: Neath – 07/12/1963
Comments: Ex Spur's full-back

**BOWS – Bowen Stuart** W.B.A.     **Defender**   0   0   1   DL$........
Born: West Bromwich – 12/12/1972
Comments: Left back, nice line in tracksuits, T.V and Video repairs

**BOWY – Bowyer Gary** Nottingham Forest     **Defender**   2   0   0   DL$........
Born: Manchester – 22/06/1971
Comments: Trainee

**BRAC – Bracewell Paul** Sunderland     **Midfield**   2   0   0   DL$........
Born: Stoke – 19/07/1962
Comments: Suffered early on from serious injury

# PLAYER GUIDE                                             90 91 92

**BRAD – Bradley Darren**  W.B.A.          **Defender**   2  1  2    DL$........
Born: Birmingham – 24/11/1965
Comments: One of many full backs used this season

**BRAR – Bradley Russell**  Halifax Town   **Midfield**   1  2  3    DL$........
Born: Birmingham – 28/03/1966
Comments: Likes to get forward from midfield

**BRCA – Bradshaw Carl**  Sheffield United **Striker**    4  3  3    DL$........
Born: Sheffield – 02/10/1968
Comments: Started his career with Sheffield Wednesday

**BRAK – Brady Kieron**  Sunderland        **Midfield**   2  2  3    DL$........
Born: Glasgow – 17/09/1971
Comments: Another skilful young Rokerite

**BRAI – Brain Simon**  Hereford           **Striker**    0  8  14   DL$........
Born: Evesham – 31/03/1966
Comments: Uses his feet more than his head, not far from the gound

**BRAG – Brannan Ged**  Tranmere Rovers    **Defender**   0  1  1    DL$........
Born: Liverpool – 15/01/1972
Comments: One of the Rovers skilled youngsters

**BRAZ – Brazil Derek**  Manchester United **Defender**   0  0  1    DL$........
Born: Dublin – 14/12/1968
Comments: Cracked the nut this season for the first time

**BRGA – Brazil Gary**  Fulham             **Striker**    3  5  16   DL$........
Born: Tunbridge Wells – 19/09/1962
Comments: Lightweight but tricky and talented

**BREA – Breacker Tim**  West Ham United   **Defender**   1  1  2    DL$........
Born: Bicester – 02/07/1965
Comments: Competitive full-back

**BREM – Bremner Kevin**  Shrewsbury Town  **Striker**    13 6  2    DL$........
Born: Banff – 07/10/1957
Comments: From Dundee

**BREN – Brennan Mark**  Manchester City   **Midfield**   3  3  4    DL$........
Born: Rossendale – 04/10/1965
Comments: Mark's been gunning in the odd goal

**BRES – Bressington Graham**  Lincoln City **Defender**  2  0  0    DL$........
Born: Eton – 08/07/1966
Comments: Club captain, who can also play in midfield

**BRIE – Brien Tony**  Chesterfield        **Defender**   3  3  0    DL$........
Born: Dublin – 10/02/1969
Comments: Long timer at the Recreation Ground

**BGAR – Briggs Gary**  Blackpool          **Defender**   4  0  0    DL$........
Born: Leeds – 08/05/1958
Comments: Trying to get a regular place

**BRIG – Bright Mark**  Crystal Palace     **Striker**    15 13 21   DL$........
Born: Stoke – 06/06/1962
Comments: Looking for Mr. Wright, very fashionable

**BRII – Brightwell Ian**  Manchester City **Midfield**   2  0  1    DL$........
Born: Lutterworth – 09/04/1968
Comments: Play's either full-back or midfield

**DREAM LEAGUE – CHAPTER 10**　　　　　　　　**90 91 92**

BRIL – **Briley Les**　Brighton & Hove A.　**Midfield**　2　1　0　DL$........
Born: Lambeth – 02/10/1956
Comments: Les can't find goal these days

BRIR – **Briscoe Robert**　Derby County　**Defender**　1　0　0　DL$........
Born: Derby – 04/09/1969
Comments: Product of the Rams Youth

BROA – **Broadbent Graham**　Halifax Town　**Striker**　0　1　0　DL$........
Born: Halifax – 20/12/1958
Comments: Striker who's missed the goal

BROK – **Brock Kevin**　Newcastle United　**Midfield**　3　5　4　DL$........
Born: Middleton Stoney – 09/09/1962
Comments: Although skilful a bit of a damp squib

BROV – **Brockie Vincent**　Doncaster Rovers　**Defender**　3　3　0　DL$........
Born: Greenock – 02/02/1969
Comments: Vinnie's now a non-contract player

BROO – **Brooks Shaun**　AFC Bournemouth　**Midfield**　4　1　0　DL$........
Born: London – 09/10/1962
Comments: Scored the "Cherries" first ever second division goal

BRGR – **Brown Grant**　Lincoln City　**Defender**　2　1　2　DL$........
Born: Sunderland – 19/11/1969
Comments: Lincoln's joint record signing

BROJ – **Brown Jon**　Exeter City　**Defender**　0　0　1　DL$........
Born: Barnsley – 08/09/1966
Comments: Versatile player, who can play anywhere across the back four

BRKE – **Brown Kenny**　West Ham United　**Defender**　0　3　3　DL$........
Born: Barking – 11/07/1967
Comments: Normally full-back but can also play in midfield

BRMI – **Brown Mike**　Bolton Wanderers　**Striker**　1　2　2　DL$........
Born: Birmingham – 08/02/1968
Comments: Exciting right winger

BRNI – **Brown Nicky**　Hull City　**Striker**　2　0　1　DL$........
Born: Hull – 16/10/1966
Comments: Plays either at full back or central defender

BRPH – **Brown Phil**　Bolton Wanderers　**Defender**　2　0　3　DL$........
Born: South Shields – 30/05/1959
Comments: Solid and reliable in defence

BROS – **Brown Steve**　Northampton Town　**Striker**　1　3　3　DL$........
Born: Northampton – 06/07/1966
Comments: On his second spell with Northampton

---

## Dream League Trivia

*Who was the first post-war footballer to score an aggregate of 100 goals in two consecutive seasons?*

Answer: Steve Bull

| PLAYER GUIDE | | 90 91 92 |

BROW – **Browne Cory**  Fulham   **Midfield**   0  0  1   DL$........
Born: Edmington – 02/07/1970
Comments: Scored on his debut – been injured since then

BRUC – **Bruce Steve**  Manchester United   **Defender**   3  15  6   DL$........
Born: Newcastle – 31/12/1960
Comments: Steve's the man for the spot kick's

BRYA – **Bryant Matthew**  Bristol City   **Defender**   0  1  2   DL$........
Born: Bristol – 21/09/1970
Comments: Product of the youth policy

BRYS – **Bryson Ian**  Sheffield United   **Midfield**   11  7  9   DL$........
Born: Kilmarnock – 26/11/1962
Comments: Experience midfield, sharp goal scorer

BUCK – **Buckle Paul**  Brentford   **Midfield**   0  0  1   DL$........
Born: Hatfield – 16/12/1970
Comments: "No neck", under-rated midfielder

BUCJ – **Buckley John**  Scunthorpe United   **Striker**   7  1  6   DL$........
Born: Glasgow – 10/05/1962
Comments: Must be a Quaker as he refuses to tackle back

BUCN – **Buckley Neil**  Hull City   **Defender**   0  3  0   DL$........
Born: Hull – 25/09/1968
Comments: Another promising young Tiger

BULG – **Bull Gary**  Barnet   **Striker**   0  0  26   DL$........
Born: West Bromwich – 12/06/1966
Comments: Cousin of Wolves goal poacher Steve

BULL – **Bull Steve**  Wolverhampton W.   **Striker**   27  26  23   DL$........
Born: Tipton – 28/03/1965
Comments: Ultimate dream player, goals guaranteed

BULW – **Bullmore Wayne**  Barnsley   **Midfield**   0  0  1   DL$........
Born: Sutton-in-Ashfield – 12/09/1970
Comments: Trainee

BUMS – **Bumstead John**  Charlton Athletic   **Midfield**   2  1  0   DL$........
Born: Rotherhithe – 27/11/1958
Comments: Veteran from Chelsea, bags of experience in midfield

BURG – **Burgess Daryl**  W.B.A.   **Defender**   0  0  2   DL$........
Born: Birmingham – 20/04/1971
Comments: Skinhead haircut belies class and pace

BURD – **Burgess Dave**  Blackpool   **Defender**   2  0  0   DL$........
Born: Liverpool – 20/01/1960
Comments: Daves stuck in his own half

BURK – **Burke David**  Bolton Wanderers   **Defender**   0  0  1   DL$........
Born: Liverpool – 06/08/1960
Comments: Dave's back where he started

BURM – **Burke Mark**  Wolverhampton W.   **Striker**   1  0  3   DL$........
Born: Solihull – 12/02/1969
Comments: Enough said

BUJA – **Burnham Jason**  Northampton Town   **Striker**   0  0  2   DL$........
Born: Mansfield – 08/05/1973
Comments: Could be one of the Cobbler's best

DREAM LEAGUE – CHAPTER 10     90 91 92

---

## Dream League Trivia

*Who was the youngest player to score five goals in one First Division game?*

Answer: Jimmy Greaves

---

**BURC** – **Burns Christopher**  Portsmouth  **Midfield**  0  0  9  DL$........
Born: Manchester – 09/11/1967
Comments: Scorches through the opposition's defence

**BURW** – **Burns Willie**  Rochdale  **Defender**  2  1  0  DL$........
Born: Motherwell – 10/12/1969
Comments: Alright on the night games

**BURA** – **Burrows Adrian**  Plymouth Argyle  **Defender**  1  4  3  DL$........
Born: Sutton – 16/01/1959
Comments: Good solid defender

**BUDA** – **Burrows David**  Liverpool  **Defender**  0  0  1  DL$........
Born: Dudley – 25/10/1968
Comments: Played for the Football League XI in 90/91

**BUTB** – **Butler Barry**  Chester City  **Defender**  5  5  6  DL$........
Born: Farnworth – 04/06/1962
Comments: Tall, hard working defender

**BUTJ** – **Butler John**  Stoke City  **Defender**  0  2  3  DL$........
Born: Liverpool – 07/02/1962
Comments: Been known to read the Sporting Life

**BUPE** – **Butler Peter**  Huddersfield Town  **Midfield**  2  3  0  DL$........
Born: Halifax – 27/08/1966
Comments: Loan

**BUTL** – **Butler Steve**  Watford  **Striker**  23  1  8  DL$........
Born: Birmingham – 27/01/1962
Comments: A battler, the man the crowd loves to hate

**BUTG** – **Butters Guy**  Portsmouth  **Defender**  3  0  3  DL$........
Born: Hillingdon – 30/10/1969
Comments: Guy's got an eye for a goal or three

**BUGA** – **Butterworth Garry**  Peterborough Utd  **Midfield**  3  0  1  DL$........
Born: Peterborough – 08/09/1969
Comments: Reliable at left-back

**BUTI** – **Butterworth Ian**  Norwich City  **Defender**  0  0  1  DL$........
Born: Crewe – 25/01/1965
Comments: Another of the Canaries central defenders

**BYRN** – **Byrne David**  Fulham  **Striker**  0  2  2  DL$........
Born: London – 05/03/1961
Comments: Loan and Talking Head

**BYRJ** – **Byrne John**  Sunderland  **Striker**  4  11  21  DL$........
Born: Manchester – 01/02/1961
Comments: John's the ideal dream striker

# PLAYER GUIDE                                           90 91 92

**CAFF** – **Caffrey Henry**   Hereford           Striker    0  0  2   DL$........
Born: Paisley – 15/02/1966
Comments: Henry's beginning to find the net

**CALD** – **Calderwood Colin**   Swindon Town   Defender   3  2  6   DL$........
Born: Stranraer – 20/01/1965
Comments: Colins a strong, goalscoring defender

**CADA** – **Caldwell Dave**   Chesterfield      Striker    0  6  0   DL$........
Born: Aberdeen – 31/07/1960
Comments: Well travelled Spireite

**CALA** – **Callaghan Aaron**   Crewe Alexandra  Defender  2  1  2   DL$........
Born: Dublin – 08/10/1966
Comments: Served a long time at Gresty Road

**CALV** – **Calvert Mark**   Hull City          Striker    0  0  1   DL$........
Born: Consett – 11/09/1970
Comments: Useful young Tiger

**CAME** – **Came Mark**   Bolton Wanderers      Defender   2  0  0   DL$........
Born: Exeter – 14/09/1961
Comments: Come back to full fitness after breaking a leg

**CAMD** – **Campbell David**   Huddersfield Town  Defender  3  0  0   DL$........
Born: Dublin – 13/09/1969
Comments: Dave's lost sight of goal in a haze of Pea and Ham

**CAMG** – **Campbell Greg**   Northampton Town  Striker    3  5  3   DL$........
Born: Portsmouth – 13/07/1965
Comments: Song of Bobby

**CAMP** – **Campbell Kevin**   Arsenal          Striker    5 10 13   DL$........
Born: Lambeth – 04/02/1970
Comments: Another product of the Gunner's youth policy

**CANH** – **Canham Tony**   York City           Midfield   4  7  6   DL$........
Born: Leeds – 08/06/1960
Comments: Yet another "God". Folk hero at Bootham Crescent

**CANT** – **Cantona Eric**   Leeds United       Striker    0  0  3   DL$........
Born: Marseille – 24/09/1966
Comments: Artist on and off the canvas

**CARB** – **Carberry Jimmy**   Wigan Athletic   Midfield   4  3  0   DL$........
Born: Liverpool – 13/10/1969
Comments: Another Liverpool born, ex Evertonion at Springfield Park

**CARE** – **Carey Brian**   Manchester Utd      Defender   0  0  1   DL$........
Born: Cork – 31/05/1968
Comments: Good young player – Ceefax!

**CARM** – **Carmichael Matt**   Lincoln City    Striker    0  2  7   DL$........
Born: Singapore – 13/05/1964
Comments: Ex-soldier, now more a defender than striker

**CARP** – **Carpenter Richard**   Gillingham    Midfield   0  1  0   DL$........
Born: Sheppey – 30/09/1972
Comments: Chisels out openings in midfield

**CARR** – **Carr Cliff**   Shrewsbury Town      Midfield   0  0  2   DL$........
Born: London – 19/06/1964
Comments: Tall, rock in midfield

**DREAM LEAGUE – CHAPTER 10**　　　　　　　**90 91 92**

CARD – **Carr Darren**　Crewe Alexandra　　**Defender**　0　1　3　DL$........
Born: Bristol – 04/09/1968
Comments: Likes to score the odd goal

CARF – **Carr Franz**　Newcastle United　　**Midfield**　0　2　2　DL$........
Born: Preston – 24/09/1966
Comments: Never fit

CART – **Carter Danny**　Leyton Orient　　**Striker**　7　6　2　DL$........
Born: Hackney – 29/06/1969
Comments: Back on the warpath after injury... Hamstring

CARJ – **Carter Jimmy**　Arsenal　　**Midfield**　3　0　0　DL$........
Born: London – 09/11/1965
Comments: Waiting for a chance

CAMA – **Carter Mark**　Barnet　　**Striker**　0　0　27　DL$........
Born: Liverpool – 17/12/1960
Comments: If Gary doesn't get them Mark does

CSTE – **Carter Steve**　Scarborough　　**Striker**　0　3　0　DL$........
Born: Sunderland – 13/04/1972
Comments: Showing promise

CARL – **Cartwright Lee**　Preston North End　**Midfield**　0　1　4　DL$........
Born: Rawtenstall – 19/09/1972
Comments: Promising young star from the Youth Team

CASC – **Cascarino Tony**　Chelsea　　**Striker**　2　10　2　DL$........
Born: St.Paul's Cray – 01/09/1962
Comments: From Celtic.

CASE – **Case Jimmy**　AFC Bournemouth　　**Midfield**　3　2　1　DL$........
Born: Liverpool – 18/05/1954
Comments: Vastly experienced team captain

CASH – **Cash Stuart**　Shrewsbury Town　　**Defender**　1　0　1　DL$........
Born: Tipton – 05/09/1965
Comments: Loan

CAST – **Castle Steve**　Leyton Orient　　**Midfield**　9　18　11　DL$........
Born: Barkingside – 17/05/1966
Comments: Another "O" coming back from injury, this time it's knees

CATO – **Caton Tommy**　Charlton Athletic　　**Defender**　1　3　0　DL$........
Born: Liverpool – 06/10/1962
Comments: Almost best centre-half in England (80)'s, almost fit

CECE – **Cecere Michele**　Walsall　　**Striker**　4　6　8　DL$........
Born: Chester – 04/01/1968
Comments: What a name, but what a striker

---

## Dream League Trivia

*Who scored nine hat tricks in one season,
the most ever?*

Answer: George Camsell – Middlesbrough 1926/27

# PLAYER GUIDE

**90 91 92**

**CHMY – Chalk Martyn**  Derby County  **Striker**  0  0  2  **DL$........**
Born: Louth – 30/08/1969
Comments: Stick like striker

**CHAL – Chalmers Paul**  Swansea City  **Striker**  6  2  8  **DL$........**
Born: Glasgow – 31/10/1963
Comments: Stylish forward who has been in and out of the first team

**CHMA – Chamberlain Mark**  Portsmouth  **Striker**  6  4  1  **DL$........**
Born: Stoke – 19/11/1961
Comments: Over shadowed as a Pompey striker

**CHAJ – Channing Justin**  Q.P.R  **Defender**  2  0  0  **DL$........**
Born: Reading – 19/11/1968
Comments: Justin's just out

**CHAG – Chapman Gary**  Exeter City  **Striker**  4  0  4  **DL$........**
Born: Leeds – 01/05/1964
Comments: Quick skilful striker regaining his touch

**CHAI – Chapman Ian**  Brighton & Hove A.  **Striker**  0  0  4  **DL$........**
Born: Brighton – 31/05/1970
Comments: Skilful product of the Youth Scheme at the Goldstone Ground

**CHAP – Chapman Lee**  Leeds United  **Striker**  12  28  20  **DL$........**
Born: Lincoln – 05/12/1959
Comments: Lay's siege to the oppositions goal, big money prospect

**CHAV – Chapman Vincent**  Rochdale  **Defender**  0  1  0  **DL$........**
Born: Newcastle – 05/12/1967
Comments: Vinnie doesn't often worry the score sheet

**CHSH – Chappell Shaun**  Swansea City  **Midfield**  0  0  3  **DL$........**
Born: Swansea – 14/02/1973
Comments: Promising young player

**CHPH – Chapple Phil**  Cambridge United  **Defender**  6  5  3  **DL$........**
Born: Norwich – 26/11/1966
Comments: Tall, strong defender, who's not afraid to get forward

**CHAR – Chard Phil**  Northampton Town  **Midfield**  2  7  4  **DL$........**
Born: Corby – 16/10/1960
Comments: Phil's the Cobbler's utility player and manager

**CHKE – Charlery Ken**  Peterborough United  **Striker**  2  10  22  **DL$........**
Born: Stepney – 28/11/1964
Comments: Probably the Posh's most consistent scorer

**CHGA – Charles Gary**  Nottingham Forest  **Defender**  0  1  1  **DL$........**
Born: London – 13/04/1970
Comments: Cup Final performance earned a England place for summer tour

**CHST – Charles Steve**  Mansfield Town  **Midfield**  7  6  8  **DL$........**
Born: Sheffield – 10/05/1960
Comments: Steve's the Stags veteran

**CHSI – Charlton Simon**  Huddersfield Town  **Defender**  0  0  1  **DL$........**
Born: Huddersfield – 25/10/1971
Comments: Promising product of the youth policy at Leed's Road

**CHEE – Cheetham Michael**  Cambridge Utd  **Midfield**  11  8  3  **DL$........**
Born: Amsterdam – 30/06/1967
Comments: Vision in midfield

DREAM LEAGUE - CHAPTER 10              90 91 92

> # Dream League Trivia
>
> *Which team has been awarded the most penalties at home in League and Cup matches?*
>
> Answer: Liverpool

**CHET – Chettle Steve**   Nottingham Forest   **Defender**   1   3   1   DL$........
Born: Nottingham – 27/09/1968
Comments: Making a great impression at the City Ground

**CHIL – Childs Gary**   Grimsby Town   **Midfield**   6   4   3   DL$........
Born: Birmingham – 19/04/1964
Comments: Skilful midfielder with an eye for goal

**CHIV – Chivers Gary**   Brighton & Hove A.   **Defender**   3   3   1   DL$........
Born: Stockwell – 15/05/1960
Comments: Experienced central defender

**CLAS – Claridge Steve**   Cambridge United   **Striker**   4   12   14   DL$........
Born: Portsmouth – 10/04/1966
Comments: Owner of a serious haircut

**CLAB – Clark Billy**   Bristol Rovers   **Defender**   0   1   1   DL$........
Born: Christchurch – 19/05/1967
Comments: Quick tackling, solid and reliable defender

**CLAL – Clark Lee**   Newcastle United   **Midfield**   0   2   5   DL$........
Born: Wallsend – 27/10/1972
Comments: Only man to injure himself in the tunnel before game

**CLAM – Clark Martin**   Mansfield Town   **Midfield**   1   0   0   DL$........
Born: Uddington – 13/10/1968
Comments: Martin never leaves the centre circle

**CLAA – Clarke Andy**   Wimbledon   **Striker**   0   3   4   DL$........
Born: London – 22/07/1967
Comments: Exciting player with blistering pace

**CLAR – Clarke Colin**   Portsmouth   **Striker**   9   17   7   DL$........
Born: Newry – 30/10/1962
Comments: Sharp striker who's always looking for a goal

**CLAD – Clarke David**   Lincoln City   **Midfield**   2   0   0   DL$........
Born: Nottingham – 03/12/1964
Comments: Save your dollars

**CLMI – Clarke Mick**   Scarborough   **Striker**   1   0   0   DL$........
Born: Birmingham – 22/12/1967
Comments: Fast becoming an Imp veteran

**CLAN – Clarke Nicky**   Mansfield Town   **Defender**   0   0   1   DL$........
Born: Walsall – 20/08/1967
Comments: Not a good investment

**CLST – Clarke Stephen**   Chelsea   **Defender**   5   1   1   DL$........
Born: Saltcoats – 29/08/1963
Comments: Solid reliable defender

# PLAYER GUIDE

**90 91 92**

CLAW – **Clarke Wayne**  Manchester City  **Striker**  1  10  1  **DL$........**
Born: Wolverhampton – 28/02/1961
Comments: Younger brother of former Leed's and England star Allan

CLPH – **Clarkson Phil**  Crewe Alexandra  **Midfield**  0  0  7  **DL$........**
Born: Hamilton – 13/11/1968
Comments: Sharpshooter for the Railwaymen

CLAG – **Clayton Gary**  Cambridge United  **Midfield**  1  0  0  **DL$........**
Born: Sheffield – 02/02/1963
Comments: Gary's forgotten where the goal is

CLOS – **Close Shaun**  Swindon Town  **Striker**  0  1  1  **DL$........**
Born: Islington – 08/09/1966
Comments: Doesn't often get close to goal

CLOU – **Clough Nigel**  Nottingham Forest  **Striker**  12  19  8  **DL$........**
Born: Sunderland – 19/03/1966
Comments: The "Red's" top scorer for five of the past six season's

COAT – **Coatsworth Gary**  Leicester City  **Defender**  0  1  1  **DL$........**
Born: Sunderland – 07/10/1968
Comments: Tall, skilful defender

COCK – **Cockerill Glenn**  Southampton  **Midfield**  5  2  6  **DL$........**
Born: Grimsby – 25/08/1959
Comments: Long timer at the Dell

COCJ – **Cockerill John**  Grimsby Town  **Midfield**  6  7  1  **DL$........**
Born: Cleethorpes – 12/07/1961
Comments: Another of the Mariners prolific midfielders

COCA – **Cockram Allan**  Reading  **Midfield**  2  3  1  **DL$........**
Born: Kensington – 08/01/1963
Comments: Rarely troubles the opposition goal

CODN – **Codner Robert**  Brighton & Hove A.  **Midfield**  10  8  7  **DL$........**
Born: Walthamstow – 23/01/1965
Comments: One of the crowds favourites at Goldstone

COSC – **Colcombe Scott**  Torquay United  **Striker**  0  0  1  **DL$........**
Born: West Bromwich – 15/12/1971
Comments: Impressive youngster, best yet to come

COLE – **Cole Andrew**  Arsenal  **Striker**  0  0  11  **DL$........**
Born: Nottingham – 15/10/1971
Comments: Loaned to Bristol City for goals

COLD – **Cole David**  Rochdale  **Defender**  5  2  0  **DL$........**
Born: Barnsley – 28/09/1962
Comments: Back home after tour of mining towns

COLC – **Coleman Chris**  Crystal Palace  **Defender**  2  0  4  **DL$........**
Born: Swansea – 10/06/1970
Comments: Mustard hot full-back turned striker

CODA – **Coleman David**  AFC Bournemouth  **Defender**  1  0  0  **DL$........**
Born: Salisbury – 08/04/1967
Comments: Product of the "Cherries" youth scheme

COLS – **Coleman Simon**  Derby County  **Midfield**  1  1  2  **DL$........**
Born: Worksop – 13/03/1968
Comments: Settled in well at the Baseball ground

**DREAM LEAGUE – CHAPTER 10**　　　　　　　**90 91 92**

COST – **Collymore Stan**   Crystal Palace    **Striker**   0   0   2   DL$........
Born: Stone – 22/01/1971
Comments: My friend Stan's the man

COLQ – **Colquhoun John**   Millwall    **Striker**   6   0   4   DL$........
Born: Stirling – 14/07/1963
Comments: From Hearts

COMS – **Comstive Paul**   Chester City    **Midfield**   2   3   3   DL$........
Born: Southport – 25/11/1961
Comments: Refuses to score more than three a season

COMY – **Comyn Andy**   Derby County    **Defender**   0   0   3   DL$........
Born: Manchester – 02/06/1968
Comments: Tall, tough tackling defender

COND – **Connelly Dean**   Barnsley    **Striker**   0   0   2   DL$........
Born: Glasgow – 06/01/1970
Comments: "Dino" is now finding his way around the box

CONC – **Connelly Karl**   Wrexham    **Striker**   0   0   9   DL$........
Born: Prescot – 09/02/1970
Comments: Karl's the Robins hit man

CONT – **Connor Terry**   Bristol City    **Striker**   3   7   2   DL$........
Born: Leeds – 09/11/1962
Comments: A recent arrival at Ashton Gate

CONR – **Conroy Mike**   Burnley    **Striker**   3   1   29   DL$........
Born: Glasgow – 31/12/1965
Comments: Mike's the Claret's strongest striker

COOA – **Cook Andy**   Exeter City    **Defender**   1   0   0   DL$........
Born: Romsey – 10/08/1969
Comments: Cookie's a strong tackling left back

COOJ – **Cook Jason**   Southend United    **Midfield**   1   0   0   DL$........
Born: Edmonton – 29/12/1969
Comments: Too many Cooks, can't score

COMI – **Cook Mitch**   Blackpool    **Midfield**   3   1   4   DL$........
Born: Scarborough – 15/10/1961
Comments: Mitch is lucky to get a look in when Bamber's about

COOK – **Cook Paul**   Wolverhampton W.    **Midfield**   2   6   8   DL$........
Born: Liverpool – 22/02/1967
Comments: Better left foot than Delia Smith

COJO – **Cooke John**   Chesterfield    **Striker**   1   2   8   DL$........
Born: Salford – 25/04/1962
Comments: John's a fave at the Recreation Ground

---

## Dream League Trivia

*Who was the First Division's top scorer in 73/74 and was still relegated?*

Answer: Mick Channon – Southampton – 21 goals

120

| PLAYER GUIDE | | | 90 | 91 | 92 | |
|---|---|---|---|---|---|---|

**COOR – Cooke Richard** AFC Bournemouth **Striker** 1 2 1 DL$........
Born: Islington – 04/09/1965
Comments: Return of an old "Cherry"

**COOC – Cooper Colin** Millwall **Defender** 2 0 2 DL$........
Born: Durham – 28/02/1967
Comments: Coming back from a ligament injury

**COOD – Cooper David** Plymouth Argyle **Striker** 0 0 2 DL$........
Born: London – 23/06/1971
Comments: Youngster with an eye for goal

**COOG – Cooper Gary** Peterborough Utd **Midfield** 4 4 5 DL$........
Born: Edgeware – 20/11/1965
Comments: High noon in midfield

**COGE – Cooper Geoff** Barnet **Defender** 0 0 1 DL$........
Born: Kingston – 27/12/1960
Comments: Signed as a forward, plays at full-back

**COGR – Cooper Graham** Halifax Town **Midfield** 3 1 4 DL$........
Born: Bolton – 18/11/1965
Comments: Likes to pop up now and then to score

**COOP – Cooper Mark** Birmingham City **Midfield** 1 11 5 DL$........
Born: Wakefield – 18/12/1968
Comments: Son of Terry, Mark's a dead ball specialist

**COMA – Cooper Mark** Leyton Orient **Striker** 12 9 7 DL$........
Born: Cambridge – 05/04/1967
Comments: Always gets a few does Mark

**CSTV – Cooper Steve** Peterborough United **Striker** 7 2 1 DL$........
Born: Birmingham – 22/06/1964
Comments: Loan

**CORD – Cordner Scott** Chesterfield **Striker** 0 1 0 DL$........
Born: Grimsby – 03/08/1972
Comments: Product of the Youth Scheme at the Recreation Ground

**CORK – Cork Alan** Sheffield United **Striker** 6 6 4 DL$........
Born: Derby – 04/03/1959
Comments: "Corky", has scored in all four League division's

**CDAI – Cork David** Darlington **Midfield** 1 12 3 DL$........
Born: Doncaster – 28/10/1962
Comments: Widely travelled midfielder

**CORN – Corner David** Darlington **Defender** 3 0 0 DL$........
Born: Sunderland – 15/05/1966
Comments: Strong tackling defender

**CORJ – Cornforth John** Swansea City **Defender** 1 0 0 DL$........
Born: Whitley Bay – 07/01/1967
Comments: John's recovering from a broken leg

**CJOH – Cornwell John** Southend United **Defender** 0 2 0 DL$........
Born: Bethnal Green – 13/10/1964
Comments: Tall, experienced defender

**COSP – Costello Peter** Peterborough United **Striker** 0 13 0 DL$........
Born: Halifax – 31/10/1969
Comments: Peter's lost his touch around goal

# DREAM LEAGUE – CHAPTER 10

## Dream League Trivia

*Who is the only player to score while playing a total of less than 90 minutes for England?*

Answer: Paul Goddard, West Ham, v. Iceland '82. Sub 40 mins.

---

**COTT – Cottee Tony**  Everton  **Striker**  15  16  9  DL$........
Born: West Ham – 11/07/1965
Comments: Everton's top scorer in the past 3 season's

**COTS – Cotterill Steve**  Wimbledon  **Striker**  1  1  0  DL$........
Born: Cheltenham – 20/07/1964
Comments: Steve's another "Don" whose lost his scoring touch

**COUG – Coughlin Russell**  Swansea City  **Midfield**  1  0  1  DL$........
Born: Swansea – 15/02/1960
Comments: Veteran member of the midfield unit

**COVO – Coverdale Drew**  Darlington  **Defender**  1  3  0  DL$........
Born: Teeside – 20/09/1969
Comments: Young full back and the clubs physiotherapist

**COWA – Cowans Gordon**  Blackburn Rovers  **Midfield**  4  1  2  DL$........
Born: Durham – 27/10/1958
Comments: Strength, experience and vision in midfield

**COWD – Cowdrill Barry**  Rochdale  **Defender**  4  1  1  DL$........
Born: Birmingham – 03/01/1957
Comments: Barry drills them home, occasionally

**CRAN – Cranson Ian**  Stoke City  **Defender**  2  0  3  DL$........
Born: Easington – 02/07/1964
Comments: Ian's another Potter who is on the comeback trail

**CROF – Croft Brian**  Chester City  **Midfield**  4  4  0  DL$........
Born: Chester – 27/09/1967
Comments: Another old boy returned home

**CROO – Crook Ian**  Norwich City  **Midfield**  0  4  1  DL$........
Born: Romford – 18/01/1963
Comments: Another refugee from White Hart Lane

**CROG – Crosby Gary**  Nottingham Forest  **Midfield**  8  5  3  DL$........
Born: Sleaford – 08/05/1964
Comments: Skilful midfielder

**CRON – Cross Nicky**  Port Vale  **Striker**  14  2  0  DL$........
Born: Birmingham – 07/02/1961
Comments: Experienced goalscorer

**CRST – Cross Steve**  Bristol Rovers  **Defender**  0  0  2  DL$........
Born: Wolverhampton – 22/12/1959
Comments: Steves found the net

**CROW – Crown David**  Gillingham  **Striker**  22  12  23  DL$........
Born: Enfield – 16/02/1958
Comments: Experienced striker, who hasn't lost his touch

## PLAYER GUIDE

                                                90 91 92

CRUM – **Crumplin John**  Brighton & Hove A.  **Midfield**  2  0  0  DL$........
Born: Bath – 26/05/1967
Comments: Experienced Seagull, who can play full back

CUGG – **Cuggy Steve**  Maidstone United  **Striker**  0  0  1  DL$........
Born: Newcastle – 18/03/1971
Comments: Young star at Watling Street

CULL – **Cullen David**  Doncaster Rovers  **Defender**  0  0  1  DL$........
Born: Durham – 10/01/1973
Comments: Product of the Youth Scheme at Belle Vue

CULT – **Cullen Tony**  Sunderland  **Striker**  1  1  0  DL$........
Born: Newcastle – 30/09/1969
Comments: Usually out on loan

CUND – **Cundy Jason**  Tottenham Hotspur  **Defender**  0  1  1  DL$........
Born: Wimbledon – 12/11/1969
Comments: One of Ken's clear outs

CUNN – **Cunningham Tony**  Rotherham Utd  **Striker**  8  14  20  DL$........
Born: Jamaica – 12/11/1957
Comments: Much travelled striker

CUNS – **Cunnington Shaun**  Grimsby Town  **Defender**  3  2  6  DL$........
Born: Bourne – 04/01/1966
Comments: Skilful defender who likes to get forward

CURB – **Curbishley Alan**  Charlton Athletic  **Midfield**  2  0  0  DL$........
Born: Forest Gate – 08/11/1957
Comments: From ranks to player-manager, cultured midfielder of his day

CURL – **Curle Keith**  Manchester City  **Defender**  3  1  5  DL$........
Born: Bristol – 14/11/1963
Comments: Curly's the man for the spot kick's

CURR – **Curran Chris**  Scarborough  **Defender**  0  0  2  DL$........
Born: Manchester – 06/01/1971
Comments: Useful young defender

CURD – **Currie David**  Barnsley  **Striker**  2  4  8  DL$........
Born: Stockton – 27/11/1962
Comments: Hot stuff is david

CUSA – **Cusack Nick**  Darlington  **Midfield**  0  0  6  DL$........
Born: Rotherham – 24/12/1965
Comments: From Motherwell

DAIS – **Daish Liam**  Cambridge United  **Defender**  1  1  0  DL$........
Born: Portsmouth – 23/09/1968
Comments: Consistent at the back

DALE – **Dale Carl**  Cardiff City  **Striker**  9  14  23  DL$........
Born: Colwyn Bay – 29/04/1966
Comments: Carl's the bluebirds No. 1 striker

DALP – **Daley Phillip**  Wigan Athletic  **Striker**  6  10  14  DL$........
Born: Walton – 12/04/1967
Comments: Phil's a productive striker who's good in the air

DATO – **Daley Tony**  Aston Villa  **Striker**  8  4  7  DL$........
Born: Birmingham – 18/10/1967
Comments: Tony's a Villa veteran at only 25, GT School for internationals

**DREAM LEAGUE – CHAPTER 10**                    **90 91 92**

DALT – **Dalton Paul**   Hartlepool United   Midfield   12 12 14   DL$........
Born: Middlesborough – 25/04/1967
Comments: Dangerous and skilful winger

DALZ – **Dalziel Ian**   Carlisle United   Defender   1   0   0   DL$........
Born: South Shields – 24/10/1962
Comments: Good in defence, poor in attack

DANI – **Daniel Ray**   Portsmouth   Midfield   1   0   0   DL$........
Born: Luton – 10/12/1964
Comments: Ray's no longer scaring goalie's

DANS – **Daniels Scott**   Exeter City   Midfield   0   0   3   DL$........
Born: Benfleet – 22/11/1969
Comments: One of the favourite's at St. James Park

DARD – **Darby Dwayne**   Torquay United   Striker   0   0   2   DL$........
Born: Waley – 17/10/1973
Comments: Skilful youngster

DARB – **Darby Julian**   Bolton Wanderers   Defender   11 13 10   DL$........
Born: Bolton – 03/10/1967
Comments: Versatile local lad who has risen up through the rank's

DAVE – **Davenport Peter**   Sunderland   Striker   3   7   6   DL$........
Born: Birkenhead – 24/03/1961
Comments: Well travelled vet

DAVA – **Davies Alan**   Swansea City   Midfield   1   3   1   DL$........
Born: Manchester – 05/12/1961
Comments: Another of the "Swan's" veteran's

DAVG – **Davies Gordon**   Wrexham   Striker   6   7   4   DL$........
Born: Merthyr – 03/08/1955
Comments: Blast from the past

DAVM – **Davies Michael**   Blackpool   Midfield   0   1   1   DL$........
Born: Stretford – 19/01/1966
Comments: Product of the Seasiders Youth Team

DAVI – **Davies Steve**   Burnley   Defender   0   0   2   DL$........
Born: Hexham – 30/10/1968
Comments: Interesting

DAVD – **Davis Darren**   Maidstone United   Defender   0   0   2   DL$........
Born: Sutton-in-Ashfield – 05/02/1967
Comments: Up and coming defender

DAVP – **Davis Paul**   Arsenal   Midfield   1   3   0   DL$........
Born: London – 09/12/1961
Comments: George's favourite player

---

## Dream League Trivia

*Who played 19 years and 9 months between scoring a goal for England?*

Answer: Stanley Matthews

124

## PLAYER GUIDE                                    90 91 92

**DSTE – Davis Steve**  Barnsley          **Defender**   1   5   0    DL$........
Born: Birmingham – 26/07/1965
Comments: Seasoned campaigner

**DAVB – Davison Bobby**  Sheffield United   **Striker**   11   1  13    DL$........
Born: S Shields – 17/07/1959
Comments: Loan, good

**DAWE – Dawes Ian**  Millwall            **Defender**   4   0   0    DL$........
Born: Croydon – 22/02/1963
Comments: Usually taken for granted

**DAWS – Daws Tony**  Scunthorpe United    **Striker**   12  14   9    DL$........
Born: Sheffield – 10/09/1966
Comments: Tiny Tony, will not pass if there is a chance of a goal kick

**DAYK – Day Keith**  Leyton Orient       **Defender**   2   1   2    DL$........
Born: Grays – 29/11/1962
Comments: Never scored more than two goal's a season since 1987

**DEAN – Deane Brian**  Sheffield United    **Striker**   23  16  17    DL$........
Born: Leeds – 07/02/1968
Comments: The Blades most consistent scorer

**DEAR – Deary John**  Burnley            **Midfield**   3   7   6    DL$........
Born: Ormskirk – 18/10/1962
Comments: Vision and scoring ability

**DEMP – Dempsey Mark**  Rotherham United   **Midfield**   3   6   0    DL$........
Born: Manchester – 14/01/1964
Comments: Still looking for Makepeace

**DEMM – Dempsey Mark**  Gillingham        **Midfield**   0   0   2    DL$........
Born: Dublin – 10/12/1972
Comments: Promising product from the Gills Youth

**DENT – Dennis Tony**  Cambridge United    **Midfield**   2   2   2    DL$........
Born: Eton – 01/12/1963
Comments: Menace from midfield

**DENN – Dennison Robert**  Wolves         **Striker**    9   5   1    DL$........
Born: Banbridge – 30/04/1963
Comments: Lost his pace, lost his way

**DEVI – Devine Steve**  Hereford         **Midfield**   1   0   1    DL$........
Born: Strabane – 11/12/1964
Comments: Steve's not a devine scorer

**DEVL – Devlin Mark**  Stoke City         **Midfield**   0   2   0    DL$........
Born: Irvine – 18/01/1973
Comments: Lost his touch around goal

**DEVO – Devonshire Alan**  Watford        **Midfield**   0   1   0    DL$........
Born: London – 13/04/1956
Comments: Only played for two clubs in sixteen years

**DEWH – Dewhurst Robert**  Blackburn Rovers **Defender**   0   0   1    DL$........
Born: Keighley – 10/09/1971
Comments: Robs no butcher

**DICA – Dickens Alan**  Chelsea           **Midfield**   1   0   0    DL$........
Born: Plaistow – 03/09/1964
Comments: Only played for two club's in his career

DREAM LEAGUE – CHAPTER 10                  90 91 92

DICK – **Dicks Julian**   West Ham United   Defender   13  5  5   DL$........
Born: Bristol – 08/08/1968
Comments: Back to his "competitive" best after injury

DILL – **Dillon Kevin**   Reading           Midfield    0  0  3   DL$........
Born: Sunderland – 18/12/1959
Comments: Adds bite and flair to the middle of the park

DIXK – **Dixon Kerry**   Chelsea            Striker    22 15  5   DL$........
Born: Luton – 24/07/1961
Comments: Golden boot's have lost their shine

DIXO – **Dixon Lee**   Arsenal              Defender    5  5  4   DL$........
Born: Manchester – 17/03/1964
Comments: Well travelled right-back, but not to Sweden

DOBB – **Dobbin Jim**   Grimsby Town        Midfield    1  0  7   DL$........
Born: Dumfermline – 17/09/1961
Comments: Jims been around a lot

DOBW – **Dobbins Wayne**   Torquay United   Midfield    0  0  1   DL$........
Born: Bromsgrove – 30/08/1968
Comments: Wayne's no cart-horse

DOMA – **Dobie Mark**   Torquay United      Midfield    0  0  2   DL$........
Born: Carlisle – 08/11/1963
Comments: Impressive in midfield

DOBS – **Dobson Paul**   Lincoln City       Striker    16  5  5   DL$........
Born: Hartlepool – 17/12/1962
Comments: Much travelled in the lower divisions

DOLA – **Dolan Eamonn**   Exeter City       Striker     3  1  0   DL$........
Born: Dagenham – 20/09/1967
Comments: Non productive for the Grecians

DOLI – **Doling Stuart**   Portsmouth       Striker     0  0  2   DL$........
Born: Newport IOW – 28/10/1972
Comments: Promising youngster

ONDO – **Donaldson O Neill**   Shrewsbury T.   Striker  0  0  2   DL$........
Born: Hansworth – 24/11/1969
Comments: Another new face this season

DONE – **Donegal Glen**   Maidstone United   Striker    0  0  1   DL$........
Born: Northampton – 20/06/1969
Comments: Glens on his way

DONO – **Donovan Kevin**   Halifax Town      Striker    0  1  2   DL$........
Born: Halifax – 17/12/1971
Comments: Loan

## Dream League Trivia

*Who holds the record for most League goals for Spurs?*

Answer: Jimmy Greaves 220 (61-70)

# PLAYER GUIDE                                              90 91 92

**DONL – Donowa Lou**  Birmingham City    **Striker**    1  3  2    DL$ ........
Born: Ipswich – 24/09/1964
Comments: Won the Midland's search for the fastest League player

**DORI – Dorigo Tony**  Leeds United    **Defender**   3  2  3    DL$ ........
Born: Australia – 31/12/1965
Comments: Skilful defender from Oz

**DOUG – Douglas Colin**  Doncaster Rovers   **Defender**   2  0  1    DL$ ........
Born: Hurlford – 09/09/1962
Comments: Served a long time at Belle Vue

**DOWI – Dowie Iain**  Southampton    **Striker**    1  4  9    DL$ ........
Born: Hatfield – 09/01/1965
Comments: Iain's been around a bit, but has bag's of experience

**DOWN – Downing Keith**  Wolves    **Midfield**   3  1  0    DL$ ........
Born: Oldbury – 23/07/1965
Comments: Psycho! Couldn't score in a motel

**DOWG – Downs Greg**  Hereford    **Defender**   1  1  2    DL$ ........
Born: Carlton – 13/12/1958
Comments: Downsies's well travelled and managing

**DOYS – Doyle Steve**  Rochdale    **Midfield**   2  0  0    DL$ ........
Born: Neath – 02/06/1958
Comments: Looking for Bodie

**DOZZ – Dozzell Jason**  Ipswich Town    **Midfield**   9  8  15   DL$ ........
Born: Ipswich – 09/12/1967
Comments: Controls the game, is always a goal threat

**DRAP – Draper Mark**  Notts County    **Midfield**   3  9  2    DL$ ........
Born: Derby – 11/11/1970
Comments: Product of the "Magpie's" youth policy

**DREY – Dreyer John**  Luton Town    **Defender**   3  3  2    DL$ ........
Born: Alnwick – 11/06/1963
Comments: Pacey centre-half, unfortunate habit of trying to be flash

**DRIN – Drinkell Kevin**  Coventry City    **Striker**    7  0  2    DL$ ........
Born: Grimsby – 18/06/1960
Comments: Strong striker

**DRIS – Driscoll Andy**  Brentford    **Midfield**   2  0  0    DL$ ........
Born: Staines – 21/10/1971
Comments: Young star who's lost his way

**DRYD – Dryden Richard**  Notts County    **Defender**   8  7  1    DL$ ........
Born: Stroud – 14/06/1969
Comments: Defender with a eye for goal

**DRYS – Drysdale Jason**  Watford    **Defender**   0  0  5    DL$ ........
Born: Bristol – 17/11/1970
Comments: One of the first graduates from the FA School

**DUBL – Dublin Dion**  Cambridge United    **Striker**   20 21 18   DL$ ........
Born: Leicester – 22/04/1969
Comments: Crowd favourite at the Abbey Stadium

**DUBK – Dublin Keith**  Watford    **Defender**   1  0  0    DL$ ........
Born: Wycombe – 29/01/1966
Comments: Often clumsy, has the distribution skills of the Mozambique government

**DREAM LEAGUE – CHAPTER 10**　　　　　　　**90 91 92**

DUFF – **Duffield Peter**　Rotherham United　**Striker**　2　5　0　DL$........
Born: Middlesborough – 04/02/1969
Comments: Peter's no duffer

DUNN – **Dunn Iain**　Chesterfield　**Striker**　2　3　1　DL$........
Born: Derwent – 01/04/1972
Comments: Iain's done the scoring... could do better

DUNP – **Dunphy Sean**　Lincoln City　**Defender**　0　0　1　DL$........
Born: Rotherham – 05/11/1970
Comments: Tall, centre half

DURI – **Durie Gordon**　Tottenham Hotspur　**Striker**　5　15　9　DL$........
Born: Paisley – 06/12/1965
Comments: Strong runner! Potent partner for Lineker? Juke box?

DURN – **Durnin John**　Oxford　**Striker**　14　10　8　DL$........
Born: Bootle – 18/08/1965
Comments: John's one of the O's potent striking force

DUXB – **Duxbury Lee**　Bradford　**Midfield**　0　5　6　DL$........
Born: Skipton – 07/10/1969
Comments: Strong scorer from the middle of the park

DYCH – **Dyche Sean**　Chesterfield　**Midfield**　2　2　3　DL$........
Born: Kettering – 26/06/1971
Comments: Seans another prolific spireite

DYER – **Dyer Alex**　Charlton Athletic　**Midfield**　0　1　0　DL$........
Born: West Ham – 14/11/1965
Comments: Midfield cum striker. Occasionally fit. Occasionally scores

DZIE – **Dziekanowski Dariuz**　Bristol City　**Striker**　8　0　6　DL$........
Born: Warsaw – 30/09/1962
Comments: Bet there having fun pronouncing this at Ashton Gate

EARL – **Earle Robbie**　Wimbledon　**Striker**　12　11　14　DL$........
Born: Newcastle – 27/01/1965
Comments: Robbie's been a revelation in the first Division

EBER – **Ebbrell John**　Everton　**Midfield**　0　6　1　DL$........
Born: Bromborough – 01/10/1969
Comments: John is a previous graduate of the F.A.'s School

EBDO – **Ebdon Marcus**　Peterborough United **Midfield**　0　0　2　DL$........
Born: Pontypool – 17/10/1970
Comments: One to watch

ECKH – **Eckhardt Jeff**　Fulham　**Defender**　2　2　7　DL$........
Born: Sheffield – 07/10/1965
Comments: Excellent in the air and firm in the tackle

---

## Dream League Trivia

*Who holds the record for most League goals for Manchester United in one season?*

Answer: Dennis Viollet 32 – (59/60)

| PLAYER GUIDE | | | 90 | 91 | 92 | |
|---|---|---|---|---|---|---|

EDIN – **Edinburgh Justin**  Tottenham Hotspur  **Defender**  0  1  0  DL$........
Born: Brentwood – 18/12/1969
Comments: Promising young full-back

EDMO – **Edmondson Darren**  Carlisle Utd  **Defender**  0  0  2  DL$........
Born: Coniston – 04/11/1971
Comments: One for the future

EDAA – **Edwards Andy**  Southend United  **Midfield**  0  1  1  DL$........
Born: Epping – 17/09/1971
Comments: Andy refuses to score more than 1 a season

EDDV – **Edwards David**  Walsall  **Striker**  0˙ 0  1  DL$........
Born: – TBA
Comments: One to watch

EDWD – **Edwards Dean**  Northampton Town  **Striker**  3  15  2  DL$........
Born: Wolverhampton – 25/02/1962
Comments: Coming back to glory

EDWK – **Edwards Keith**  Plymouth Argyle  **Striker**  5  5  0  DL$........
Born: Stockton – 16/07/1957
Comments: Loan

EDRO – **Edwards Robert**  Crewe Alexandra  **Striker**  0  11  9  DL$........
Born: Manchester – 23/02/1970
Comments: Favourite at Gresty Road

EELE – **Eeles Tony**  Gillingham  **Midfield**  2  0  1  DL$........
Born: Chatham – 15/11/1970
Comments: Slippery midfielder

EKOK – **Ekoko Efan**  AFC Bournemouth  **Striker**  0  5  11  DL$........
Born: Manchester – 08/06/1967
Comments: Tall fast striker

ELIR – **Eli Roger**  Burnley  **Defender**  3  10  12  DL$........
Born: Bradford – 11/09/1965
Comments: Strong, positive, scoring defender

ELKI – **Elkins Gary**  Wimbledon  **Defender**  0  0  1  DL$........
Born: Wallingford – 04/05/1966
Comments: Reliable and versatile utility player

ELLM – **Elliot Matthew**  Scunthorpe United  **Defender**  4  6  8  DL$........
Born: Surrey – 01/11/1968
Comments: Sony player of the year 91....

ELLP – **Elliott Paul**  Chelsea  **Defender**  0  0  3  DL$........
Born: London – 18/03/1964
Comments: Skilful defender

ELMA – **Ellis Mark**  Halifax Town  **Striker**  0  4  0  DL$........
Born: Bradford – 06/01/1962
Comments: Mark's lost his touch

ELLN – **Ellis Neil**  Maidstone United  **Striker**  0  2  0  DL$........
Born: Bebington – 30/04/1969
Comments: another Ellis who's lost it

ELLT – **Ellis Tony**  Stoke City  **Striker**  6  9  5  DL$........
Born: Salford – 20/10/1964
Comments: Steve was the Potter's second highest scorer last season

| DREAM LEAGUE – CHAPTER 10 | | 90 91 92 |

ETON – **Ellison Lee**   Darlington   **Striker**   0   3   11   DL$........
Born: Bishop Auckland – 13/01/1973
Comments: Exciting product from the Youth policy at Feethams

ELSE – **Elsey Karl**   Gillingham   **Midfield**   5   1   3   DL$........
Born: Swansea – 20/11/1958
Comments: Well travelled around the lower leagues

EVAC – **Evans Ceri**   Oxford   **Defender**   2   1   0   DL$........
Born: Christchurch – 02/10/1963
Comments: Solid and reliable

EVAD – **Evans David**   Halifax Town   **Striker**   0   2   0   DL$........
Born: Bromwich – 20/05/1958
Comments: Daves lost the knack

EVNI – **Evans Nicky**   Barnet   **Striker**   0   0   4   DL$........
Born: Bedford – 06/07/1958
Comments: Much loved by the Bee's fans

EVAR – **Evans Richard**   Bristol Rovers   **Striker**   0   0   1   DL$........
Born: Ebbw Vale – 12/04/1968
Comments: Product of non-league football

EVAS – **Evans Stewart**   Crewe Alexandra   **Striker**   5   10   6   DL$........
Born: Maltby – 15/11/1960
Comments: Good target man for high crosses with no wind

EVAN – **Evans Terry**   Brentford   **Defender**   4   3   9   DL$........
Born: London – 12/04/1965
Comments: Big Tel, a long serving Bee. Highly thought of iron man

EYRE – **Eyres David**   Blackpool   **Striker**   9   6   10   DL$........
Born: Liverpool – 26/02/1964
Comments: David's got an eye for goal

FAIC – **Fairclough Chris**   Leeds United   **Defender**   9   5   2   DL$........
Born: Nottingham – 12/04/1964
Comments: Another of the White's skilful defence

FAID – **Fairclough David**   Wigan Athletic   **Striker**   1   1   0   DL$........
Born: Liverpool – 05/01/1957
Comments: How the mighty have fallen

FAIR – **Fairclough Wayne**   Mansfield Town   **Defender**   0   6   3   DL$........
Born: Nottingham – 27/04/1968
Comments: Strong defender at the Field Mill Ground

FAIW – **Fairweather Carlton**   Wimbledon   **Striker**   2   1   0   DL$........
Born: London – 22/09/1961
Comments: Laid-back player who is both graceful and skilfull

---

## Dream League Trivia

*How many goals did John Aldridge score for Oxford in 84/85?*

Answer: 30, a club record

# PLAYER GUIDE                                       90 91 92

**FALC – Falco Mark**  Millwall            Striker      5   6   4   DL$........
Born: Hackney – 22/10/1960
Comments: Another old boy who still pops them in

**FALW – Falconer Willie**  Middlesbrough  Defender    3   5   5   DL$........
Born: Aberdeen – 05/04/1966
Comments: Versatile player who can play either in midfield or defence

**FARR – Farrell Andy**  Burnley           Defender    2   2   3   DL$........
Born: Colchester – 07/10/1965
Comments: Another of the Clarets scoring defence

**FARS – Farrell Sean**  Fulham            Midfield    0   2  11   DL$........
Born: Watford – 28/02/1969
Comments: Centre forward, but not quite the finished article

**FARM – Farrington Mark**  Brighton & H.A.  Striker   0   0   1   DL$........
Born: Liverpool – 15/06/1965
Comments: Mark's found the net at last

**FASH – Fashanu John**  Wimbledon         Striker    14  20  20   DL$........
Born: Kensington – 18/09/1962
Comments: Even frightens his own manager

**FAJU – Fashanu Justin**  Torquay United  Striker     0   0  10   DL$........
Born: Kensington – 18/08/1962
Comments: Was once the youngest £1 million player

**FEEG – Fee Greg**  Mansfield Town        Defender    0   0   5   DL$........
Born: Halifax – 24/06/1964
Comments: Finding the net at last

**FENS – Fensom Andy**  Cambridge United   Midfield    0   0   1   DL$........
Born: Northampton – 18/02/1969
Comments: Andy's found the net

**FENW – Fenwick Terry**  Tottenham Hotspur  Defender  1   1   0   DL$........
Born: Camden, Co. Durham – 17/11/1959
Comments: Tough tackling, "competitive" right-back

**FERD – Ferdinand Les**  Queens Park Rangers  Striker  2  10  10   DL$........
Born: Camden Co Durham – 17/11/1959
Comments: Les is in contention for the number 1 striker's spot

**FERE – Fereday Wayne**  W.B.A.           Midfield    0   0   2   DL$........
Born: Warley – 16/06/1963
Comments: Maybe at his best when running forward from full back

**FINL – Finley Alan**  Stockport County   Defender    1   3   1   DL$........
Born: Liverpool – 10/12/1967
Comments: Tall, tough tackling defender

**FIKE – Finney Kevin**  Lincoln City      Striker     0   0   2   DL$........
Born: Newcastle – 19/10/1969
Comments: Played in a number of positions on the park

**FIST – Finney Stephen**  Preston North End  Striker  0   0   1   DL$........
Born: – TBA
Comments: Watch this space

**FIOR – Flore Mark**  Plymouth Argyle     Midfield    1   4   4   DL$........
Born: Southwark – 18/11/1969
Comments: Mark's a left-winger, but can play anywhere on the left side

# DREAM LEAGUE – CHAPTER 10     90 91 92

**FISN – Fisher Neal**  Bolton Wanderers   **Striker**   0  0  1   DL$........
Born: St.Helens – 07/11/1970
Comments: Just beginning to break into the first team

**FITS – Fitzgerald Scott**  Wimbledon   **Defender**  0  0  1   DL$........
Born: London – 13/08/1969
Comments: Successful product of Wimbledon's youth policy

**FITZ – Fitzpatrick Paul**  Leicester City   **Midfield**  4  0  4   DL$........
Born: Liverpool – 05/10/1965
Comments: Paul scores 4 or nothing

**FLEC – Fleck Robert**  Norwich City   **Striker**  12  9  19   DL$........
Born: Glasgow – 11/08/1965
Comments: Has been the "Canaries" leading scorer for three season's

**FLEM – Fleming Craig**  Oldham Athletic   **Defender**  0  0  1   DL$........
Born: Calder – 06/10/1971
Comments: Can either play full-back or in midfield

**FLMA – Fleming Mark**  Brentford   **Defender**  0  1  0   DL$........
Born: Hammersmith – 11/08/1969
Comments: Good at the back, lost the knack up front

**FLEP – Fleming Paul**  Mansfield Town   **Defender**  2  0  0   DL$........
Born: Halifax – 06/09/1967
Comments: Yet to make an impact

**FLEA – Fletcher Andrew**  Scarborough   **Striker**  0  1  5   DL$........
Born: Saltburn – 12/08/1971
Comments: Promising youngster

**FLES – Fletcher Steve**  Hartlepool United   **Striker**  0  2  3   DL$........
Born: Hartlepool – 26/06/1972
Comments: Trying to keep his first team place

**FLOU – Flounders Andy**  Rochdale   **Striker**  19  29  18   DL$........
Born: Hull – 13/12/1963
Comments: Another of those Dream strikers

**FLYN – Flynn Brian**  Wrexham   **Midfield**  2  1  0   DL$........
Born: Port Talbot – 12/10/1955
Comments: Aged midfield star

**FLYM – Flynn Mike**  Preston North End   **Defender**  1  1  4   DL$........
Born: Oldham – 23/02/1969
Comments: Back to his best after injury

**FLYS – Flynn Sean**  Coventry City   **Midfield**  0  0  2   DL$........
Born: Birmingham – 13/03/1968
Comments: Promising young player

---

## Dream League Trivia

*How many goals did England cede in the 1982 cup?*

Answer: 1

| PLAYER GUIDE | | 90 | 91 | 92 | |
|---|---|---|---|---|---|

**FOLE – Foley Steve**  Stoke City    Midfield    4   7   1    DL$........
Born: Liverpool – 04/10/1962
Comments: Recent arrival at the Victoria Ground

**FORD – Ford Gary**  Mansfield Town    Midfield    2   1   3    DL$........
Born: York – 08/02/1961
Comments: Needs no escort to score a goal

**FORM – Ford Mike**  Oxford    Defender    2   1   1    DL$........
Born: Bristol – 09/02/1966
Comments: Product of the Youth Scheme at the Manor Ground

**FORT – Ford Tony**  Grimsby Town    Striker    8   5   1    DL$........
Born: Grimsby – 14/05/1959
Comments: Tony's lost sight of goal lately

**FORS – Forsyth Mike**  Derby County    Defender    0   0   2    DL$........
Born: Liverpool – 20/03/1966
Comments: Tall, tough defender

**FOSA – Foster Adrian**  W.B.A    Striker    1   0   1    DL$........
Born: Kidderminster – 20/07/1971
Comments: Maybe a little out of his depth at the present time

**FOSC – Foster Colin**  West Ham United    Defender    1   4   1    DL$........
Born: Chislehurst – 16/07/1964
Comments: Competitive central defender, who can also score

**FOST – Foster Steve**  Oxford    Defender    4   5   2    DL$........
Born: Portsmouth – 24/09/1957
Comments: Age and experience at the back, also poaches the odd goal

**FOXR – Fox Ruel**  Norwich City    Midfield    3   4   2    DL$........
Born: Ipswich – 14/01/1968
Comments: Making a first team come-back

**FOYL – Foyle Martin**  Port Vale    Striker    3   15   15    DL$........
Born: Salisbury – 02/05/1963
Comments: Club's record signing, who is an experienced goalscorer

**FRAI – Frain David**  Stockport County    Striker    2   3   4    DL$........
Born: Sheffield – 11/10/1962
Comments: Can't refrain David from scoring

**FRAJ – Frain John**  Birmingham City    Midfield    1   3   5    DL$........
Born: Birmingham – 08/10/1968
Comments: Product of the youth scheme, who can also play left-back

**FRDA – France Darren**  Hull City    Striker    0   0   4    DL$........
Born: Hull – 08/08/1967
Comments: Another young tiger to watch

**FRAN – Francis John**  Burnley    Striker    4   15   10    DL$........
Born: Dewsbury – 21/11/1963
Comments: Good solid striker

**FRAK – Francis Kevin**  Stockport County    Striker    1   5   17    DL$........
Born: Moseley – 06/12/1967
Comments: One of county's tallest at 6'7"

**FRAL – Francis Lee**  Chesterfield    Defender    0   1   1    DL$........
Born: London – 24/10/1969
Comments: Youngster with an eye for a goal

**DREAM LEAGUE – CHAPTER 10**                    **90 91 92**

FRAT – **Francis Trevor**  Sheffield Wednesday  **Striker**    0   6   3   DL$........
Born: Plymouth – 19/04/1954
Comments: Player-manager, not often seen these day's

FROG – **Froggart Steven**  Aston Villa         **Midfield**   0   0   1   DL$........
Born: Lincoln – 09/03/1973
Comments: Brilliant product of the youth policy

FRYC – **Fry Chris**  Hereford                   **Striker**   1   0   4   DL$........
Born: Cardiff – 23/10/1969
Comments: Chris pans the opposition

FURL – **Furlong Paul**  Coventry City           **Striker**   0   0   5   DL$........
Born: N.London – 01/10/1968
Comments: Canters along

FUTC – **Futcher Ron**  Crewe Alexandra          **Striker**  11  19   6   DL$........
Born: Chester – 25/09/1956
Comments: Age and experience in front of goal

FYFE – **Fyfe Tony**  Carlisle United            **Striker**   0   3   6   DL$........
Born: Carlisle – 23/02/1962
Comments: 6 & two 3's

GABB – **Gabbiadini Marco**  Derby County        **Striker**  25  11  19   DL$........
Born: Nottingham – 20/01/1968
Comments: Marco knows where goal is

GABR – **Gabbiadini Ricardo**  Scarborough       **Striker**   2   0   4   DL$........
Born: Newport – 11/03/1970
Comments: Flash name for a duff striker

GAGE – **Gage Kevin**  Sheffield United          **Defender**  3   0   1   DL$........
Born: Chiswick – 21/04/1964
Comments: Kevins not green in defence

GALT – **Gale Tony**  West Ham United            **Defender**  1   1   0   DL$........
Born: London – 19/11/1959
Comments: Ex midfielder who is now firmly established in defence

GALM – **Gall Mark**  Brighton & Hove A.         **Striker**  20  13  16   DL$........
Born: London – 14/05/1963
Comments: Prolific goal scorer

GALB – **Gallacher Bernard**  Brighton & H.A. **Defender**    0   0   1   DL$........
Born: Johnstone – 22/03/1967
Comments: No, not the golfer

GALJ – **Gallacher John**  Newcastle United      **Striker**   7   0   0   DL$........
Born: Glasgow – 26/01/1969
Comments: Injured all season

---

## Dream League Trivia

*For which club did 'Pongo' Waring score 49 division one goals?*

Answer: Aston Villa 1930/31

# PLAYER GUIDE                                    90 91 92

**GALL – Gallacher Kevin**  Coventry City    **Striker**    3  16  10    **DL$........**
Born: Cyldebank – 23/11/1966
Comments: Supporters 'Player of the Year' 90/91

**GANJ – Gannon Jim**  Stockport County    **Defender**   1  6  17    **DL$........**
Born: London – 07/09/1968
Comments: One of the best Dream defenders

**GANN – Gannon John**  Sheffield United    **Midfield**   3  0  1    **DL$........**
Born: Wimbledon – 18/12/1966
Comments: Back to his best after injury

**GARD – Gardiner Mark**  Crewe Alexandra    **Striker**   8  11  7    **DL$........**
Born: Cirencester – 25/12/1966
Comments: Busy striker

**GARN – Garner Andy**  Blackpool    **Striker**   10  14  5    **DL$........**
Born: Chesterfield – 08/03/1966
Comments: Andy's yet to regain previous goalscoring touch

**GADA – Garner Darren**  Plymouth Argyle    **Midfield**   0  1  0    **DL$........**
Born: Plymouth – 10/12/1971
Comments: Promising product of the youth policy

**GARS – Garner Simon**  Blackburn Rovers    **Striker**   18  2  5    **DL$........**
Born: Boston – 23/11/1959
Comments: Long time server at Ewood Park

**GASH – Garnett Shaun**  Tranmere Rovers    **Midfield**   0  1  0    **DL$........**
Born: Wallasey – 22/11/1969
Comments: Shauns a rock in midfield

**GASC – Gascoigne Paul**  Spurs    **Midfield**   7  19  0    **DL$........**
Born: Gateshead – 27/05/1967
Comments: England, tears and ligaments, Lazio or London by Christmas?

**GATT – Gatting Steve**  Charlton Athletic    **Defender**   0  1  3    **DL$........**
Born: Park Royal – 29/05/1959
Comments: Buy of the season (free). Solid and reliable

**GAUG – Gaughan Steve**  Darlington    **Midfield**   1  0  0    **DL$........**
Born: Doncaster – 14/04/1970
Comments: Steve's lost sight of goal again

**GAVI – Gavin Mark**  Bristol City    **Midfield**   4  0  1    **DL$........**
Born: Bailleston – 10/12/1963
Comments: Gavin's on his second spell with the Robin's

**GAVP – Gavin Pat**  Peterborough United    **Striker**   1  5  4    **DL$........**
Born: Hammersmith – 05/06/1967
Comments: Consistent goal scorer

**GAYB – Gayle Brian**  Sheffield United    **Defender**   0  4  4    **DL$........**
Born: London – 06/03/1965
Comments: One of several Blades, rejoined with Mr Bassett

**GAYL – Gayle Howard**  Blackburn Rovers    **Midfield**   5  4  1    **DL$........**
Born: Liverpool – 18/05/1958
Comments: Age and experience, Howards a well travelled midfielder

**GAYJ – Gayle John**  Birmingham City    **Striker**   1  6  1    **DL$........**
Born: Birmingham – 30/07/1964
Comments: Best remembered for the two goals in the L/DAF Final 91

## Dream League Trivia

*Who scored against Reading in three different games, for three different clubs in the same season, 1982/83?*

Answer: Kevin Bremner – Wrexham, Plymouth and Millwall

**GAYM – Gayle Marcus**  Brentford   **Midfield**  0  6  5  DL$........
Born: Hammersmith – 27/09/1970
Comments: Fast, but sometimes forgets the ball.

**GAYN – Gaynor Tommy**  Nottingham Forest   **Striker**  1  3  3  DL$........
Born: Limerick – 29/01/1963
Comments: There once was a thirty year old from Limerick

**GEEP – Gee Phil**  Leicester City   **Striker**  1  0  6  DL$........
Born: Pelshall – 19/12/1964
Comments: One of two ex Derby strikers now in the squad

**GEMM – Gemmill Scot**  Nottingham Forest   **Midfield**  0  0  10  DL$........
Born: Paisley – 02/01/1971
Comments: Skilful son of Archie

**GERN – Gernon Irvin**  Northampton Town   **Defender**  1  0  0  DL$........
Born: Birmingham – 30/12/1962
Comments: Irvin's played for England at U-21 level

**GIBB – Gibbins Roger**  Cardiff City   **Striker**  1  5  2  DL$........
Born: Enfield – 06/09/1955
Comments: Rogers on his second spell at Ninian Park

**GIBN – Gibbs Nigel**  Watford   **Defender**  0  0  1  DL$........
Born: St.Albans – 20/11/1965
Comments: Nice place, St. Albans

**GIBC – Gibson Colin**  Leicester City   **Defender**  1  1  3  DL$........
Born: Bridport – 06/04/1960
Comments: 'Gibo' scores the odd goal between injuries

**GIBS – Gibson Terry**  Swindon Town   **Striker**  9  5  1  DL$........
Born: Walthamstow – 23/12/1962
Comments: Well travelled and experienced striker... On loan

**GIGG – Giggs Ryan**  Manchester United   **Striker**  0  1  7  DL$........
Born: Cardiff – 29/11/1973
Comments: Silent star at Old Trafford

**GILB – Gilbert David**  Grimsby Town   **Midfield**  12  13  3  DL$........
Born: Lincoln – 22/06/1963
Comments: Clever on the ball, the Mariners free kick expert

**GILK – Gilkes Michael**  Southampton   **Striker**  3  1  0  DL$........
Born: Hackney – 20/07/1965
Comments: Very fast, raiding winger with quick dribbling skills. Loan

**GILL – Gill Gary**  Cardiff City   **Defender**  0  9  2  DL$........
Born: Middlesbrough – 28/11/1964
Comments: Settling down to life as a Bluebird

# PLAYER GUIDE

**90 91 92**

**GILJ – Gilligan Jimmy** Swansea City **Striker** 5 18 9 DL$........
Born: London – 24/01/1964
Comments: Jimmy's getting back to his best after back surgery

**GITT – Gittens Jon** Middlesbrough **Defender** 4 0 0 DL$........
Born: Moseley – 22/01/1964
Comments: Loan

**GLEG – Gleghorn Nigel** Birmingham City **Midfield** 12 6 22 DL$........
Born: Seaham – 12/08/1962
Comments: Nigel's also the emergency goalie

**GLOV – Glover Dean** Port Vale **Defender** 4 1 1 DL$........
Born: West Bromwich – 29/12/1963
Comments: Classy central defender

**GLOL – Glover Lee** Nottingham Forest **Striker** 0 1 2 DL$........
Born: Kettering – 24/04/1970
Comments: Product of the "Red's" youth policy

**GOAT – Goater Shaun** Rotherham United **Striker** 2 4 9 DL$........
Born: Bermuda – 25/02/1970
Comments: Good pace, good first touch shows a lot of promise

**GODD – Goddard Paul** Ipswich Town **Striker** 4 6 4 DL$........
Born: Harlington – 12/10/1959
Comments: One of Lyall's 'old boys'. Holds an international record

**GODF – Godfrey Kevin** Brentford **Striker** 3 6 6 DL$........
Born: Kennington – 24/02/1960
Comments: Ageing striker still popping them in

**GOLM – Goldsmith Martin** Walsall **Striker** 0 3 0 DL$........
Born: Walsall – 04/11/1969
Comments: Tall, striker usually out on loan

**GOOM – Gooding Mick** Reading **Striker** 3 7 4 DL$........
Born: Newcastle – 12/04/1959
Comments: Well travelled striker

**GOOW – Goodison Wayne** Rochdale **Defender** 6 1 0 DL$........
Born: Wakefield – 23/09/1964
Comments: At the Wrong park

**GOOD – Goodman Don** Sunderland **Striker** 21 8 20 DL$........
Born: Leeds – 09/05/1966
Comments: Might heve made the difference in the Cup Final

**GOOJ – Goodman Jon** Millwall **Striker** 0 5 3 DL$........
Born: Walthamstow – 02/06/1971
Comments: Talented youngster

**GOOS – Goodwin Shaun** Rotherham United **Midfield** 6 4 7 DL$........
Born: Rotherham – 14/06/1969
Comments: Product of the "Merry Millers" youth policy. Very talented

**GORD – Gordon Colin** Leicester City **Striker** 3 1 5 DL$........
Born: Stourbridge – 17/01/1963
Comments: Well travelled and experienced striker

**GORM – Gorman Paul** Shrewsbury Town **Defender** 1 0 0 DL$........
Born: Dublin – 06/08/1963
Comments: Pushing hard to make the left-back spot his own

# DREAM LEAGUE – CHAPTER 10                    90 91 92

**GORP – Gorman Paul**   Charlton Athletic       **Striker**    0  2  3   DL$........
Born: Macclesfield – 18/09/1968
Comments: Lethal striker on the way up, one to watch

**GOED – Gormley Eddie**   Doncaster Rovers    **Midfield**   0  6  5   DL$........
Born: Dublin – 23/10/1968
Comments: Couldn't call Eddie gormless

**GOSS – Goss Jeremy**   Norwich City           **Midfield**   0  3  1   DL$........
Born: Cyprus – 11/05/1965
Comments: Recently recalled to the first team squad

**GOUC – Gouck Andy**   Blackpool               **Midfield**   1  0  2   DL$........
Born: Blackpool – 08/06/1972
Comments: Product of the Youth policy at Bloomfield Road

**GRAD – Graham Deniol**   Barnsley             **Striker**    0  0  1   DL$........
Born: Cannock – 04/10/1969
Comments: Graham's found the net

**GRAJ – Graham Jimmy**   Rochdale              **Defender**   0  1  0   DL$........
Born: Glasgow – 15/11/1969
Comments: Tall, tough tackling defender

**GRAM – Graham Mike**   Carlisle United        **Defender**   0  0  1   DL$........
Born: Lancaster – 24/02/1959
Comments: Aged back player

**GRAH – Graham Tommy**   Halifax Town          **Striker**    2  4  0   DL$........
Born: Glasgow – 31/03/1958
Comments: The Shaymen's most experienced player

**GRKI – Grant Kim**   Charlton Athletic         **Striker**    0  2  1   DL$........
Born: Ghana – 25/09/1972
Comments: From youth team, compensates experience with enthusiasm

**GRAA – Gray Andy**   Tottenham Hotspur        **Midfield**   8  4  7   DL$........
Born: Lambeth – 22/02/1964
Comments: Trying to get a first team place

**GRAY – Gray Frank**   Darlington               **Defender**   0  8  0   DL$........
Born: Glasgow – 27/10/1954
Comments: The Quakers manager

**GRAK – Gray Kevin**   Mansfield Town           **Midfield**   0  1  1   DL$........
Born: Sheffield – 07/01/1972
Comments: Product of the Stags Youth policy

**GRAP – Gray Philip**   Luton Town              **Striker**    0  0  6   DL$........
Born: Belfast – 02/10/1968
Comments: Powerful, seems to enjoy winding up the opposition

---

## Dream League Trivia

*Who scored the first goal in the 1986 Cup Final?*

Answer: Gary Lineker

| PLAYER GUIDE | | | 90 | 91 | 92 | |
|---|---|---|---|---|---|---|
| **GRAS – Gray Stuart** Southampton<br>Born: Withernsea – 19/04/1960<br>Comments: Another newcomer to the Dell | Defender | 3 | 1 | 1 | DL$........ |
| **GRSI – Grayson Simon** Leicester City<br>Born: Ripon – 16/12/1969<br>Comments: Young midfielder whose lost sight of goal | Midfield | 2 | 0 | 0 | DL$........ |
| **GREA – Grealish Tony** Walsall<br>Born: Paddington – 21/09/1956<br>Comments: Well travelled veteran of the centre circle | Midfield | 0 | 1 | 0 | DL$........ |
| **GRER – Green Richard** Gillingham<br>Born: Wolverhampton – 22/11/1967<br>Comments: Richy's not green at poaching goals | Defender | 1 | 0 | 4 | DL$........ |
| **GRSC – Green Scott** Bolton Wanderers<br>Born: Walsall – 15/01/1970<br>Comments: Scott's not been so hot this season | Striker | 2 | 6 | 3 | DL$........ |
| **GREC – Greenall Colin** Preston North End<br>Born: Billinge – 30/12/1963<br>Comments: Defender who likes it up front | Defender | 0 | 0 | 6 | DL$........ |
| **GREN – Greenwood Nigel** Preston N.E.<br>Born: Preston – 27/11/1966<br>Comments: Product from the Youth scheme at Deepdale | Striker | 0 | 1 | 4 | DL$........ |
| **GREG – Gregory David** Ipswich Town<br>Born: Sudbury – 23/01/1970<br>Comments: Promising product from the Youth system | Midfield | 0 | 1 | 0 | DL$........ |
| **GRET – Gregory Tony** Halifax Town<br>Born: Doncaster – 21/03/1968<br>Comments: One hundred and eighty | Midfield | 0 | 2 | 0 | DL$........ |
| **GRIF – Griffith Cohen** Cardiff City<br>Born: Georgetown – 26/12/1962<br>Comments: Just rememberd where the goals is | Striker | 9 | 14 | 1 | DL$........ |
| **GRIB – Griffiths Bryan** Wigan Athletic<br>Born: Prescot – 26/01/1965<br>Comments: Tricky left winger with a 100% penalty taking record | Striker | 9 | 15 | 6 | DL$........ |
| **GRIC – Griffiths Carl** Shrewsbury Town<br>Born: Coventry – 15/07/1971<br>Comments: Product of the YTS scheme | Striker | 4 | 5 | 8 | DL$........ |
| **GRIA – Grimes Ashly** Stoke City<br>Born: Dublin – 02/08/1957<br>Comments: The old warhorse is back | Striker | 0 | 0 | 1 | DL$........ |
| **GRIT – Gritt Steve** Charlton Athletic<br>Born: Bournemouth – 31/10/1957<br>Comments: Player-manager. Gritty has seen it all. | Midfield | 0 | 0 | 1 | DL$........ |
| **GROV – Groves Paul** Blackpool<br>Born: Derby – 28/02/1966<br>Comments: One of the Dream League favourites | Midfield | 2 | 13 | 12 | DL$........ |
| **GROP – Groves Perry** Arsenal<br>Born: Bow,London – 19/04/1965<br>Comments: Perry was George's first signing for Arsenal | Striker | 5 | 6 | 1 | DL$........ |

DREAM LEAGUE – CHAPTER 10

> # Dream League Trivia
> *Who scored the winning goal for Arsenal in the FA Cup Final of 1971?*
>
> Answer: Charlie George

| | | | | | | |
|---|---|---|---|---|---|---|
| GUNB – **Gunn Bryn**   Chesterfield | **Defender** | 9 | 2 | 0 | DL$........ |
| Born: Kettering – 21/08/1958 | | | | | | |
| Comments: Bryn's lost his shot | | | | | | |

GUNB – **Gunn Bryn**   Chesterfield — **Defender**   9  2  0   DL$........
Born: Kettering – 21/08/1958
Comments: Bryn's lost his shot

GURI – **Gurinovich Igor**   Brighton & Hove A.   **Midfield**   0  2  0   DL$........
Born: Minsk – 05/03/1960
Comments: Exotic name on South coast

GYNN – **Gynn Mick**   Coventry City   **Midfield**   1  11  3   DL$........
Born: Peterborough – 18/08/1961
Comments: Mini Micky's a favourite at Highfield Road

HAAG – **Haag Kelly**   Fulham   **Striker**   0  3  6   DL$........
Born: Enfield – 06/10/1970
Comments: Has a reputation for finding the net

HACK – **Hackett Gary**   West Bromwich Albion   **Striker**   2  1  0   DL$........
Born: Stourbridge – 11/10/1962
Comments: One of many tried in this postion

HAIL – **Hails Julian**   Fulham   **Striker**   0  0  1   DL$........
Born: Lincoln – 20/11/1967
Comments: One to watch

HALE – **Hales Kevin**   Leyton Orient   **Defender**   2  0  0   DL$........
Born: Dartford – 13/01/1961
Comments: Kevin's the longest serving "O"

HALD – **Hall Derek**   Hereford   **Midfield**   5  0  0   DL$........
Born: Manchester – 05/01/1965
Comments: Derek hasn't cost anybody anything

HALG – **Hall Gareth**   Chelsea   **Defender**   1  0  0   DL$........
Born: Croydon – 20/03/1969
Comments: Not often seen on the park

HALP – **Hall Paul**   Torquay United   **Striker**   0  0  3   DL$........
Born: Manchester – 03/07/1972
Comments: Skilful product of the Gulls youth policy

HALR – **Hall Richard**   Southampton   **Defender**   0  0  5   DL$........
Born: Ipswich – 14/03/1972
Comments: Brilliant youngster, one to watch

HALW – **Hall Wayne**   York City   **Midfield**   3  1  4   DL$........
Born: Rotherham – 25/10/1968
Comments: "Hoof". Specializes in long aimless balls from half-way line

HAJO – **Halpin John**   Rochdale   **Midfield**   0  1  3   DL$........
Born: Broxburn – 15/11/1961
Comments: No relation to Sir Ralph

# PLAYER GUIDE                                                    90 91 92

**HALS – Halsall Mick**   Peterborough United   **Midfield**   11   8   8   DL$........
Born: Bootle – 21/07/1961
Comments: The Posh's team captain

**HAMI – Hamilton David**   Burnley   **Defender**   0   1   0   DL$........
Born: South Shields – 07/11/1960
Comments: Should stick to playing records

**HAMG – Hamilton Gary**   Darlington   **Midfield**   0   0   2   DL$........
Born: Rossendale – 04/10/1965
Comments: Hang on, Gary's remembered where the net is

**HAIA – Hamilton Ian**   Scunthorpe United   **Striker**   6   2   10   DL$........
Born: Stevenage – 14/12/1967
Comments: Alleged midfield supplier, strange arm action!

**HARB – Harbey Graham**   W.B.A   **Defender**   0   1   1   DL$........
Born: Chesterfield – 29/08/1964
Comments: Still inclined to launch moonshots. Enjoys cult status

**HARD – Harding Paul**   Notts County   **Midfield**   0   0   1   DL$........
Born: Barnet – 06/03/1964
Comments: Now a regular in the first team

**HARJ – Hardy Jason**   Halifax Town   **Midfield**   1   0   0   DL$........
Born: Burnley – 14/12/1969
Comments: Loan

**HAPA – Hardyman Paul**   Sunderland   **Defender**   2   0   3   DL$........
Born: Portsmouth – 11/03/1964
Comments: Defender with an eye for goal

**HARF – Harford Mick**   Luton Town   **Striker**   4   11   16   DL$........
Born: Sunderland – 12/02/1959
Comments: 'God'. At his best was the best in the country

**HARG – Hargreaves Christian**   Grimsby T.   **Striker**   4   4   0   DL$........
Born: Cleethorpes – 12/05/1972
Comments: Product of the Youth scheme at Blundell Park

**HARK – Harkes John**   Sheffield Wednesday   **Midfield**   0   3   3   DL$........
Born: New Jersey, USA – 08/03/1967
Comments: Occasional scorchers from this 'flying eagle' from New Joysea

**HARL – Harle David**   Doncaster Rovers   **Midfield**   0   2   1   DL$........
Born: Denaby – 15/08/1963
Comments: Rarely threatens the goal

**HADA – Harmon Darren**   Shrewsbury Town   **Striker**   0   0   2   DL$........
Born: Northampton – 30/01/1973
Comments: Another youngster to watch out for

**HAAL – Harper Alan**   Everton   **Defender**   0   2   0   DL$........
Born: Liverpool – 01/11/1960
Comments: Mr. Utility

**HSTE – Harper Steve**   Burnley   **Striker**   10   0   7   DL$........
Born: Stoke – 03/02/1969
Comments: Steve's now a regular at Turf Moor

**HARR – Harris Mark**   Swansea City   **Defender**   2   1   4   DL$........
Born: Reading – 15/07/1963
Comments: "Chopper", who can also score the odd spectacular goal

# DREAM LEAGUE – CHAPTER 10        90 91 92

HAGE – **Harrison Gerry**   Bristol City   **Midfield**   0 0 1   DL$........
Born: Lambeth – 15/04/1972
Comments: Ex Chelsea youngster, finding his feet

HART – **Hart Nigel**   York City   **Defender**   2 0 0   DL$........
Born: Golborne – 01/10/1958
Comments: Nigel's forgotten where the opposition's net is

HARV – **Harvey Jimmy**   Tranmere Rovers   **Midfield**   7 3 1   DL$........
Born: Lurgan – 02/05/1958
Comments: Age and experience in the middle of the park

HLEE – **Harvey Lee**   Leyton Orient   **Midfield**   7 4 1   DL$........
Born: Harlow – 21/12/1966
Comments: Injuries have limited Lee's career at Brisbane Road

HARI – **Harvey Richard**   Luton Town   **Defender**   0 1 2   DL$........
Born: Letchworth – 17/04/1969
Comments: Steady dependable left back, one of the best in the league

HATH – **Hathaway Ian**   Rotherham United   **Striker**   1 1 0   DL$........
Born: Worsley – 22/08/1968
Comments: Tricky winger with good ball control

HAUS – **Hauser Thomas**   Sunderland   **Striker**   6 2 1   DL$........
Born: West Germany – 10/04/1965
Comments: Struggling to regain and keep 1st team place

HAWK – **Hawke Warren**   Chesterfield   **Midfield**   1 0 2   DL$........
Born: Durham – 20/09/1970
Comments: Pounces in for the odd goal

HAWP – **Hawker Phil**   West Bromwich Albion   **Defender**   1 0 0   DL$........
Born: Solihull – 07/12/1962
Comments: Now a fading memory at the Hawthorns

HAMA – **Hayes Martin**   Wimbledon   **Striker**   3 0 0   DL$........
Born: Walthamstow – 21/03/1966
Comments: Ex Arsenal and Celtic, back to the land of the living

HAYL – **Haylock Garry**   Huddersfield Town   **Midfield**   0 4 0   DL$........
Born: Bradford – 31/12/1970
Comments: Been in and out of the senior squad

HAYP – **Haylock Paul**   Maidstone United   **Defender**   0 0 1   DL$........
Born: Lowestoft – 24/03/1963
Comments: Pauls left the stack to score

HAZA – **Hazard Mike**   Swindon Town   **Midfield**   1 8 7   DL$........
Born: Sunderland – 05/02/1960
Comments: Penalties are not that easy for this one

---

## Dream League Trivia

*Who scored from 40 yards against Newcastle in the Cup for non-league Hereford?*

Answer: Ronnie Radford

| PLAYER GUIDE | | | 90 | 91 | 92 | |
|---|---|---|---|---|---|---|

HAZE – **Hazel Desmond**  Rotherham United  **Striker**  3  5  8  DL$........
Born: Bradford – 15/07/1967
Comments: Good honest club man

HEAN – **Heaney Neil**  Cambridge United  **Striker**  0  0  2  DL$........
Born: Middlesbrough – 03/11/1971
Comments: Loan

HEAR – **Heard Pat**  Cardiff City  **Defender**  3  3  1  DL$........
Born: Hull – 17/03/1960
Comments: Pats heard he used to be a goal scorer

HEAA – **Heath Adrian**  Stoke City  **Striker**  2  1  2  DL$........
Born: Stoke – 11/01/1961
Comments: Adrian's back to the place where he started

HEAT – **Heathcote Mike**  Cambridge United  **Defender**  0  6  5  DL$........
Born: Durham – 10/09/1965
Comments: Another of Uniteds back's who likes to score

HEBB – **Hebberd Trevor**  Chesterfield  **Midfield**  5  1  0  DL$........
Born: Winchester – 19/06/1958
Comments: Bin around, knows the score

HELL – **Helliwell Ian**  Scunthorpe United  **Striker**  15  7  14  DL$........
Born: Rotherham – 07/12/1962
Comments: Human telegraph pole, difficulty controlling ball with feet

HENJ – **Hendrie John**  Middlesbrough  **Striker**  5  4  5  DL$........
Born: Lennoxtown – 24/10/1963
Comments: Winger with an eye for goal

HEND – **Hendry Colin**  Blackburn Rovers  **Defender**  4  3  5  DL$........
Born: Keith – 07/12/1965
Comments: Tall, tough tackling defender

HEJO – **Hendry John**  Tottenham Hotspur  **Striker**  5  2  2  DL$........
Born: Glasgow – 06/01/1970
Comments: Promising young striker

HENL – **Henry Liburd**  Maidstone United  **Striker**  1  2  8  DL$........
Born: Dominica – 29/08/1967
Comments: Well travelled member of the Stones strike force

HENN – **Henry Nick**  Oldham Athletic  **Midfield**  1  4  7  DL$........
Born: Liverpool – 21/02/1969
Comments: Another from the youth policy at Boundary Park

HENT – **Henry Tony**  Shrewsbury Town  **Striker**  0  0  7  DL$........
Born: Sunderland – 26/11/1957
Comments: Returned to these shores from a spell in Japan

HENS – **Henshaw Gary**  Bolton Wanderers  **Midfield**  2  0  0  DL$........
Born: Leeds – 18/02/1965
Comments: Cross Pennine loyalties

HERI – **Heritage Peter**  Hereford  **Striker**  9  1  9  DL$........
Born: Bexhill – 08/11/1960
Comments: Back to nine after a lapse

HESS – **Hessenthaler Andy**  Watford  **Midfield**  0  0  2  DL$........
Born: Gravesend – 17/08/1965
Comments: New Hornet who is a Barny Rubble lookalike. Good in the air

# Dream League Trivia

*Which two players both scored five goals on the same day in Division One in 1983?*

Answer: Tony Woodcock – Arsenal, Ian Rush – Liverpool

HEJA – **Hewitt Jamie**  Chesterfield   Defender  7  0  3   DL$........
Born: Chesterfield – 17/05/1968
Comments: A member of the Spireites Youth Squad

HICK – **Hicks Martin**  Birmingham City   Defender  2  2  1   DL$........
Born: Stratford-on-Avon – 27/02/1957
Comments: Veteran defender

HICS – **Hicks Stuart**  Scunthorpe United   Defender  0  2  0   DL$........
Born: Peterborough – 30/05/1967
Comments: Will never kick the ball if a header will do

HIGG – **Higgins Dave**  Tranmere Rovers   Defender  1  2  1   DL$........
Born: Liverpool – 19/08/1961
Comments: But can Dave play snooker?

HIGN – **Hignett Craig**  Crewe Alexandra   Midfield  8  15  17   DL$........
Born: Whiston – 12/01/1970
Comments: Long time star at Gresty Road. Valuable!

HILA – **Hilaire Vince**  Exeter City   Striker  0  2  4   DL$........
Born: Forest Hill – 10/10/1959
Comments: Famous old timer now at St. James Park

HILD – **Hildersley Ron**  Halifax Town   Striker  0  0  1   DL$........
Born: Fife – 06/04/1965
Comments: Hilda's found the net

HILM – **Hilditch Mark**  Rochdale   Striker  9  2  0   DL$........
Born: Royton – 20/08/1960
Comments: Mark's not the striker he used to be

HILE – **Hiley Scott**  Exeter City   Midfield  0  2  1   DL$........
Born: Plymouth – 27/09/1968
Comments: Scott loves to attack from any position

HILL – **Hill Andy**  Manchester City   Defender  2  1  4   DL$........
Born: Maltby – 20/01/1965
Comments: Dreamed of being famous at Old Trafford

HILC – **Hill Colin**  Leicester City   Defender  0  0  1   DL$........
Born: Hillingdon – 12/11/1963
Comments: Loan

HIDA – **Hill David**  Scunthorpe United   Midfield  0  1  5   DL$........
Born: Nottingham – 06/06/1966
Comments: Ferocious midfield scuffler, in on the off ball action

HILK – **Hill Keith**  Blackburn Rovers   Defender  0  3  0   DL$........
Born: Bolton – 17/05/1969
Comments: From Apprentice, a dependable central defender

**PLAYER GUIDE**  **90 91 92**

HDAV – **Hillier David** Arsenal **Midfield** 0 0 1 **DL$**........
Born: Blackheath – 19/12/1969
Comments: Hard tackling midfielder who can also play at full-back

HIMS – **Himsworth Gary** Scarborough **Striker** 4 1 5 **DL$**........
Born: Appleton – 19/12/1969
Comments: Gary's lightweight, but not around the box

HINC – **Hinchcliffe Andy** Everton **Defender** 2 1 0 **DL$**........
Born: Manchester – 05/02/1969
Comments: Another of the "Toffee's" impressive defender's

HIND – **Hindmarch Rob** Wolverhampton W. **Defender** 0 2 0 **DL$**........
Born: Stannington – 27/04/1961
Comments: Lightning is not his middle name

HINE – **Hine Mark** Scunthorpe United **Midfield** 4 6 0 **DL$**........
Born: Middlesbrough – 18/05/1964
Comments: Claim to fame being sent off after two minutes

HIRS – **Hirst David** Sheffield Wednesday **Striker** 16 29 20 **DL$**........
Born: Barnsley – 07/12/1967
Comments: Number one goal getter for the Owl's

HIRL – **Hirst Lee** Scarborough **Defender** 0 2 3 **DL$**........
Born: Sheffield – 26/01/1969
Comments: Useful product of the youth scheme at McCain

HOBS – **Hobson Gordon** Exeter City **Midfield** 8 7 0 **DL$**........
Born: Sheffield – 27/11/1957
Comments: Hobson Choice was to score goals

HOCK – **Hockaday David** Hull City **Defender** 0 1 0 **DL$**........
Born: Billingham – 09/11/1957
Comments: Can play either right back or midfield

HOCA – **Hoddle Carl** Barnet **Midfield** 2 0 1 **DL$**........
Born: Harlow – 08/03/1967
Comments: Younger brother of you know who

HOJO – **Hodge John** Exeter City **Striker** 0 0 1 **DL$**........
Born: Liverpool – 01/04/1969
Comments: John's a speedy and skilful winger

HODG – **Hodge Steve** Leeds United **Midfield** 14 3 7 **DL$**........
Born: Nottingham – 25/10/1962
Comments: Refugee from Mr. Clough

HODA – **Hodges David** Torquay United **Midfield** 1 0 1 **DL$**........
Born: Hereford – 17/01/1970
Comments: No longer at the club

HOGL – **Hodges Glyn** Sheffield United **Striker** 9 4 3 **DL$**........
Born: Streatham – 30/04/1963
Comments: Glyns taken time to settle in at Bramall Lane

HODK – **Hodges Kevin** Torquay United **Midfield** 4 3 0 **DL$**........
Born: Bridport – 12/06/1960
Comments: Long time serving Pilgrim... On Loan

HOLR – **Holden Rick** Oldham Athletic **Striker** 9 6 5 **DL$**........
Born: Skipton – 09/09/1964
Comments: Rick's on the goal trail again

**DREAM LEAGUE – CHAPTER 10**  90 91 92

HDAD – **Holdsworth David**  Watford  **Defender**  3  2  2  DL$........
Born: London – 08/11/1968
Comments: Superb, unassuming defender who's a great hit with the ladies

HOLD – **Holdsworth Dean**  Brentford  **Striker**  24  8  34  DL$........
Born: London – 08/11/1968
Comments: Another "God", rated at £1m by Brentford and $25+ in Dream League!

HOLL – **Holland Paul**  Mansfield Town  **Midfield**  0  0  6  DL$........
Born: Lincoln – 08/07/1973
Comments: Skilful and productive result of the Stags Youth

HOLI – **Holloway Ian**  Queens Park Rangers  **Midfield**  8  7  0  DL$........
Born: Kingswood – 12/03/1963
Comments: Ian's lost his touch around goal

HLDA – **Holmes David**  Scarborough  **Striker**  0  0  1  DL$........
Born: Derby – 22/11/1972
Comments: Another youngster on his way up

HMAT – **Holmes Matt**  AFC Bournemouth  **Midfield**  2  2  3  DL$........
Born: Luton – 01/08/1969
Comments: Good steady midfielder

HOMI – **Holmes Micky**  Carlisle United  **Midfield**  3  2  5  DL$........
Born: Blackpool – 09/09/1965
Comments: Micky's a recent arrival at Brunton Park

HOLM – **Holmes Paul**  Birmingham City  **Defender**  2  1  2  DL$........
Born: Wortley – 18/02/1968
Comments: Impressive Yorkshireman

HOLZ – **Holzman Mark**  Reading  **Striker**  0  0  1  DL$........
Born: Bracknell – 22/02/1973
Comments: One of the Royals youngsters on the move

HONB – **Honour Brian**  Hartlepool United  **Midfield**  0  5  6  DL$........
Born: Horden – 16/02/1964
Comments: Industrious, crowd favourite at the Victoria Ground

HOPK – **Hopkins Jeff**  Bristol Rovers  **Defender**  4  0  0  DL$........
Born: Swansea – 14/04/1964
Comments: Hoppy from the Palace

HOPR – **Hopkins Robert**  Shrewsbury Town  **Midfield**  6  3  4  DL$........
Born: Birmingham – 25/10/1961
Comments: Well travelled and experienced veteran

HORB – **Horne Barry**  Southampton  **Midfield**  6  2  4  DL$........
Born: St.Asaph – 18/05/1962
Comments: Barry's the most consistant outfield player for Wales

---

## Dream League Trivia

*Who scored the first goal in the 1986 World Cup?*

Answer: Emilio Butragueno – Spain

# PLAYER GUIDE   90 91 92

**HORP – Horner Philip**  Blackpool   **Defender**  3  7  5   DL$........
Born: Leeds – 10/11/1966
Comments: Tall, bustling defender

**HORT – Horton Duncan**  Barnet   **Defender**  0  0  3   DL$........
Born: Maidstone – 18/02/1967
Comments: Duncan's been in and out of League football

**HOUC – Houchen Keith**  Port Vale   **Striker**  8  0  4   DL$........
Born: Middlesbrough – 25/07/1960
Comments: Back from across the border

**HOUD – Hough David**  Swansea City   **Defender**  1  0  0   DL$........
Born: Crewe – 20/02/1966
Comments: Good solid club man

**HOUG – Houghton Ray**  Liverpool   **Midfield**  1  10  10   DL$........
Born: Glasgow – 09/01/1962
Comments: Well travelled, veteran midfielder

**HOUS – Houghton Scott**  Tottenham Hotspur  **Midfield**  0  1  2   DL$........
Born: Hitchin – 22/10/1971
Comments: Promising product of the youth policy

**HOWA – Howard Jonathan**  Rotherham Utd  **Striker**  0  0  3   DL$........
Born: Sheffield – 07/10/1971
Comments: Yet another "Millers" youth, strong player on the ball

**HOWT – Howard Terence**  Leyton Orient   **Defender**  8  4  5   DL$........
Born: Stepney – 26/02/1966
Comments: Only missed one game since Orient won promotion

**HOWD – Howell David**  Barnet   **Defender**  0  0  3   DL$........
Born: London – 10/10/1958
Comments: Central defender who has represented England as a semi-pro

**HOWE – Howells David**  Tottenham Hotspur   **Striker**  7  4  2   DL$........
Born: Guildford – 15/12/1967
Comments: Outstanding player who has risen through the rank's

**HOWS – Howey Steve**  Newcastle United   **Midfield**  0  0  2   DL$........
Born: Sunderland – 26/10/1971
Comments: Tall young striker – heads well

**HOWL – Howlett Gary**  York City   **Midfield**  4  3  2   DL$........
Born: Dublin – 02/04/1963
Comments: Gary howls around midfield

**HOYL – Hoyland Jamie**  Sheffield United   **Midfield**  16  0  5   DL$........
Born: Sheffield – 23/01/1966
Comments: Skilful, scoring midfielder

**HUGA – Hughes Adrian**  Preston North End  **Defender**  1  1  0   DL$........
Born: Billinge – 19/12/1970
Comments: Powerful young defender whose lost sight of goal

**HUGC – Hughes Ceri**  Luton Town   **Midfield**  0  1  0   DL$........
Born: Pontypridd – 26/02/1971
Comments: Cultured, "competitive".

**HUGD – Hughes Darren**  Port Vale   **Defender**  1  0  2   DL$........
Born: Prescot – 06/10/1965
Comments: Fast moving left back who loves to join the attack

**DREAM LEAGUE – CHAPTER 10**          **90 91 92**

HUGH – **Hughes Mark**  Manchester United  **Striker**  14 18 12  **DL$........**
Born: Wrexham – 01/11/1963
Comments: Sparky's always in the hunt for goal's

HUGM – **Hughes Mark**  Tranmere Rovers  **Defender**  4  2  1  **DL$........**
Born: Port Talbot – 03/02/1962
Comments: No, not that Mark Hughes but a skilful defender

HUMI – **Hughes Michael**  Manchester City  **Striker**  0  0  1  **DL$........**
Born: Larne – 02/08/1971
Comments: Just recently made it to the first team from trainee

HULM – **Hulme Kevin**  Bury  **Striker**  0  7  4  **DL$........**
Born: Farnworth – 02/12/1967
Comments: Now making regular appearance's for the senior squad

HUME – **Humes Tony**  Wrexham  **Defender**  3  2  0  **DL$........**
Born: Blyth – 19/03/1966
Comments: Tough tackling all-rounder

HUMP – **Humphrey John**  Crystal Palace  **Defender**  0  1  0  **DL$........**
Born: Paddington – 31/01/1961
Comments: Wingers watch out when Humphrey's about

HUMG – **Humphries Glenn**  Scunthorpe Utd  **Defender**  0  1  4  **DL$........**
Born: Hull – 11/08/1964
Comments: All furrowed brows and injuries

HUNA – **Hunt Andy**  Newcastle United  **Striker**  0  2  11  **DL$........**
Born: Thurrock – 09/06/1970
Comments: Unpredictable forward, very skilful, good poacher in time

HUNG – **Hunter Geoff**  Wrexham  **Defender**  3  3  1  **DL$........**
Born: Hull – 27/10/1959
Comments: Traps the odd goal

HURO – **Hunter Roy**  West Bromwich Albion  **Striker**  0  0  1  **DL$........**
Born: Middlesbrough – 29/10/1973
Comments: Another younster tried upfront

HURL – **Hurlock Terry**  Southampton  **Midfield**  2  0  0  **DL$........**
Born: Hackney – 22/09/1958
Comments: From Rangers, "competitive" in midfield

HUTC – **Hutchings Chris**  Rotherham Utd  **Defender**  5  2  4  **DL$........**
Born: Winchester – 05/07/1957
Comments: Widely travelled with bags of experience

HUTD – **Hutchinson Donald**  Liverpool  **Striker**  2  0  0  **DL$........**
Born: Gateshead – 09/05/1971
Comments: Rarely seen striker

---

## Dream League Trivia

*Who scored the fastest own goal?*

Answer: The legendary Pat Kruse, Torquay – 6 secs.

| PLAYER GUIDE | | 90 | 91 | 92 | |
|---|---|---|---|---|---|

HUTI – **Hutchinson Ian**  Halifax Town     **Defender**   0   0   1   DL$........
Born: Teeside – 07/11/1972
Comments: Young defender from the trainees

HUTO – **Hutchison Tommy**  Swansea City   **Midfield**   2   0   0   DL$........
Born: Cardenden – 22/09/1947
Comments: Will he play when he's in his 50's

INCE – **Ince Paul**  Manchester United     **Midfield**   2   3   3   DL$........
Born: Ilford – 21/10/1967
Comments: Bustling midfielder, trainee referee

IRON – **Irons Kenny**  Tranmere Rovers     **Striker**   0   7   10  DL$........
Born: Liverpool – 04/11/1970
Comments: Beginning to show his talent

IRVI – **Irvine Alan**  Blackburn Rovers    **Striker**   1   2   0   DL$........
Born: Glasgow – 12/07/1958
Comments: Well travelled, experienced striker

IRWI – **Irwin Denis**  Manchester United    **Defender**   1   0   4   DL$........
Born: Cork – 31/07/1965
Comments: Denis is now on the goal hunt

JACM – **Jackson Matthew**  Everton         **Defender**   0   0   1   DL$........
Born: Leeds – 19/10/1971
Comments: Impressive young defender

JACP – **Jackson Peter**  Huddersfield Town  **Defender**   2   1   1   DL$........
Born: Bradford – 06/04/1961
Comments: Terrier's team captain

JACR – **Jackson Robbie**  Walsall           **Striker**   0   2   0   DL$........
Born: Altrincham – 09/02/1973
Comments: Young saddler, rarely seen

JACO – **Jacobs Wayne**  Hull City            **Defender**   3   1   0   DL$........
Born: Sheffield – 03/02/1969
Comments: Tough tackling Yorkshireman

JAKU – **Jakub Joe**  Burnley                **Midfield**   5   3   0   DL$........
Born: Falkirk – 07/12/1956
Comments: Diminutive veteran

JALK – **Jalkin Nico**  Port Vale             **Midfield**   0   0   1   DL$........
Born: Rotterdam – 22/06/1964
Comments: Highly rated midfielder, who can also take penalties

JAMJ – **James Julian**  Luton Town           **Midfield**   1   1   2   DL$........
Born: Tring – 22/03/1970
Comments: Right-back, lost form completely in recent months

JAMM – **James Martin**  Preston North End   **Midfield**   0   2   4   DL$........
Born: Formby – 18/05/1971
Comments: Rated a great prospect

JAMR – **James Robbie**  Bradford             **Striker**   4   4   3   DL$........
Born: Swansea – 23/03/1957
Comments: Vastly experienced club captain

JAMT – **James Tony**  Leicester City         **Defender**   2   9   0   DL$........
Born: Sheffield – 27/06/1967
Comments: Will he recover to reproduce 1991 form?

# Dream League Trivia

*Who scored the most goals in a World Cup Finals tournament?*

Answer: Just Fontaine, 13, France

**JASP – Jasper Dale**  Crewe Alexandra    **Defender**  0  1  0   DL$........
Born: Croydon – 14/01/1964
Comments: Over 100 apearences for the Railwaymen

**JEFF – Jeffels Simon**  Carlisle United    **Defender**  0  3  2   DL$........
Born: Darton – 18/01/1966
Comments: Tall, competitive defender

**JEFJ – Jeffers John**  Port Vale    **Striker**  1  2  3   DL$........
Born: Liverpool – 05/10/1968
Comments: Skilful left-winger who on his day can be devastating

**JEMI – Jeffrey Micheal**  Doncaster Rovers    **Striker**  0  0  6   DL$........
Born: Liverpool – 11/08/1971
Comments: Very skilful young rover

**JEMS – Jemson Nigel**  Sheffield Wednesday    **Striker**  6  13  5   DL$........
Born: Preston – 10/08/1969
Comments: A gem from Forest

**JENL – Jenkinson Leigh**  Hull City    **Striker**  0  0  9   DL$........
Born: Thorne – 09/07/1969
Comments: Owner of the 'Jenkinson Jinx'

**JEPS – Jepson Ron**  Preston North End    **Striker**  5  3  5   DL$........
Born: Stoke – 12/05/1963
Comments: Tall, strongly built striker

**JEWE – Jewell Paul**  Bradford    **Striker**  2  5  6   DL$........
Born: Liverpool – 28/09/1964
Comments: A diamond upfront

**JOBL – Jobling Kevin**  Grimsby Town    **Midfield**  1  0  2   DL$........
Born: Sunderland – 01/01/1968
Comments: One of the favourites at Blundell Park

**JOBS – Jobson Richard**  Oldham Athletic    **Defender**  2  1  3   DL$........
Born: Hull – 09/05/1963
Comments: One of the best centre-back's in the League

**JOHL – Johnrose Lenny**  Hartlepool United    **Striker**  3  8  4   DL$........
Born: Preston – 29/11/1969
Comments: Experienced striker

**JOHA – Johnson Alan**  Wigan Athletic    **Defender**  2  5  4   DL$........
Born: Ince – 19/02/1971
Comments: Strong in the air, likes to come forward and score

**JOHD – Johnson David A**  Sheffield Wed.    **Striker**  0  0  3   DL$........
Born: Sheffield – 29/10/1970
Comments: Good prospect from the youth policy

| PLAYER GUIDE | | | 90 91 92 | |
|---|---|---|---|---|

**JOHG – Johnson Gavin**  Ipswich Town   **Defender**   0  0  6   **DL$........**
Born: Eye – 10/10/1970
Comments: Looking forward to the Premier League

**JNIG – Johnson Nigel**  Rotherham United   **Defender**   2  2  2   **DL$........**
Born: Rotherham – 23/06/1964
Comments: Tall lynch pin of the defence

**JOHN – Johnson Tommy**  Derby County   **Striker**   18 19 15   **DL$........**
Born: Newcastle – 15/01/1971
Comments: Should help the Rams go up next year

**JMAU – Johnston Maurice**  Everton   **Striker**   0  0  7   **DL$........**
Born: Glasgow – 30/04/1963
Comments: Another of the "Toffee's" well travelled staff. From Rangers

**JOAN – Jones Andy**  Leyton Orient   **Striker**   4 11 7   **DL$........**
Born: Wrexham – 09/01/1963
Comments: Could prosper from Nuge's departure

**JODA – Jones David**  Doncaster Rovers   **Striker**   12 3 0   **DL$........**
Born: Harrow – 03/07/1964
Comments: Left his boots in his locker

**JONJ – Jones Joey**  Wrexham   **Defender**   1 2 0   **DL$........**
Born: Llandudno – 04/03/1955
Comments: No more overlapping runs I am afraid

**JONE – Jones Keith**  Southend United   **Midfield**   2 9 6   **DL$........**
Born: Dulwich – 14/10/1964
Comments: Fairly recent arrival at Roots Hall

**JONL – Jones Lee**  Liverpool   **Striker**   0 5 5   **DL$........**
Born: Wrexham – 29/05/1973
Comments: Very promising recruit to the Anfield ranks

**JOLI – Jones Linden**  Reading   **Defender**   3 2 0   **DL$........**
Born: Tredegar – 05/03/1961
Comments: "The Welsh Wonder", always gives one hundred per cent

**JONM – Jones Mark**  Cardiff City   **Midfield**   0 1 2   **DL$........**
Born: Berinsfield – 22/06/1961
Comments: Stocky, scoring midfielder

**JOMU – Jones Murray**  Grimsby Town   **Striker**   0 3 4   **DL$........**
Born: Bexley – 07/10/1964
Comments: Too good to hurry, Murray's been around alot

**JOPH – Jones Philip**  Wigan Athletic   **Midfield**   0 1 2   **DL$........**
Born: Liverpool – 01/12/1969
Comments: Phil's a fearsome, tough tackling, competetive midfielder

**JONR – Jones Richard**  Hereford   **Defender**   6 1 1   **DL$........**
Born: Pontypool – 26/04/1969
Comments: Long timer at Edgar Street

**JORO – Jones Rob M**  Liverpool   **Defender**   0 1 0   **DL$........**
Born: Wrexham – 05/11/1971
Comments: Outstanding defender should the shins recover

**JROB – Jones Robert**  Wrexham   **Midfield**   0 1 0   **DL$........**
Born: Liverpool – 12/11/1971
Comments: There Jones' are becoming complicated

| DREAM LEAGUE – CHAPTER 10 | | | 90 91 92 | |

JONT – **Jones Tommy**  Swindon Town   Midfield   2  0  4   DL$........
Born: Aldershot – 07/10/1964
Comments: It's not unusual to find a goal or two

JONV – **Jones Vaughan**  Bristol Rovers   Defender   2  1  0   DL$........
Born: Tonyrefail – 02/09/1959
Comments: Long serving "Pirate"

JOVI – **Jones Vinny**  Chelsea   Midfield   5  2  4   DL$........
Born: Watford – 05/01/1965
Comments: One of football's "hard" men

JOYJ – **Joyce Joe**  Scunthorpe United   Defender   0  0  2   DL$........
Born: Consett – 18/03/1961
Comments: Typical Geordie "skipper" sprays the ball around the terraces

JOYS – **Joyce Sean**  Torquay United   Midfield   5  3  1   DL$........
Born: Doncaster – 15/02/1967
Comments: Tough tackling midfielder

JOYC – **Joyce Warren**  Plymouth   Midfield   12  9  7   DL$........
Born: Oldham – 20/01/1965
Comments: Captain with a good eye for goal

JULE – **Jules Mark**  Scarborough   Striker   0  0  9   DL$........
Born: Bradford – 05/09/1971
Comments: Diamond by the sea

JURY – **Juryeff Ian**  Halifax Town   Striker   3  11  5   DL$........
Born: Gosport – 24/11/1962
Comments: Eight clubs in ten years, can't he settle down?

KABI – **Kabia Jason**  Lincoln City   Striker   0  0  4   DL$........
Born: Sutton – 28/05/1969
Comments: Non-Contract Player, paid by the goal?

KAMC – **Kamara Chris**  Luton Town   Midfield   1  0  0   DL$........
Born: Middlesbrough – 25/12/1957
Comments: Midfield hard man, slight tendency towards two footed tackles

KANC – **Kanchelskis Andrej**  Manchester Utd   Midfield   0  0  8   DL$........
Born: Kirowgrad – 23/01/1969
Comments: Cultured midfielder

KEAN – **Keane Roy**  Nottingham Forest   Midfield   0  11  12   DL$........
Born: Cork – 10/08/1971
Comments: Prolific goal scorer

KEAR – **Kearney Mark**  Bury   Defender   4  1  1   DL$........
Born: Ormskirk – 12/06/1962
Comments: Good club man

---

## Dream League Trivia

*Who was the last player to score against Wales in a World Cup Finals tournament?*

Answer: Pele

| | | | 90 | 91 | 92 | |
|---|---|---|---|---|---|---|

KEEN – **Keen Kevin**   West Ham United   **Midfield**   11   1   1   **DL$**........
Born: Amersham – 25/02/1967
Comments: Kevin's come through the rank's to first team status

KELL – **Kelly David**   Newcastle United   **Striker**   8   15   13   **DL$**........
Born: Birmingham – 25/11/1965
Comments: Has got an eye for goal in Division 2. What can he do in Div. 1

KELM – **Kelly Mark**   Portsmouth   **Striker**   0   1   0   **DL$**........
Born: Sutton – 27/11/1969
Comments: Overshadowed by other Pompey strikers

KEMA – **Kelly Mark**   Fulham   **Midfield**   1   0   1   **DL$**........
Born: Blackpool – 07/10/1966
Comments: Sparkling midfielder but struggles to sustain it for 90 mins

KELT – **Kelly Tom**   Exeter City   **Defender**   2   1   5   **DL$**........
Born: Bellshill – 28/03/1964
Comments: Team captain, coming back after fitness and injury problems

KETO – **Kelly Tony**   Hull City   **Midfield**   0   4   5   **DL$**........
Born: Meridan – 14/02/1966
Comments: Loan

KTON – **Kelly Tony G**   Bolton Wanderers   **Midfield**   5   7   3   **DL$**........
Born: Prescot – 01/10/1964
Comments: Well travelled around the lower division's

KAND – **Kennedy Andy**   Watford   **Striker**   13   3   2   **DL$**........
Born: Stirling – 08/10/1964
Comments: Tall strong striker

KENM – **Kennedy Mick**   Stoke City   **Midfield**   0   3   0   **DL$**........
Born: Salford – 09/04/1961
Comments: Well travelled and experienced penalty taker

KENT – **Kent Kevin**   Port Vale   **Striker**   3   0   0   **DL$**........
Born: Stoke – 19/03/1965
Comments: Kevin has now appeared in all four divisions of the League

KERN – **Kernaghan Alan**   Middlesbrough   **Striker**   5   0   4   **DL$**........
Born: Otley – 25/04/1967
Comments: Long time favourite at Ayresome Park

KERR – **Kerr Dylan**   Blackpool   **Defender**   0   0   2   **DL$**........
Born: Valetta – 14/01/1967
Comments: Loan

KERP – **Kerr Paul**   Millwall   **Striker**   1   2   13   **DL$**........
Born: Portsmouth – 09/06/1964
Comments: Wouldn't want to play in Italy...Whose asking anyway

KERS – **Kerslake David**   Swindon Town   **Midfield**   0   0   1   **DL$**........
Born: London – 19/06/1966
Comments: Steady, dependable club man

KEVA – **Kevan David**   Stoke City   **Midfield**   0   0   1   **DL$**........
Born: Wigtown – 31/08/1968
Comments: Fighting for a first team place

KILC – **Kilcline Brian**   Newcastle United   **Defender**   2   4   0   **DL$**........
Born: Nottingham – 07/05/1962
Comments: One of Kevin's bargains?

# DREAM LEAGUE - CHAPTER 10

> ## Dream League Trivia
> 
> *Name three players who have scored hat tricks with each goal conceded by a different goalkeeper*
> 
> Answer: 1966 – David Herd, 1972 – Brian Clarke, 1986 – Alvin Martin

KILN – **Kilner Andy**  Rochdale   Striker   0 11 3   DL$........
Born: Bolton – 11/10/1966
Comments: Loan

KIMB – **Kimble Alan**  Cambridge United   Defender   8 5 0   DL$........
Born: Poole – 06/08/1966
Comments: Reliable servant at Abbey Stadium

KIMG – **Kimble Garry**  Peterborough United   Striker   0 1 6   DL$........
Born: Poole – 06/08/1966
Comments: Gary's been around a bit

KINP – **King Phil**  Sheffield Wednesday   Defender   0 0 1   DL$........
Born: Bristol – 28/12/1967
Comments: Long serving Owl, as long as he listens to Trevor

KITS – **Kitson Paul**  Derby County   Striker   1 0 13   DL$........
Born: Co Durham – 09/01/1971
Comments: Paul's on the Ball when it comes to scoring

KIWO – **Kiwomya Chris**  Ipswich Town   Striker   0 11 17   DL$........
Born: Huddersfield – 02/12/1969
Comments: "Benson's" an impressive striker with pace

KNIL – **Knill Alan**  Bury   Defender   1 1 1   DL$........
Born: Slough – 08/10/1964
Comments: Alan's on the comeback after injury

KRIS – **Kristensen Bjorn**  Newcastle United   Defender   3 1 0   DL$........
Born: Malling – 10/10/1963
Comments: Benny 'Bjorn Again' Kristensen, regular scorer when fit

KRUS – **Kruszynski Detsi**  Brentford   Midfield   2 2 0   DL$........
Born: Divschav – 14/10/1961
Comments: Loan

KUHL – **Kuhl Martin**  Portsmouth   Midfield   10 13 4   DL$........
Born: Frimley – 10/01/1965
Comments: Martin's lost his touch around goal

LAKM – **Lake Michael**  Sheffield United   Midfield   0 0 5   DL$........
Born: Manchester – 06/11/1966
Comments: Now first team regular

LAKE – **Lake Paul**  Manchester City   Midfield   1 0 0   DL$........
Born: Manchester – 28/10/1968
Comments: Paul's coming back from a serious knee injury

LAMM – **Lambert Matthew**  Preston N. End   Defender   0 0 2   DL$........
Born: Morecombe – 28/09/1971
Comments: Could jump higher to greater success

| PLAYER GUIDE | | | 90 | 91 | 92 | |
|---|---|---|---|---|---|---|

**LANC – Lancashire Graham** Burnley — Striker — 0  0  10 — DL$........
Born: Blackpool – 19/10/1972
Comments: Young, skilful and prolific

**LAND – Lancaster Dave** Chesterfield — Striker — 0  5  8 — DL$........
Born: Preston – 08/09/1961
Comments: Drops the Spireites bombs

**LANK – Langley Kevin** Wigan Athletic — Midfield — 0  2  2 — DL$........
Born: St Helens – 24/05/1964
Comments: Kev's the team captain, inplace of the injured Rimmer

**LAWN – Law Nicky** Rotherham United — Defender — 0  2  0 — DL$........
Born: London – 08/09/1961
Comments: Another widely travelled "Miller"

**LAWR – Lawrence George** AFC Bournemouth — Striker — 3  2  1 — DL$........
Born: London – 14/09/1962
Comments: Another well travelled "Cherry"

**LAWS – Laws Brian** Nottingham Forest — Defender — 3  0  0 — DL$........
Born: Wallsend – 14/10/1961
Comments: Veteran defender

**LESA – Le Saux Graeme** Chelsea — Defender — 1  5  3 — DL$........
Born: Jersey – 17/10/1968
Comments: Full-back who can also play in midfield

**LETI – Le Tissier Matthew** Southampton — Striker — 24 23  8 — DL$........
Born: Guernsey – 14/10/1968
Comments: Matt's been the "Saint's" best until this year

**LEAB – Leaburn Carl** Charlton Athletic — Striker — 0  1  14 — DL$........
Born: Lewisham – 30/03/1969
Comments: Scoring after years of hazy knowledge of opposition net

**LEAD – Leadbitter Chris** Cambridge United — Striker — 7  4  1 — DL$........
Born: Middlesbrough – 17/10/1967
Comments: Chris has had lead boots this season

**LEEC – Lee Chris** Scarborough — Midfield — 0  0  1 — DL$........
Born: Halifax – 18/06/1971
Comments: Hardly ventures out of the centre of the park

**LEED – Lee Dave** Southampton — Midfield — 8  15  1 — DL$........
Born: Manchester – 05/11/1967
Comments: Was the "Shaker's" leading scorer in 90/91

**LEDA – Lee David** Plymouth Argyle — Defender — 1  2  6 — DL$........
Born: Kingswood – 26/11/1969
Comments: Loan

**LEEJ – Lee Jason** Lincoln City — Striker — 0  3  7 — DL$........
Born: Newham – 09/05/1971
Comments: Quick and aggressive forward

**LEER – Lee Raymond** Scarborough — Midfield — 0  0  1 — DL$........
Born: Bristol – 19/09/1970
Comments: Another of the youngsters breaking through at Seamer Road

**LERO – Lee Robert** Charlton Athletic — Striker — 2  13  12 — DL$........
Born: West Ham – 01/02/1966
Comments: Blindingly brilliant, or big nance...the jury's still out

**DREAM LEAGUE – CHAPTER 10**                     **90 91 92**

---

LEGG – **Legg Andy**   Swansea City          **Midfield**    3   7   9    **DL$**........
Born: Neath – 28/07/1966
Comments: Andy's got a good long throw, and speed down the wing

LEMO – **Lemon Paul**   Chesterfield         **Striker**     0   2   2    **DL$**........
Born: Middlesbrough – 03/06/1966
Comments: Not yellow at going for goal

LENN – **Lennon Neil**   Crewe Alexandra     **Defender**    0   3   0    **DL$**........
Born: Lurgan – 25/06/1971
Comments: Neil imagines he's a scorer

LEON – **Leonard Mark**   Rochdale           **Striker**     7   5   2    **DL$**........
Born: St Helens – 27/09/1962
Comments: Tall sharp shooter

LEVE – **Lever Mark**   Grimsby Town         **Defender**    2   2   0    **DL$**........
Born: Beverley – 29/03/1970
Comments: Another of the Mariners promising youngsters

LEWM – **Lewis Mickey**   Oxford             **Midfield**    1   1   4    **DL$**........
Born: Birmingham – 15/02/1965
Comments: Micky's improving his good scoring

LIGH – **Lightfoot Chris**   Chester City    **Midfield**    1   2   5    **DL$**........
Born: Wimwick – 01/04/1970
Comments: Promising product of the youth scheme

LILL – **Lillis Jason**   Maidstone United   **Midfield**    14  1   4    **DL$**........
Born: Chatham – 01/10/1969
Comments: Regular member of the Stones Squad

LILM – **Lillis Mark**   Stockport County    **Striker**     16  14  2    **DL$**........
Born: Manchester – 17/01/1960
Comments: Has played for some of the elite

LIMB – **Limber Nicholas**   Manchester City **Midfield**    0   0   1    **DL$**........
Born: Doncaster – 23/01/1974
Comments: Nicky's limbered up to get a goal

LIMP – **Limpar Anders**   Arsenal           **Striker**     0   13  4    **DL$**........
Born: Solna,Sweden – 24/09/1965
Comments: Can play on either wing or midfield

LINA – **Linacre Phil**   Darlington         **Striker**     0   3   0    **DL$**........
Born: Middlesbrough – 17/05/1962
Comments: Not enjoying his best patch

LINE – **Lineker Gary**   Tottenham Hotspur  **Striker**     26  19  33   **DL$**........
Born: Leicester – 30/11/1960
Comments: Off to the land of the rising yen. Not a good Dream buy

---

## Dream League Trivia

*Which player scored four goals in one match in the 1986 World Cup Finals?*

Answer: Emilio Butragueno

# PLAYER GUIDE  90 91 92

LING – **Ling Martin**  Swindon Town  **Striker**  10  0  3  DL$........
Born: West Ham – 15/07/1966
Comments: Small but perfectly formed!

LINI – **Linighan Andy**  Arsenal  **Defender**  2  0  0  DL$........
Born: Hartlepool – 18/06/1962
Comments: Valuble deputy for Tony Adam's

LIND – **Linighan David**  Ipswich Town  **Defender**  0  3  3  DL$........
Born: Hartlepool – 09/01/1965
Comments: A central reason for winning the 2nd division

LIST – **Lister Steve**  Scunthorpe United  **Midfield**  1  1  1  DL$........
Born: Doncaster – 18/11/1961
Comments: Own goal specialist and penalty misser

LITT – **Littlejohn Adrian**  Sheffield United  **Striker**  0  1  0  DL$........
Born: Wolverhampton – 26/09/1970
Comments: Fighting to retain first team place

LIVI – **Livingstone Steve**  Blackburn Rovers  **Striker**  8  9  1  DL$........
Born: Middlesbrough – 08/09/1969
Comments: Best remembered for winning goal in 87 F.A Youth Final

LLOY – **Lloyd Philip**  Torquay United  **Defender**  2  0  0  DL$........
Born: Hemsworth – 26/12/1964
Comments: Back from long term injury

LOCK – **Locke Adam**  Southend United  **Midfield**  0  4  0  DL$........
Born: Croydon – 20/08/1970
Comments: The Shrimpers key in midfield

LOGA – **Logan David**  Scarborough  **Defender**  4  1  0  DL$........
Born: Middlesbrough – 05/12/1963
Comments: Dave's the berry in defence

LORA – **Loram Mike**  Stockport County  **Striker**  14  7  9  DL$........
Born: Brixham – 13/08/1967
Comments: Loan

LORM – **Lormor Tony**  Lincoln City  **Striker**  8  13  9  DL$........
Born: Ashington – 29/10/1970
Comments: Tony's consistently No. 1 goal getter for the imps

LOUG – **Loughlan Anthony**  Notts Forest  **Midfield**  0  1  0  DL$........
Born: Surrey – 19/01/1970
Comments: Trainee

LOVE – **Lovell Steve**  Gillingham  **Striker**  17  20  17  DL$........
Born: Swansea – 16/07/1960
Comments: Love's putting the ball in the back of the net

LOVS – **Lovell Stuart**  Reading  **Midfield**  0  2  6  DL$........
Born: Sydney – 09/01/1972
Comments: A strong player with a nose for goal

LOWE – **Lowe David**  Port Vale  **Striker**  13  0  3  DL$........
Born: Liverpool – 30/08/1965
Comments: Loan

LOWK – **Lowe Kenny**  Barnet  **Midfield**  0  0  3  DL$........
Born: Sedgefield – 06/11/1964
Comments: Talent and skill in midfield

**DREAM LEAGUE – CHAPTER 10**

---

## Dream League Trivia

*Who scored the most goals in a Football League career?*

Answer: Arthur Rowley, 434. Everybody should know this one.

---

**LOWN – Lowndes Steve**  Hereford  **Striker**  5  1  4  DL$........
Born: Cwmbran – 17/06/1960
Comments: Dependable up front

**LUKE – Luke Noel**  Peterborough United  **Midfield**  5  2  0  DL$........
Born: Birmingham – 28/12/1964
Comments: Longest serving player at London Road

**LUND – Lund Gary**  Notts County  **Striker**  9  5  3  DL$........
Born: Grimsby – 13/09/1964
Comments: Another of County's veteran's

**LUNS – Lundon Sean**  Chester City  **Defender**  2  0  0  DL$........
Born: Liverpool – 07/03/1969
Comments: Pass

**LUSC – Luscombe Lee**  Brentford  **Striker**  0  0  3  DL$........
Born: Guernsey – 06/07/1971
Comments: Models Toby Jugs in his spare time

**LYNC – Lynch Tommy**  Shrewsbury Town  **Midfield**  0  2  2  DL$........
Born: Limerick – 10/10/1964
Comments: Has also been known to play in defence

**LYNE – Lyne Neil**  Shrewsbury Town  **Striker**  0  6  11  DL$........
Born: Leicester – 04/04/1970
Comments: Skilful striker

**LYDA – Lyons Darren**  Bury  **Striker**  0  0  4  DL$........
Born: TBA
Comments: Non Contract Player, goalscoring for wages

**MABB – Mabbutt Gary**  Tottenham Hotspur  **Defender**  1  3  2  DL$.......
Born: Bristol – 23/08/1961
Comments: Deadly left knee in the penalty area

**MCDK – MacDonald Kevin**  Walsall  **Striker**  1  0  3  DL$........
Born: Inverness – 22/12/1960
Comments: Experience and vision in the middle of the park

**MACS – MacKenzie Steve**  Shrewsbury Town  **Midfield**  1  2  1  DL$........
Born: Romford – 23/11/1961
Comments: Not wanted by Mr Francis

**MACL – MacLaren Ross**  Swindon Town  **Midfield**  5  1  1  DL$........
Born: Edinburgh – 14/04/1962
Comments: Name fits Swindons home strip

**MACD – Macdonald Gary**  Hartlepool United  **Striker**  2  0  0  DL$........
Born: Middlesbrough – 26/03/1962
Comments: Where did all the goals go?

# PLAYER GUIDE                                             90 91 92

**MACR – Mackenzie Roger** Doncaster Rovers   **Striker**   0   0   1   DL$........
Born: Sheffield – 27/01/1973
Comments: Rising star at the Belle Vue Ground

**MCPJ – Macphail John**   Hartlepool United   **Defender**   2   1   1   DL$........
Born: Dundee – 07/12/1955
Comments: Experience in defence, John's also the Pool's team captain

**MADA – Madden David**   Maidstone United   **Defender**   1   0   0   DL$........
Born: London – 06/01/1963
Comments: David's a hard man to pin down

**MADL – Madden Lawrie** Wolverhampton W.   **Defender**   0   0   1   DL$........
Born: London – 28/09/1955
Comments: Guaranteed a goal every 3 years

**MADD – Maddix Danny**   Queens Park Rangers   **Defender**   3   3   0   DL$........
Born: Ashford – 11/10/1967
Comments: Danny's lost sight of goal this season

**MAGI – Magilton John**   Oxford   **Midfield**   0   8   13   DL$........
Born: Belfast – 06/05/1969
Comments: Been under the watchful eye of several scouts

**MAIL – Mail David**   Hull City   **Defender**   2   1   1   DL$........
Born: Bristol – 12/09/1962
Comments: Skilful centre back

**MAKE – Makel Lee**   Newcastle United   **Midfield**   0   0   1   DL$........
Born: Sunderland – 11/01/1973
Comments: Silliest name in squad – still a fringe player

**MALK – Malkin Chris**   Tranmere Rovers   **Striker**   22   4   5   DL$........
Born: Bebington – 04/06/1967
Comments: Tall, powerhouse upfront

**MANU – Manuel Billy**   Brentford   **Defender**   4   0   1   DL$........
Born: Hackney – 28/06/1969
Comments: "Billy the Pitbull"

**MAST – Mardenborough Steve**   Darlington   **Midfield**   0   1   6   DL$........
Born: Birmingham – 11/09/1964
Comments: Well travelled striker who might have found his roost

**MARK – Marker Nick**   Plymouth Argyle   **Defender**   1   3   1   DL$........
Born: Exeter – 03/05/1965
Comments: Team captain, strong, reliable always give's 100%

**MACH – Marsden Chris**   Huddersfield Town   **Midfield**   2   5   1   DL$........
Born: Sheffield – 03/01/1969
Comments: Long time serving Terrier

**MCHR – Marsh Chris**   Walsall   **Midfield**   0   2   1   DL$........
Born: Dudley – 14/01/1970
Comments: Promising product from the Youth Scheme at Bescot Crescent

**MACO – Marshall Colin**   Scarborough   **Midfield**   0   0   1   DL$........
Born: Glasgow – 01/11/1969
Comments: Loan

**MADW – Marshall Dwight**   Plymouth Argyle   **Striker**   0   0   14   DL$........
Born: Jamaica – 03/10/1965
Comments: Has provided much needed striking power for the Pilgrims

**DREAM LEAGUE – CHAPTER 10**            **90 91 92**

MAGA – **Marshall Gary**   Exeter City        **Striker**    3   3   4   DL$........
Born: Bristol – 20/04/1964
Comments: Shoots his way along either wing. Good crosser of the ball

MARS – **Marshall Ian**   Oldham Athletic    **Striker**    6  17  10  DL$........
Born: Oxford – 20/03/1966
Comments: Was the Latic's leading scorer when listed as a defender!

MARJ – **Marshall John**   Fulham            **Defender**   5   2   0   DL$........
Born: Surrey – 18/08/1964
Comments: A one club man, because no-one want's him

MARA – **Martin Alvin**   West Ham United    **Defender**   1   1   0   DL$........
Born: Bootle – 29/07/1958
Comments: Very prone to being injured

MARD – **Martin David**   Non League Team    **Defender**   5  12   1   DL$........
Born: East Ham – 25/04/1963
Comments: On loan to Colchester so watch out

MADE – **Martin Dean**   Scunthorpe United   **Midfield**   0   1   1   DL$........
Born: Halifax – 09/09/1967
Comments: Whole hearted and competitve player

MALE – **Martin Lee**   Manchester United    **Defender**   1   0   0   DL$........
Born: Hyde – 05/02/1968
Comments: Last goal was 1990 Cup Final winner

MDAV – **Martindale Dave**   Tranmere Rovers **Midfield**   2   0   0   DL$........
Born: Liverpool – 09/04/1964
Comments: Wheres the goal's gone Dave

MARW – **Marwood Brian**   Sheffield United  **Midfield**   6   2   1   DL$........
Born: Seaham Harbour – 05/02/1960
Comments: Skilful in midfield or on the wings

MASK – **Maskell Craig**   Reading           **Striker**   19  10  16  DL$........
Born: Aldershot – 10/04/1968
Comments: Good touch and has ability to turn opposition players

MATM – **Matthews Mike**   Hull City         **Midfield**   3   1   2   DL$........
Born: Hull – 25/09/1960
Comments: Back to his best after a broken leg

MATN – **Matthews Neil**   Stockport County  **Striker**   13  14   1   DL$........
Born: Grimsby – 19/09/1966
Comments: Neil must be happy not to be out on loan

MANE – **Matthews Neil**   Cardiff City      **Defender**   0   1   0   DL$........
Born: Manchester – 03/12/1967
Comments: Neil hasn't been across the centre line this year

---

## Dream League Trivia

*Who scored 9 goals in an FA Cup Tie in 1971?*


Answer: Ted MacDougal, Bournemouth v Margate

---

160

| PLAYER GUIDE | | | 90 | 91 | 92 | |
|---|---|---|---|---|---|---|

MARO – **Matthews Rob**   Notts County   **Striker**   0   0   3   DL$........
Born: – TBA
Comments: Robs one for the future

MATR – **Matthewson Trevor**   Birmingham City   **Defender**   1   3   6   DL$........
Born: Sheffield – 12/02/1963
Comments: Long time serving Blue

MAUC – **Mauchlen Ally**   Leeds United   **Midfield**   1   1   1   DL$........
Born: Kilwinning – 29/06/1960
Comments: Loan

MAUG – **Mauge Ron**   Manchester City   **Defender**   2   8   1   DL$........
Born: Islington – 10/03/1969
Comments: Loan. Big Dream League prospect lost

MAYA – **May Andy**   Bristol City   **Midfield**   0   3   2   DL$........
Born: Bury – 26/02/1964
Comments: Andy may score but then again

MAYD – **May David**   Blackburn Rovers   **Defender**   0   1   0   DL$........
Born: Oldham – 24/06/1970
Comments: From Youth team

MCAG – **McAllister Gary**   Leeds United   **Midfield**   10   5   5   DL$........
Born: Motherwell – 25/12/1964
Comments: You can count Gary's goal's on one hand

MCAV – **McAvennie Frank**   West Ham United   **Striker**   0   11   7   DL$........
Born: Glasgow – 22/11/1959
Comments: That hat-trck was a bit late for both the Hammers and Frank

MCST – **McCall Steve**   Plymouth Argyle   **Midfield**   0   2   1   DL$........
Born: Carlisle – 15/10/1960
Comments: Another Francis reject

MCCM – **McCarrick Mark**   Tranmere Rovers   **Defender**   5   2   0   DL$........
Born: Livepool – 04/02/1962
Comments: Local job

MCCD – **McCarrison Dugald**   Darlington   **Striker**   0   0   2   DL$........
Born: Lanark – 22/12/1969
Comments: On loan from Celtic

MCCJ – **McCarthy Jon**   York City   **Defender**   0   2   9   DL$........
Born: Middlesbrough – 18/08/1970
Comments: "Brains".All the way from Nottingham Polytechnic

MCMI – **McCarthy Mick**   Millwall   **Defender**   0   0   2   DL$........
Born: Barnsley – 07/02/1959
Comments: Player-manager, might prefer the office to the net

MCCA – **McCarthy Sean**   Bradford   **Striker**   12   15   15   DL$........
Born: Bridgend – 12/09/1967
Comments: Prolific bantam

MCCL – **McClair Brian**   Manchester United   **Striker**   8   17   23   DL$........
Born: Bellshill – 08/12/1963
Comments: Brian's been red hot this season, a dollar a goal?

MCCC – **McClean Christian**   Northampton Town   **Striker**   4   0   5   DL$........
Born: Colchester – 17/10/1963
Comments: Big, strong cobbler

161

**DREAM LEAGUE – CHAPTER 10**　　　　　　**90 91 92**

# Dream League Trivia

*Who scored the most goals in one League match?*

Answer: Joe Payne, Luton v Bristol in 1936

MCBR – **McCord Brian**　Barnsley　　　**Midfield**　1　1　0　DL$........
Born: Derby – 24/08/1968
Comments: At home either as right-back or midfield

MCDJ – **McDermott John**　Grimsby Town　**Defender**　0　0　1　DL$........
Born: Middlesbrough – 03/02/1969
Comments: Long time server at Blundell Park

MCDN – **McDonald Neil**　Oldham Athletic　**Midfield**　1　4　1　DL$........
Born: Wallsend – 02/11/1965
Comments: At home at right-back or in midfield

MCDR – **McDonald Rod**　Walsall　　　**Striker**　0　6　20　DL$........
Born: London – 20/03/1967
Comments: Could prove a good buy for someone, potential Dream League star

MCDA – **McDonough Darron**　Newcastle United　**Defender**　5　0　0　DL$........
Born: Antwerp – 07/11/1962
Comments: Darron must be homesick, he can't score

MCGO – **McGee Owen**　Scarborough　**Defender**　0　1　0　DL$........
Born: Teesside – 29/04/1970
Comments: Young defender lost touch

MCGE – **McGee Paul**　Wimbledon　　**Striker**　1　7　3　DL$........
Born: Dublin – 17/05/1968
Comments: Skilful natural winger

MCGH – **McGhee Mark**　Reading　　　**Striker**　25　6　5　DL$........
Born: Glasgow – 25/05/1957
Comments: Player/Manager was once a prolific goal scorer

MCGI – **McGinlay John**　Millwall　　**Striker**　24　9　8　DL$........
Born: Inverness – 08/04/1964
Comments: Struggling to find a first team place

MCED – **McGoldrick Eddie**　Crystal Palace　**Midfield**　0　0　3　DL$........
Born: London – 30/04/1965
Comments: Claplinesque till he shaved his "tashe" off

MCLL – **McGrath Lloyd**　Coventry City　**Midfield**　0　0　2　DL$........
Born: Birmingham – 24/02/1965
Comments: Long serving at Highfield Road

MCGP – **McGrath Paul**　Aston Villa　　**Defender**　1　0　1　DL$........
Born: Greenford – 04/12/1959
Comments: Villa vet who's found the net

MCGU – **McGugan Paul**　Chesterfield　**Defender**　0　1　3　DL$........
Born: Glasgow – 17/07/1964
Comments: Tall, defender who likes to push forward

| PLAYER GUIDE | | | 90 | 91 | 92 | |
|---|---|---|---|---|---|---|

MCJA – **McJannet Les**  Darlington    **Defender**  4  4  0  DL$........
Born: Cumnock – 02/08/1961
Comments: Ever-present Mr Reliable

MCKE – **McKearney David**  Crewe Alexandra  **Midfield**  1  2  4  DL$........
Born: Crosby – 20/06/1968
Comments: Dave's getting better

MCKG – **McKeown Gary**  Shrewsbury Town  **Midfield**  0  0  1  DL$........
Born: Oxford – 19/10/1970
Comments: Loan

MCLJ – **McLaughlin Joe**  Watford    **Defender**  0  1  1  DL$........
Born: Greenock – 02/06/1960
Comments: Paul Young lookalike

MCLO – **McLoughlin Alan**  Portsmouth  **Midfield**  16  1  3  DL$........
Born: Manchester – 20/04/1967
Comments: Likes to move around the coast

MCLP – **McLoughlin Paul**  Mansfield Town  **Striker**  4  0  8  DL$........
Born: Bristol – 23/12/1963
Comments: Paul's another whose getting better

MCMA – **McMahon Steve**  Manchester City  **Midfield**  6  3  1  DL$........
Born: Liverpool – 20/08/1961
Comments: Vision in midfield, reducing on the goal front

MCMS – **McManaman Steven**  Liverpool  **Striker**  0  0  11  DL$........
Born: Liverpool – 11/02/1972
Comments: Has played in midfield and attack

MAND – **McMillan Andy**  York City    **Defender**  0  1  1  DL$........
Born: Bloemfontein, S.Africa – 22/06/1968
Comments: Being watched by famous "names"

MCMT – **McMinn Ted**  Derby County  **Midfield**  3  0  3  DL$........
Born: Castle Douglas – 28/09/1962
Comments: Watch out for his transfer

MCNA – **McNab Neil**  Huddersfield Town  **Midfield**  1  3  0  DL$........
Born: Greenock – 04/06/1957
Comments: Loan

MCNB – **McNally Bernard**  W. Bromwich Albion  **Midfield**  6  1  2  DL$........
Born: Shrewsbury – 17/02/1963
Comments: Likes to play in the middle.....but doesn't

MCPA – **McParland Ian**  Walsall    **Striker**  5  8  0  DL$........
Born: Edinburgh – 04/10/1961
Comments: Could emulate famous 'Peter'

MCPH – **McPherson Keith**  Reading    **Defender**  1  3  1  DL$........
Born: Greenwich – 11/09/1963
Comments: Good, solid dependable defender and team captain

MEAD – **Meade Raphael**  Brighton & Hove A.  **Striker**  0  0  12  DL$........
Born: Islington – 22/11/1962
Comments: Prolific striker, back from European football

MEAS – **Measham Ian**  Burnley    **Defender**  0  0  1  DL$........
Born: Barnsley – 14/12/1964
Comments: Long time in defence for the clarets

**DREAM LEAGUE - CHAPTER 10**　　　　　　　　**90 91 92**

MEGS – **Megson Gary**   Manchester City　　**Midfield**　0　1　0　DL$........
Born: Manchester – 02/05/1959
Comments: Aged, well travelled midfielder

MEGK – **Megson Kevin**   Halifax Town　　**Striker**　1　0　0　DL$........
Born: Halifax – 01/07/1971
Comments: Lost the scoring habit

MEHE – **Mehew David**   Bristol Rovers　　**Striker**　19　8　11　DL$........
Born: Camberley – 29/10/1967
Comments: Pirate upfront

MELV – **Melville Andy**   Oxford　　**Defender**　7　4　4　DL$........
Born: Swansea – 29/11/1968
Comments: Tall, skilful defender who likes to score

MEND – **Mendonca Clive**   Grimsby Town　　**Striker**　15　12　4　DL$........
Born: Tullington – 09/09/1968
Comments: Clives trying to add to the Mariners attack

MERS – **Merson Paul**   Arsenal　　**Striker**　7　16　13　DL$........
Born: London – 20/03/1968
Comments: Brilliant product of the Gunner's youth policy

METH – **Methven Colin**   Walsall　　**Defender**　4　1　2　DL$........
Born: India – 10/12/1955
Comments: It's a long way from India to Bescot Crescent

MEYE – **Meyer Adrian**   Scarborough　　**Defender**　2　1　5　DL$........
Born: Bristol – 22/09/1970
Comments: Sparkling product from the Boro's Youth Policy

MICK – **Micklewhite Gary**   Derby County　　**Midfield**　2　3　2　DL$........
Born: Southwark – 21/03/1961
Comments: Been a ram for a long time

MIAD – **Mike Adrian**   Manchester City　　**Striker**　0　0　1　DL$........
Born: TBA
Comments: One to watch

MILP – **Millar Paul**   Cardiff City　　**Striker**　0　1　2　DL$........
Born: Belfast – 16/11/1966
Comments: Paul's not afraid to shoot

MILK – **Millen Keith**   Brentford　　**Defender**　1　2　1　DL$........
Born: Croydon – 26/09/1966
Comments: Up through the ranks

MILD – **Miller David**   Stockport County　　**Midfield**　3　4　0　DL$........
Born: Burnley – 08/01/1964
Comments: Done the rounds in the lower divisions

---

## Dream League Trivia

*Who has scored the most international goals?*

Answer: Pele, 97 between 1957 and 1971

# PLAYER GUIDE

**90 91 92**

**MILI – Miller Ian**  Scunthorpe United  **Striker**  1  0  0  DL$........
Born: Perth – 13/05/1955
Comments: Would have more success in a windmill

**MIPA – Miller Paul**  Wimbledon  **Striker**  0  0  2  DL$........
Born: Bisley – 31/01/1968
Comments: "Maggot's" is now getting first team glory

**MPAU – Miller Paul**  Swansea City  **Defender**  1  0  0  DL$........
Born: London – 11/10/1959
Comments: Well stricken in years

**MILL – Milligan Mike**  Oldham Athletic  **Midfield**  8  1  4  DL$........
Born: Manchester – 20/02/1967
Comments: Skilful midfielder

**MILB – Mills Brian**  Port Vale  **Striker**  0  2  1  DL$........
Born: Swynnerton – 26/12/1971
Comments: Highly rated product of the "Valiants" youth policy

**MILG – Mills Gary**  Leicester City  **Midfield**  4  5  7  DL$........
Born: Northampton – 11/11/1961
Comments: Major contributor to City's end of season run

**MILS – Mills Simon**  Port Vale  **Defender**  1  0  4  DL$........
Born: Sheffield – 16/08/1964
Comments: Skilful right-back with an excellent passing ability

**MIAN – Milner Andy**  Rochdale  **Striker**  4  7  14  DL$........
Born: Kendal – 10/02/1967
Comments: Andy's getting carried away scoring

**MILT – Milton Simon**  Ipswich Town  **Midfield**  10  7  8  DL$........
Born: London – 23/08/1963
Comments: Prefers his goals to fly in from no less than 20 yards

**MIST – Milton Steve**  Fulham  **Striker**  9  0  0  DL$........
Born: Fulham – 13/04/1963
Comments: Seems to have gone back to Mothercare

**MINT – Minto Scott**  Charlton Athletic  **Defender**  2  2  2  DL$........
Born: Cheshire – 06/08/1971
Comments: Best product from youths. Possible million in the bank

**MIJE – Minton Jeffrey**  Tottenham Hotspur  **Striker**  0  0  1  DL$........
Born: Hackney – 28/12/1973
Comments: Product of the Spur's youth policy

**MITC – Mitchell Brian**  Bradford  **Defender**  2  0  1  DL$........
Born: Stonehaven – 16/07/1963
Comments: Solid dependable bantam

**MITD – Mitchell David**  Swindon Town  **Striker**  0  1  8  DL$........
Born: Glasgow – 13/06/1962
Comments: Might be a 'gooden' for next season

**MOCK – Mockler Andrew**  Scarborough  **Midfield**  0  5  5  DL$........
Born: Stockton – 18/11/1970
Comments: One of the Boro's younsters

**MOHA – Mohan Nicky**  Middlesbrough  **Defender**  0  0  2  DL$........
Born: Middlesbrough – 06/10/1970
Comments: Nicky's making a comeback after serious injury

DREAM LEAGUE – CHAPTER 10    90 91 92

> # Dream League Trivia
>
> *Who is the youngest Cup Final goalscorer?*
>
> Answer: Norman Whiteside – Manchester United

**MOLB** – **Molby Jan**   Liverpool         **Midfield**   1   9   4   DL$........
Born: Kolding,Denmark – 04/07/1963
Comments: Now regaining previous form and team place in centre circle

**MONC** – **Moncur John**   Swindon Town   **Midfield**   1   0   0   DL$........
Born: Stepney – 22/09/1966
Comments: Glenda's brought a refugee from White Hartland

**MONI** – **Monington Mark**   Burnley     **Midfield**   0   0   1   DL$........
Born: Bilsthorpe – 21/10/1970
Comments: Tall midfielder

**MONK** – **Monkou Kenneth**   Chelsea     **Defender**   1   1   3   DL$........
Born: Surinam – 29/11/1964
Comments: Familiar figure in defence

**MOON** – **Mooney Brian**   Sunderland    **Midfield**   9   0   0   DL$........
Born: Dublin – 02/02/1966
Comments: Where's the goals Brian

**MOOT** – **Mooney Tommy**   Scarborough   **Striker**    0  13  11   DL$........
Born: Teesside North – 11/08/1971
Comments: 1992-3 could be his season. A good Dream League investment

**MDAR** – **Moore Darren**   Torquay United  **Striker**  0   0   1   DL$........
Born: Hansworth – 22/04/1974
Comments: Very promising newcomer

**MOOR** – **Moore Gary**   Maidstone United **Striker**   0   1   0   DL$........
Born: Greenwich – 29/12/1968
Comments: Stick to playing the guitar Gary

**MOOJ** – **Moore John**   Scarborough     **Striker**    0   0   1   DL$........
Born: Consett – 01/10/1966
Comments: League glory from non league

**MOOK** – **Moore Kevin**   Southampton    **Defender**   1   1   0   DL$........
Born: Grimsby – 29/04/1958
Comments: Long time serving "Saint"

**MORK** – **Moran Kevin**   Blackburn Rovers **Defender** 2   1   3   DL$........
Born: Dublin – 29/04/1956
Comments: Established in making Cup records

**MORP** – **Moran Paul**   Tottenham Hotspur **Striker**  1   0   0   DL$........
Born: Enfield – 22/05/1968
Comments: Not often seen

**MORA** – **Moran Steve**   Exeter City    **Striker**   15   8  20   DL$........
Born: Croydon – 10/01/1961
Comments: More than the average striker, worth a gamble to Christmas

| PLAYER GUIDE | | | 90 | 91 | 92 | |
|---|---|---|---|---|---|---|

MORG – **Morgan Nicky**  Bristol City  **Striker**  5  17  5  **DL$**........
Born: East Ham – 30/10/1959
Comments: Experienced striker who's losing his touch

MORS – **Morgan Simon**  Fulham  **Defender**  2  0  3  **DL$**........
Born: Birmingham – 05/09/1966
Comments: Never commited a foul, as he tells refs whenever pulled up

MOST – **Morgan Steve**  Rochdale  **Midfield**  1  3  0  **DL$**........
Born: Wrexham – 28/12/1970
Comments: Lost sight of the net

MGAN – **Morgan Steve**  Plymouth Argyle  **Defender**  1  3  2  **DL$**........
Born: Oldham – 19/09/1968
Comments: Strong tackling versitile player

MORT – **Morgan Trevor**  Exeter City  **Striker**  12  3  1  **DL$**........
Born: Forest Gate – 30/09/1956
Comments: Long in year's, short in goals

MORL – **Morley Trevor**  West Ham United  **Striker**  12  17  5  **DL$**........
Born: Nottingham – 20/03/1961
Comments: Highest scorer for the "Hammer's" (90/91)

MOPA – **Morrell Paul**  AFC Bournemouth  **Defender**  0  1  2  **DL$**........
Born: Poole – 23/03/1961
Comments: One of the "Cherries" longest serving players

MOAN – **Morris Andy**  Chesterfield  **Striker**  1  8  3  **DL$**........
Born: Sheffield – 17/11/1967
Comments: At 6ft 4 lives up to the club's nickname

MODA – **Morris David**  AFC Bournemouth  **Midfield**  0  0  2  **DL$**........
Born: Plumstead – 19/11/1971
Comments: Rarely seen midfielder

MORM – **Morris Mark**  AFC Bournemouth  **Defender**  3  0  1  **DL$**........
Born: Morden – 26/09/1962
Comments: Missing his old mentor Dave Bassett

MRRI – **Morrison Andy**  Plymouth Argyle  **Midfield**  1  2  4  **DL$**........
Born: Inverness – 30/07/1970
Comments: Big and strong in the tackle

MORR – **Morrissey John**  Tranmere Rovers  **Midfield**  4  10  6  **DL$**........
Born: Liverpool – 08/03/1965
Comments: No flowers in his back pocket

MOGR – **Morrow Grant**  Doncaster Rovers  **Striker**  2  1  0  **DL$**........
Born: Glasgow – 04/10/1970
Comments: Tomorrow Grant may score

MORH – **Mortensen Henrik**  Norwich City  **Striker**  0  1  0  **DL$**........
Born: Odder, Denmark – 12/02/1968
Comments: Bet the Yokels are having fun with this at Carrow Road

MRTI – **Mortimer Paul**  Crystal Palace  **Midfield**  5  7  3  **DL$**........
Born: London – 08/05/1968
Comments: £500,000 Villa Park misfit

MORN – **Morton Neil**  Chester City  **Striker**  0  7  2  **DL$**........
Born: Congleton – 21/12/1968
Comments: Exciting player from Non League

**DREAM LEAGUE – CHAPTER 10**　　　　　　　　　90 91 92

MOUL – **Moulden Paul**　Oldham Athletic　**Striker**　0　4　1　DL$........
Born: Farnwoth – 06/09/1967
Comments: Mould's growing on the boots that onced scored many at the Lads' Club

MOUN – **Mountfield Derek** Wolverhampton W.　**Defender**　7　4　1　DL$........
Born: Liverpool – 02/11/1962
Comments: "Mounty"'s found the net again but not his won for once

MUDD – **Mudd Paul**　Scarborough　**Defender**　0　0　1　DL$........
Born: Hull – 13/11/1970
Comments: Here's mud in your eye, Paul's scored

MUIR – **Muir Ian**　Tranmere Rovers　**Striker**　27　13　5　DL$........
Born: Coventry – 05/05/1963
Comments: Scoring consistently fewer thanks to injury

MUIJ – **Muir John**　Stockport County　**Striker**　4　14　1　DL$........
Born: Sedgley – 26/04/1963
Comments: Inconsistent is his middle name

MUMB – **Mumby Peter**　Burnley　**Striker**　6　7　0　DL$........
Born: Bradford – 22/02/1969
Comments: Free gift to Burnley from Shamrock Rovers

MUNS – **Munday Stuart**　Brighton & Hove A.　**Defender**　0　0　1　DL$........
Born: Shoeburyness – 28/09/1972
Comments: Trainee

MUND – **Mundee Denny**　AFC Bournemouth　**Midfield**　0　2　4　DL$........
Born: Swindon – 10/10/1968
Comments: Versatile utility player

MUNG – **Mungall Steve**　Tranmere Rovers　**Defender**　1　1　0　DL$........
Born: Bellshill – 22/05/1958
Comments: Don't count on him scoring too many next year

MURP – **Murphy Aidan**　Crewe Alexandra　**Midfield**　5　2　1　DL$........
Born: Manchester – 17/09/1967
Comments: Over 100 apearances for the Railwaymen

MURF – **Murphy Frank**　Barnet　**Striker**　0　0　5　DL$........
Born: Glasgow – 01/06/1959
Comments: Another of the Bee's vet's

MURS – **Murray Shaun**　Portsmouth　**Striker**　0　1　0　DL$........
Born: Newcastle – 07/02/1970
Comments: Some striker!

MUST – **Mustoe Robbie**　Middlesbrough　**Midfield**　7　7　3　DL$........
Born: Oxford – 28/08/1968
Comments: Scores well from midfield

## Dream League Trivia

*Who scored the most goals in a League Cup competition?*

Answer: Clive Allen, 12 – 1986/87

| PLAYER GUIDE | | | 90 | 91 | 92 | |
|---|---|---|---|---|---|---|

MUTC – **Mutch Andy**  Wolverhampton W.  **Striker**  12  8  10  DL$........
Born: Liverpool – 28/12/1963
Comments: Mutch of a Mutchness and good value

MYER – **Myers Andy**  Chelsea  **Midfield**  0  0  1  DL$........
Born: Hounslow – 03/11/1973
Comments: Product of the Blue's youth policy

MYEC – **Myers Chris**  Torquay United  **Midfield**  0  2  4  DL$........
Born: Yeovil – 01/04/1969
Comments: Young star at Plainmoor

NARB – **Narbett Jon**  Hereford  **Midfield**  5  12  10  DL$........
Born: Birmingham – 21/11/1968
Comments: Ignore his form at your peril

NAUG – **Naughton Willie**  Walsall  **Striker**  5  1  0  DL$........
Born: Catrine – 20/03/1962
Comments: Last season at least

NAYI – **Nayim Mohamed Amar**  Spurs  **Midfield**  3  5  1  DL$........
Born: Morocco – 05/11/1966
Comments: Gritty member of the "Spur"s side with a great dive

NAYD – **Naylor Dominic**  Barnet  **Defender**  1  0  1  DL$........
Born: Watford – 12/08/1970
Comments: Back this season from a spell in Hong Kong

NAYG – **Naylor Glenn**  York City  **Striker**  0  5  8  DL$........
Born: York – 11/08/1972
Comments: Skilful striker

NAYT – **Naylor Tony**  Crewe Alexandra  **Striker**  0  1  24  DL$........
Born: Manchester – 29/03/1967
Comments: Need one say more

NDLO – **Ndlovu Peter**  Coventry City  **Striker**  0  0  2  DL$........
Born: Bulawayo – 25/02/1973
Comments: Don't underestimate this fellow

NEIL – **Neill Warren**  Portsmouth  **Defender**  0  1  0  DL$........
Born: Acton – 21/11/1962
Comments: Dependable in defence

NEIA – **Neilson Alan**  Newcastle United  **Defender**  0  0  1  DL$........
Born: Wegberg – 26/09/1972
Comments: Promising defender

NELS – **Nelson Garry**  Charlton Athletic  **Striker**  6  5  6  DL$........
Born: Braintree – 16/01/1961
Comments: Hardest working, least productive striker in team

NETS – **Nethercott Stewart**  Barnsley  **Defender**  0  0  1  DL$........
Born: Chadwell Heath – 21/03/1973
Comments: Loan

NEVP – **Nevin Pat**  Everton  **Striker**  1  9  2  DL$........
Born: Glasgow – 06/09/1963
Comments: Can be devastating along the wing

NEWE – **Newell Mike**  Blackburn Rovers  **Striker**  10  7  13  DL$........
Born: Liverpool – 27/01/1965
Comments: All depends on whether he fulfills his potential

DREAM LEAGUE – CHAPTER 10                90 91 92

> # Dream League Trivia
>
> Who scored the Northern Ireland goal to beat Spain in the 1982 World Cup?
>
> Answer: Gerry Armstrong

**NEWH – Newhouse Aidan**  Wimbledon  **Midfield**  0  1  1  DL$........
Born: Wallasey – 23/05/1972
Comments: Another young "Don" trying to get a regular place

**NERI – Newman Rickey**  Maidstone United  **Midfield**  0  0  1  DL$........
Born: Guilford – 05/08/1970
Comments: Loan

**NEWM – Newman Rob**  Norwich City  **Defender**  9  8  9  DL$........
Born: Bradford-on-Avon – 13/12/1963
Comments: Has a reputation for scoring from midfield

**NEWS – Newsome Jon**  Leeds United  **Defender**  0  0  2  DL$........
Born: Sheffield – 06/09/1970
Comments: Scored the 2nd against Sheffield Utd in the 'Big One'

**NEMA – Newson Mark**  Fulham  **Defender**  0  1  3  DL$........
Born: Stepney – 07/12/1960
Comments: "Noose". Play's well for 89 minutes then drops a right ricket

**NEED – Newton Edward**  Chelsea  **Midfield**  0  0  5  DL$........
Born: Hammersmith – 13/12/1971
Comments: Highly rated at the Bridge

**NICH – Nicholas Peter**  Watford  **Midfield**  0  0  1  DL$........
Born: Newport – 10/11/1959
Comments: Most capped Welshman, but is going bald in the reserves

**NICM – Nicholson Max**  Doncaster Rovers  **Striker**  0  0  2  DL$........
Born: Leeds – 03/10/1971
Comments: Another youngster showing potential at Belle Vue

**NICS – Nicholson Shane**  Lincoln City  **Defender**  1  4  1  DL$........
Born: Newark – 03/06/1970
Comments: Strong left back, product of the Imps Youth policy

**NICO – Nicol Steve**  Liverpool  **Defender**  9  3  1  DL$........
Born: Irvine – 11/12/1961
Comments: Probably the "Red's" most versitile player

**NILS – Nilsson Roland**  Sheffield Wednesday  **Defender**  0  0  1  DL$........
Born: Helsingborg, Sweden – 27/11/1963
Comments: Coming back from a bad injury

**NIXP – Nixon Paul**  Bristol Rovers  **Striker**  5  1  0  DL$........
Born: Seaham – 23/09/1963
Comments: Paul's a dried up pirate

**NOGA – Nogan Kurt**  Luton Town  **Striker**  2  0  2  DL$........
Born: Cardiff – 09/09/1970
Comments: Capable of missing open goals from anywhere in the area

# PLAYER GUIDE                                    90 91 92

**NOGL – Nogan Lee**  Watford          **Striker**   0  6 10   DL$........
Born: Cardiff – 21/05/1969
Comments: 'Noggin the Nog', prolific goal scorer by Watfords standards

**NOLA – Nolan Ian**  Tranmere Rovers   **Striker**   0  0  1   DL$........
Born: Liverpool – 09/07/1970
Comments: Could it be the first of many?

**NORB – Norbury Mick**  Cambridge United  **Striker**   0  0  2   DL$........
Born: Hemsworth – 22/01/1969
Comments: Could be Dion's replacement

**NORR – Norris Steve**  Chesterfield   **Striker**   3 32 18   DL$........
Born: Coventry – 22/09/1961
Comments: Worth at least another season in many Dream Teams

**NORT – North Marc**  Leicester City   **Striker**   6  2  0   DL$........
Born: Ware – 29/05/1966
Comments: Suddenly dried up

**NORD – Norton David**  Hull City      **Midfield**   1  0  2   DL$........
Born: Cannock – 03/03/1965
Comments: Been known to captain the Tigers

**NOTE – Noteman Kevin**  Mansfield Town  **Striker**   4  8 11   DL$........
Born: Preston – 15/10/1969
Comments: Guaranteed to double his score next year

**NTAM – Ntamark Charlie**  Walsall    **Midfield**   0  3  5   DL$........
Born: Cameroon – 22/07/1964
Comments: Highly rated international yet to acclimatise, surprise, surprise

**NUGE – Nugent Kevin**  Plymouth Argyle  **Striker**   0  9 17   DL$........
Born: Edmonton – 10/04/1969
Comments: Prolific goal scorer recently signed and then injured

**OBRI – O'Brien Liam**  Newcastle United  **Midfield**   3  3  4   DL$........
Born: Dublin – 05/09/1964
Comments: Lack of energy to reach opponents box, long distance scorer

**OCAL – O'Callaghan Kevin**  Southend United  **Striker**   0  2  0   DL$........
Born: London – 19/10/1961
Comments: Small, neat, experienced player

**OCOB – O'Connell Brendan**  Barnsley   **Striker**   1  9  5   DL$........
Born: London – 12/11/1966
Comments: Was the Oakwell Supporter's "Player of the Year" 90/91

**OCON – O'Connor Mark**  Gillingham    **Midfield**   1  3  3   DL$........
Born: Rochdale – 10/03/1963
Comments: Mark cant break three

**ODOH – O'Doherty Ken**  Huddersfield Town  **Defender**   1  0  0   DL$........
Born: Dublin – 30/03/1963
Comments: Loan

**ODRI – O'Driscoll Sean**  AFC Bournemouth  **Midfield**   0  2  1   DL$........
Born: Wolverhampton – 01/07/1957
Comments: Another long serving "Cherry"

**OHAR – O'Hara Steve**  Walsall       **Midfield**   0  0  3   DL$........
Born: Lanark – 21/02/1971
Comments: Nothing scarlet about Steve

## DREAM LEAGUE – CHAPTER 10              90 91 92

**OLEA – O'Leary David**   Arsenal   **Defender**   0   1   0   DL$........
Born: London – 02/05/1958
Comments: Longest ever serving Gunner with consistent scoring record

**OREG – O'Regan Kieran**   Huddersfield Town   **Midfield**   3   12   5   DL$........
Born: Cork – 09/11/1963
Comments: Kieran's the clever one, can play anywhere including in goal

**OREI – O'Reilly Gary**   Brighton & Hove A.   **Defender**   2   0   3   DL$........
Born: Isleworth – 21/03/1961
Comments: Tall strong central defender

**ORIO – O'Riordan Don**   Notts County   **Midfield**   0   3   0   DL$........
Born: Dublin – 14/05/1957
Comments: Irishman who's not sure where the goal is anymore

**OSHA – O'Shaughnessy Steve**   Darlington   **Defender**   10   3   1   DL$........
Born: Wrexham – 13/10/1967
Comments: He might have another strikers season

**OSHE – O'Shea Danny**   Cambridge United   **Defender**   0   0   1   DL$........
Born: Kennington – 26/03/1963
Comments: Danny's found the net at last

**OSHT – O'Shea Tim**   Gillingham   **Defender**   2   0   0   DL$........
Born: London – 12/11/1966
Comments: Lost touch fro the Gills

**OAKS – Oakes Scott**   Luton Town   **Midfield**   0   0   2   DL$........
Born: Leicester – 05/08/1972
Comments: Showaddy what! Yet to show signs of musical talent

**OGHA – Oghani George**   Scarborough   **Striker**   4   16   0   DL$........
Born: Manchester – 02/09/1960
Comments: What happened? Age

**OGLE – Ogley Mark**   York City   **Defender**   0   0   1   DL$........
Born: Barnsley – 10/03/1967
Comments: Clinging to the professional game

**OKAI – Okai Steve**   Leyton Orient   **Striker**   0   0   1   DL$........
Born: Ghana – 03/12/1973
Comments: Skilful right-winger

**OKEN – Okenie Folorunso**   Birmingham City   **Striker**   0   0   1   DL$........
Born: Nigeria – 09/10/1967
Comments: Foli to his friends

**OLDF – Oldfield David**   Leicester City   **Striker**   7   7   4   DL$........
Born: Perth, Australia – 30/05/1968
Comments: Tubular striker from Oz

---

## Dream League Trivia

*Who was the first player to miss a penalty in a FA Cup Final?*

Answer: John Aldridge, 1988

---

172

# PLAYER GUIDE           90 91 92

**OLIV – Oliver Gavin**  Bradford          **Defender**  0  6  0   DL$........
Born: Felling – 06/09/1962
Comments: Bradford's Player of the season in 90/91

**OLNE – Olney Ian**  Aston Villa          **Striker**   2  3  2   DL$........
Born: Luton – 17/12/1969
Comments: Striker whose most often found lurking around sub's bench

**OLSS – Olsson Paul**  Hartlepool United  **Midfield**  2  1  6   DL$........
Born: Hull – 24/12/1965
Comments: Regular scorer from midfield

**ONUO – Onuora Iffy**  Huddersfield Town  **Striker**   4  8  13  DL$........
Born: Glasgow – 28/07/1967
Comments: Brainy boy Ifem, came from University

**ONWE – Onwere Udo**  Fulham              **Midfield**  0  1  3   DL$........
Born: Hammersmith – 09/11/1971
Comments: Busy midfielder who suffers a little in confidence

**ORLY – Orlygsson Thorvaldur**  Notts Forest  **Midfield**  1  0  0   DL$........
Born: Odense – 02/08/1966
Comments: Icelandic International left out in the cold

**ORMO – Ormondroyd Ian**  Leicester City  **Striker**   6  3  11  DL$........
Born: Bradford – 22/09/1964
Comments: Returning to the good old days

**ORMS – Ormsby Brendan**  Doncaster Rovers  **Defender**  0  5  3   DL$........
Born: Birmingham – 01/10/1960
Comments: Tough tackling no-nonsense defender

**OSBS – Osborn Simon**  Crystal Palace    **Midfield**  0  0  2   DL$........
Born: New Addington – 19/01/1972
Comments: Pocket battleship,"Ozzy" moonlights with Black Sabbath

**OSBO – Osborne Lawrence**  Gillingham    **Defender**  0  5  4   DL$........
Born: London – 20/10/1967
Comments: Could be a good bet for a few more

**OSBB – Osborne Steve**  Peterborough     **Striker**   5  1  0   DL$........
Born: Middlesbrough – 03/03/1969
Comments: Lost his way upfront

**OSMA – Osman Russell**  Bristol City     **Defender**  6  1  2   DL$........
Born: Repton – 14/02/1959
Comments: Experienced defender who is lighting up Ashton Park

**OTTO – Otto Ricky**  Leyton Orient       **Midfield**  0  0  5   DL$........
Born: London – 09/11/1967
Comments: One to watch

**OVER – Overson Vince**  Stoke City       **Defender**  0  2  3   DL$........
Born: Kettering – 15/05/1962
Comments: Tall central defender with an eye for goal

**OWEN – Owen Gareth**  Wrexham            **Midfield**  0  2  7   DL$........
Born: Chester – 21/10/1971
Comments: Useful young midfielder, from the Robins Youth

**OWER – Owers Gary**  Sunderland          **Midfield**  9  2  4   DL$........
Born: Newcastle – 03/10/1968
Comments: Strong midfielder whose shots usually go long and wide

**DREAM LEAGUE – CHAPTER 10**

---

# Dream League Trivia

*Who scored in every round of the FA Cup in 1969/70?*

Answer: Peter Osgood, Chelsea

---

OXBR – **Oxbrow Darren**  Maidstone United  **Defender**  0  1  1  DL$........
Born: Ipswich – 01/09/1969
Comments: Well at least he's found it

PAGE – **Page Don**  Rotherham United  **Striker**  2  14  13  DL$........
Born: Manchester – 18/01/1964
Comments: Bit of a teaser for your Dream League Team

PAIN – **Painter Robert**  Burnley  **Midfield**  5  5  7  DL$........
Born: Ince – 26/01/1971
Comments: Better scoring record than a lot of them

PALI – **Palin Leigh**  Hull City  **Midfield**  1  5  1  DL$........
Born: Worcester – 12/09/1965
Comments: Ever present at Boothferry Park

PALL – **Pallister Gary**  Manchester United  **Defender**  3  0  1  DL$........
Born: Ramsgate – 30/06/1965
Comments: Skilful in defence, occasionally surprises with a goal

PALM – **Palmer Carlton**  Sheffield Wednesday  **Midfield**  0  3  5  DL$........
Born: West Bromwich – 05/12/1965
Comments: Shows promise for the senior England squad in 94

PALC – **Palmer Charlie**  Notts County  **Defender**  5  1  0  DL$........
Born: Aylesbury – 10/07/1963
Comments: Long time serving "Magpie"

PALE – **Palmer Lee**  Gillingham  **Defender**  3  1  0  DL$........
Born: Gillingham – 19/09/1970
Comments: Product of the Youth Team at Priestfield

PALR – **Palmer Roger**  Oldham Athletic  **Striker**  20  9  5  DL$........
Born: Manchester – 30/01/1959
Comments: Reads the ball well

PALS – **Palmer Steve**  Ipswich Town  **Midfield**  0  1  0  DL$........
Born: Brighton – 31/03/1968
Comments: Brains of the team. Degree in electrical engineering

PARD – **Pardew Alan**  Charlton Athletic  **Midfield**  7  1  2  DL$........
Born: Wimbledon – 18/07/1961
Comments: Best remembered for semi-final winner Palace v Liverpool

PARI – **Paris Alan**  Notts County  **Defender**  4  1  0  DL$........
Born: Slough – 15/08/1964
Comments: Experience in midfield

PARG – **Parker Garry**  Aston Villa  **Midfield**  7  8  3  DL$........
Born: Oxford – 07/09/1965
Comments: Experienced and skilful midfielder with an eye for goal

| | | | 90 | 91 | 92 | |
|---|---|---|---|---|---|---|

PARP – **Parker Paul**  Manchester United  **Defender**  0  1  0  DL$........
Born: Essex – 04/04/1964
Comments: Can play anywhere along the back four and stays there

PARS – **Parkin Steve**  West Bromwich Albion  **Defender**  1  0  0  DL$........
Born: Mansfield – 07/11/1965
Comments: Could be another full back

PART – **Parkin Tim**  Port Vale  **Defender**  1  0  0  DL$........
Born: Penrith – 31/12/1957
Comments: Tall, experienced central defender who doesn't like to score

PAGA – **Parkinson Gary**  Middlesbrough  **Defender**  3  1  1  DL$........
Born: Middlesbrough – 10/01/1968
Comments: Long time serving right-back

PARJ – **Parkinson Joe**  Wigan Athletic  **Midfield**  3  0  3  DL$........
Born: Eccles – 11/06/1971
Comments: Tough tackler who can play either midfield or at full-back

PPHI – **Parkinson Philip**  Bury  **Midfield**  2  2  0  DL$........
Born: Chorley – 01/12/1967
Comments: Mr.Reliable

PARA – **Parlour Ray**  Arsenal  **Midfield**  0  0  1  DL$........
Born: Romford – 07/03/1973
Comments: Shooting star from the reserve team squad

PARR – **Parris George**  West Ham United  **Defender**  2  8  1  DL$........
Born: Ilford – 11/09/1964
Comments: On the come-back trail

PASC – **Pascoe Colin**  Sunderland  **Striker**  2  5  2  DL$........
Born: Port Talbot – 09/04/1965
Comments: Long server at Roker Park

PASK – **Paskin John**  Wrexham  **Striker**  2  1  7  DL$........
Born: Capetown – 01/02/1962
Comments: 5 years ago maybe

PATE – **Paterson Jamie**  Halifax Town  **Striker**  0  0  2  DL$........
Born: Dumfries – 26/04/1973
Comments: Tiny Jamie, smallest member of the Shaymen's squad

PATT – **Patterson Darren**  Wigan Athletic  **Defender**  1  5  4  DL$........
Born: Belfast – 15/10/1969
Comments: Was once a "super-sub", now is the first choice centre-half

PATM – **Patterson Mark**  Bolton Wanderers  **Striker**  4  8  1  DL$........
Born: Darwen – 24/05/1965
Comments: Mark's lost his touch around goal

PAMA – **Patterson Mark**  Derby County  **Midfield**  0  1  3  DL$........
Born: Leeds – 13/09/1968
Comments: Patters about the park

PAYD – **Payne Derek**  Barnet  **Midfield**  0  0  1  DL$........
Born: Edgware – 26/04/1967
Comments: Diminutive midfielder

PAYM – **Payne Mark**  Rochdale  **Striker**  6  0  2  DL$........
Born: Cheltenham – 03/08/1960
Comments: Mark's feeling his way back

DREAM LEAGUE - CHAPTER 10                     90 91 92

PAYT - **Payton Andy**   Middlesbrough        **Striker**    18 25 11   DL$........
Born: Burnley – 23/10/1966
Comments: Prolific goal scorer, good buy, due Div 1. status

PEAD - **Peacock Darren**  Queens Park Rangers  **Defender**   4  0  1   DL$........
Born: Bristol – 03/02/1968
Comments: Strut's around in defence

PEAC - **Peacock Gavin**   Newcastle United   **Midfield**    4  7 20   DL$........
Born: Kent – 18/11/1967
Comments: Definitely more calibre than a pea shooter, hot property

PEAA - **Peake Andy**   Middlesbrough         **Midfield**    0  4  1   DL$........
Born: Market Harborough – 01/11/1961
Comments: Did Andy Peake in 90/91?

PEAJ - **Peake Jason**   Hartlepool United    **Midfield**    0  1  1   DL$........
Born: Leicester – 29/09/1971
Comments: Has Jason reached the summit of his goal scoring ability?

PEAK - **Peake Trevor**   Luton Town          **Defender**    0  1  0   DL$........
Born: Nuneaton – 10/02/1957
Comments: Veteran defender, able to charm his way out of red cards

PAND - **Pearce Andy**   Coventry City        **Defender**    0  1  2   DL$........
Born: Bradford – 20/04/1966
Comments: Tall, aerial attack potential

PEAR - **Pearce Stuart**   Nottingham Forest  **Defender**    7 16  8   DL$........
Born: London – 24/04/1962
Comments: Long time favourite at the City Ground, injury a set back

PEJO - **Pearson John**   Barnsley            **Striker**     0  6  2   DL$........
Born: Sheffield – 01/09/1963
Comments: Well travelled Tyke

PEAN - **Pearson Nigel**   Sheffield Wednesday  **Defender**  1 12  2   DL$........
Born: Nottingham – 21/08/1963
Comments: The Owl's team captain

PEEL - **Peel Nathan**   Preston North End    **Striker**     0  1  0   DL$........
Born: Blackburn – 17/05/1972
Comments: A lot to prove at new club

PEER - **Peer Dean**   Birmingham City        **Midfield**    3  0  4   DL$........
Born: Dudley – 08/08/1969
Comments: Engine-room, who never stops running when fit

PEJI - **Pejic Mel**   Wrexham                **Defender**    7  2  2   DL$........
Born: Chesterton – 27/04/1959
Comments: Great to see yet another old stager in Wales

---

## Dream League Trivia

*Whose uncle scored a goal in the FA Cup Final then broke
a leg and watched the rest of the game on TV?*

Answer: Elton John, Nephew of Roy Dwight

| PLAYER GUIDE | | | 90 91 92 |

PEMB – **Pemberton John**   Sheffield United   **Defender**   1   0   1   DL$........
Born: Oldham – 18/11/1964
Comments: Not a lot can be said

PEMM – **Pembridge Mark**   Derby   **Defender**   0   1   4   DL$........
Born: Methyr Tydfil – 29/11/1970
Comments: Competitive, no respect for reputations-will kick anybody

PEND – **Pender John**   Burnley   **Defender**   0   0   3   DL$........
Born: Luton – 19/11/1963
Comments: Tall, experienced defender

PENN – **Penney David**   Oxford   **Striker**   2   4   5   DL$........
Born: Wakefield – 17/08/1964
Comments: In for a Penney, in for a ...

PENG – **Pennyfather Glenn**   Ipswich Town   **Midfield**   1   0   0   DL$........
Born: Billericay – 11/02/1963
Comments: Been fighting to retain a first team place

PENR – **Penrice Gary**   Queens Park Rangers   **Striker**   14   5   5   DL$........
Born: Bristol – 23/03/1964
Comments: Skilful striker

PEPP – **Pepper Nigel**   York City   **Midfield**   1   4   4   DL$........
Born: Rotherham – 25/04/1968
Comments: Used to play rugby...most of his shots go over the bar

PETE – **Peters Rob**   Brentford   **Defender**   0   1   0   DL$........
Born: Kensington – 18/05/1971
Comments: Yet to produce the goods

PHEL – **Phelan Mike**   Manchester United   **Defender**   1   1   0   DL$........
Born: Nelson – 24/09/1962
Comments: Skilful in defence but prefers midfield

PHET – **Phelan Terry**   Wimbledon   **Defender**   0   0   1   DL$........
Born: Manchester – 16/03/1967
Comments: One of the fastest players in the League

PHID – **Phillips David**   Norwich City   **Midfield**   4   4   2   DL$........
Born: Wegberg – 29/07/1963
Comments: Midfielder who can also play at full-back

PHIJ – **Phillips Jimmy**   Middlesbrough   **Defender**   0   2   1   DL$........
Born: Bolton – 08/02/1966
Comments: Key left-back

PHJU – **Phillips Justin**   Derby County   **Defender**   0   1   0   DL$........
Born: Derby – 17/12/1971
Comments: Justin's always out

PHLE – **Phillips Les**   Oxford   **Midfield**   0   1   0   DL$........
Born: Lambeth – 07/01/1963
Comments: Long time favourite at the Manor Ground

PHIW – **Phillips Wayne**   Wrexham   **Defender**   0   0   5   DL$........
Born: Bangor – 15/12/1970
Comments: Will he improve is the question?

PHIL – **Philliskirk Tony**   Bolton Wanderers   **Striker**   23   26   18   DL$........
Born: Sunderland – 10/02/1965
Comments: Tony's been the Trotter's leading scorer for two seasons

DREAM LEAGUE – CHAPTER 10         90 91 92

## Dream League Trivia

*Who is the only player to score a hat trick in a Wembley FA Cup Final?*

Answer: Stan Mortenson, Blackpool 1953

PLEE – **Philpott Lee**   Cambridge United   **Midfield**   7   6   5   DL$........
Born: Barnet – 21/02/1970
Comments: Plays either midfield or wing

PICK – **Pickard Owen**   Plymouth Argyle   **Striker**   0   1   0   DL$........
Born: Barnstable – 18/11/1969
Comments: Promising young player

PICN – **Pickering Nick**   Darlington   **Midfield**   3   0   5   DL$........
Born: Newcastle – 04/08/1963
Comments: Nicks supplied a few by picking up a few

PIKE – **Pike Chris**   Cardiff City   **Striker**   20   15   21   DL$........
Born: Cardiff – 19/10/1961
Comments: Plenty of life in this 'old' dog yet

PIKM – **Pike Martin**   Fulham   **Defender**   2   4   2   DL$........
Born: South Shields – 21/10/1964
Comments: Gells well with the back four, also uses a lot on his hair

PILL – **Pilling Andy**   Wigan Athletic   **Midfield**   6   3   3   DL$........
Born: Wigan – 30/06/1969
Comments: Andy can play all over the park

PITC – **Pitcher Darren**   Charlton Athletic   **Defender**   0   3   2   DL$........
Born: London – 12/10/1969
Comments: Product of the FA school of excellence.....!

PLAN – **Platnauer Nicky**   Leicester City   **Defender**   0   1   0   DL$........
Born: Leicester – 10/06/1961
Comments: Regular in defence but not on the score sheet

PLUM – **Plummer Clavin**   Chesterfield   **Striker**   9   4   0   DL$........
Born: Nottingham – 14/02/1963
Comments: Oops!

POIN – **Pointon Neil**   Manchester City   **Defender**   1   1   1   DL$........
Born: Church Warsop – 28/11/1964
Comments: Neil's making the left-back position his own

POLL – **Pollock Jamie**   Middlesbrough   **Midfield**   0   0   1   DL$........
Born: Stockton – 16/02/1974
Comments: Trainee

POLS – **Polston John**   Norwich City   **Defender**   1   4   1   DL$........
Born: London – 10/06/1968
Comments: In contention for the central defensive postion

POOG – **Poole Gary**   Barnet   **Midfield**   0   0   2   DL$........
Born: Stratford – 11/09/1967
Comments: Joined with Gary Bull

178

# PLAYER GUIDE  90 91 92

**PORA – Porter Andy**  Port Vale  **Midfield**  1  0  1  DL$........
Born: Manchester – 17/09/1968
Comments: Tigerish midfielder

**PORT – Porter Gary**  Watford  **Midfield**  5  4  9  DL$........
Born: Sunderland – 06/03/1966
Comments: Subbuteo sized player, accurate left foot at set pieces

**POTT – Potts Steven**  West Ham United  **Defender**  0  1  0  DL$........
Born: Hartford (USA) – 07/05/1967
Comments: Struggled early on at Upton Park, now a regular on first team

**POUN – Pounder Tony**  Bristol Rovers  **Striker**  0  3  3  DL$........
Born: Yeovil – 11/03/1966
Comments: Tony can either play on the flanks or as a central striker

**POWE – Powell Chris**  Southend United  **Defender**  0  1  0  DL$........
Born: Lambeth – 08/09/1969
Comments: Often found on loan at Aldershot

**POWD – Powell Darryl**  Portsmouth  **Striker**  0  0  6  DL$........
Born: Lambeth – 15/01/1971
Comments: Should benefit from Darren's departure

**POWG – Powell Gary**  Wigan Athletic  **Striker**  0  5  8  DL$........
Born: Holylake – 02/04/1969
Comments: Fast and skilful, another of the ex Everton posse

**POWL – Power Lee**  Norwich City  **Striker**  0  3  1  DL$........
Born: Lewisham – 30/06/1972
Comments: From trainee

**PREE – Preece Andy**  Stockport County  **Midfield**  1  7  15  DL$........
Born: Evesham – 27/03/1967
Comments: Don't worry, we've all spotted him

**PRED – Preece David**  Luton Town  **Midfield**  2  1  3  DL$........
Born: Bridgnorth – 28/05/1963
Comments: Good passer of the ball, inclined to run round in circles

**PRER – Preece Roger**  Chester City  **Midfield**  1  0  0  DL$........
Born: Much Wenlock – 09/06/1969
Comments: Attacking right sided player, whose lost sight of goal

**PRIC – Price Chris**  Blackburn Rovers  **Defender**  1  1  3  DL$........
Born: Hereford – 30/03/1960
Comments: Too many chances have just skimmed off the top

**PRIM – Price Mark**  Scarborough  **Striker**  0  0  1  DL$........
Born: Keithly – 15/10/1973
Comments: Give him a chance

**PRIO – Prior Spencer**  Southend United  **Defender**  1  0  1  DL$........
Born: Rochford – 22/04/1971
Comments: Product of the youth scheme at Roots Hall

**PROC – Proctor Mark**  Middlesbrough  **Midfield**  4  0  2  DL$........
Born: Middlesborough – 30/01/1961
Comments: Currently in his second spell with the club

**PROU – Proudlock Paul**  Carlisle United  **Striker**  8  8  3  DL$........
Born: Hartlepool – 25/10/1965
Comments: Proud Pauls trying to regain past glorys

| DREAM LEAGUE – CHAPTER 10 | | 90 91 92 |

PUCK – **Puckett David**   AFC Bournemouth   **Striker**   18 26 8   DL$........
Born: Southampton – 29/10/1960
Comments: Prolific goal scorer at Aldershot at least

PUGH – **Pugh David**   Chester City   **Midfield**   0 3 0   DL$........
Born: Liverpool – 19/09/1964
Comments: Dave's made left-back his own

PURN – **Purnell Philip**   Swansea City   **Striker**   2 0 1   DL$........
Born: Bristol – 16/09/1964
Comments: Loan

PUTN – **Putney Trevor**   Watford   **Midfield**   0 1 2   DL$........
Born: Harold Hill – 11/02/1961
Comments: Joker of the pack, valuable and experienced

PUTT – **Puttnam David**   Lincoln City   **Midfield**   1 6 7   DL$........
Born: Leicester – 03/02/1967
Comments: Big budget moves from midfield

QUIP – **Quinlan Philip**   Everton   **Striker**   0 2 0   DL$........
Born: Madrid – 17/04/1971
Comments: Struggling to find his place on the first team

QUIJ – **Quinn Jimmy**   AFC Bournemouth   **Striker**   13 9 23   DL$........
Born: Belfast – 18/11/1959
Comments: Well travelled veteran, could we bargain

QUIM – **Quinn Mick**   Newcastle United   **Striker**   34 20 7   DL$........
Born: Liverpool – 02/05/1962
Comments: The original immoveable object but scores lots of goals

QUIN – **Quinn Niall**   Manchester City   **Striker**   4 21 15   DL$........
Born: Dublin – 06/10/1966
Comments: Proved there's life after Arsenal

QUOW – **Quow Trevor**   Northampton Town   **Midfield**   1 0 0   DL$........
Born: Peterborough – 28/09/1960
Comments: What can one say about his scoring record

RAEA – **Rae Alex**   Millwall   **Midfield**   0 10 13   DL$........
Born: Glasgow – 30/09/1969
Comments: Been told to get more tackles in, gets sent off

RAMA – **Ramage Craig**   Derby County   **Striker**   2 3 2   DL$........
Born: Derby – 30/03/1970
Comments: Ramage is doing some damage!

RAMM – **Rammell Andy**   Barnsley   **Striker**   0 12 7   DL$........
Born: Nuneaton – 10/02/1967
Comments: Andy's getting back on the goal trail

---

## Dream League Trivia

*How many League goals did Clive Allen score in the 1986/87 season?*

Answer: Thirty Three

| | | | 90 | 91 | 92 | |
|---|---|---|---|---|---|---|

RAMS – **Ramsey Paul**  Cardiff City  **Defender**  3  0  3  DL$........
Born: Londonderry – 03/09/1962
Comments: Adding strength at the back at Ninian Park

RAND – **Randall Adrian**  Burnley  **Midfield**  2  10  2  DL$........
Born: Amesbury – 10/11/1968
Comments: Saved from the dole, was at Aldershot

RANK – **Rankine Mark**  Wolverhampton W.  **Midfield**  2  3  5  DL$........
Born: Doncaster – 30/09/1969
Comments: Made his mark last season

RATS – **Ratcliffe Simon**  Brentford  **Defender**  2  2  2  DL$........
Born: Davyhulme – 08/02/1967
Comments: Two's enough for Simon

RATH – **Rathbone Mike**  Preston North End  **Defender**  0  1  0  DL$........
Born: Birmingham – 06/11/1958
Comments: Bone of contention maybe but quietly slipping away

RAVE – **Raven Paul**  Doncaster Rovers  **Defender**  0  0  1  DL$........
Born: Salisbury – 28/07/1970
Comments: On loan

RAYN – **Raynor Paul**  Cambridge United  **Striker**  8  5  2  DL$........
Born: Nottingham – 29/04/1966
Comments: Seems to have lost the knack

RECK – **Reck Sean**  Wrexham  **Midfield**  1  1  0  DL$........
Born: Oxford – 05/05/1967
Comments: May find him washed up on the Welsh coast

REDD – **Reddish Shane**  Doncaster Rovers  **Midfield**  0  0  2  DL$........
Born: Bolsover – 05/05/1971
Comments: Tasty player

REDF – **Redfearn Neil**  Barnsley  **Midfield**  3  15  5  DL$........
Born: Dewsbury – 20/06/1965
Comments: Neil's ready for past glories

REDI – **Redford Ian**  Ipswich Town  **Midfield**  2  6  0  DL$........
Born: Perth – 05/04/1960
Comments: Lost sight of goal

REDK – **Redknapp Jamie**  Liverpool  **Midfield**  0  0  1  DL$........
Born: Barton on Sea – 25/06/1973
Comments: Talented youngster

REDM – **Redmond Steven**  Manchester City  **Defender**  0  3  1  DL$........
Born: Liverpool – 02/11/1967
Comments: Product of the youth scheme at Maine Road

REEC – **Reece Andy**  Bristol Rovers  **Midfield**  3  1  4  DL$........
Born: Shrewsbury – 05/09/1962
Comments: Long serving skilful midfielder

REET – **Rees Tony**  Grimsby Town  **Striker**  13  10  5  DL$........
Born: Merthyr Tydfil – 01/08/1964
Comments: Tony's lost a little of his touch around goal

REEV – **Reeves Alan**  Rochdale  **Defender**  2  0  3  DL$........
Born: Birkenhead – 19/11/1967
Comments: Defender with an eye for goal

| DREAM LEAGUE – CHAPTER 10 | 90 91 92 |

## Dream League Trivia

*Which player scored for both teams in the 1981 FA Cup Final?*

Answer: Tommy Hutchinson – Manchester City

**RDAV – Reeves David**  Bolton Wanderers   **Striker**   11 11 11   DL$........
Born: Birkenhead – 19/11/1967
Comments: Mr. Consistency around goal

**REGI – Regis Cyrille**  Aston Villa   **Striker**   5 7 11   DL$........
Born: French Guyana – 09/02/1958
Comments: Cyrille's been born again at Villa Park

**REGD – Regis Dave**  Plymouth Argyle   **Striker**   0 15 2   DL$........
Born: Paddington – 03/03/1964
Comments: Most of his career has been spent in non-league football

**REIN – Reid Nicky**  Blackburn Rovers   **Midfield**   4 2 1   DL$........
Born: Ormston – 30/10/1960
Comments: Can play in midfield or back four

**REIP – Reid Paul**  Bradford   **Striker**   9 2 0   DL$........
Born: Warley – 19/01/1968
Comments: Loan

**REPE – Reid Peter**  Manchester City   **Midfield**   0 0 1   DL$........
Born: Huyton – 20/06/1956
Comments: Could be after the odd bottle or two of Grecian

**REIS – Reid Shaun**  York City   **Midfield**   4 0 1   DL$........
Born: Huyton – 13/10/1965
Comments: "Terminator 3"?

**RENN – Rennie David**  Birmingham City   **Midfield**   4 2 4   DL$........
Born: Edinburgh – 29/08/1964
Comments: Shouldn't play on a full stomach

**RICH – Richards Carl**  Maidstone United   **Striker**   4 4 2   DL$........
Born: Jamaica – 12/01/1960
Comments: Almost scores in formation

**RICD – Richards Dean**  Bradford   **Striker**   2 0 1   DL$........
Born: Bradford – 09/06/1974
Comments: Not the rugby player

**RICS – Richards Steve**  Halifax Town   **Defender**   5 3 1   DL$........
Born: Dundee – 24/10/1961
Comments: Losing his goal scoring ability

**RICK – Richardson Kevin**  Aston Villa   **Midfield**   0 0 6   DL$........
Born: Newcastle – 04/12/1962
Comments: Well travelled midfielder

**RICL – Richardson Lee**  Blackburn Rovers   **Midfield**   1 2 1   DL$........
Born: Halifax – 12/03/1969
Comments: Lee doesn't trouble the scoring sheet often

| PLAYER GUIDE | | | | 90 | 91 | 92 | |
|---|---|---|---|---|---|---|---|

**RICN – Richardson Neil**  Rotherham United  **Defender**  0  2  2   DL$........
Born: Sunderland – 03/03/1968
Comments: Big strong defender with a good touch on the ball

**RINI – Richardson Nick**  Halifax Town  **Midfield**  6  4  9   DL$........
Born: Halifax – 11/04/1967
Comments: Interesting form to consider

**RICP – Richardson Steve**  Reading  **Defender**  0  0  1   DL$........
Born: Slough – 11/02/1962
Comments: Loyal Royal

**RILE – Riley David**  Peterborough United  **Striker**  5  9  11   DL$........
Born: Northampton – 08/12/1960
Comments: Riley's wily infront of goal

**RIMN – Rimmer Neill**  Wigan Athletic  **Midfield**  2  4  1   DL$........
Born: Southport – 12/10/1964
Comments: Inspirational in midfield, out of action through knee injury

**RIMM – Rimmer Stuart**  Chester City  **Striker**  12  1  15   DL$........
Born: Southport – 12/10/1964
Comments: Well needed boost to the Blues strike force

**RIPL – Ripley Stuart**  Middlesbrough  **Striker**  1  6  4   DL$........
Born: Middlesbrough – 20/11/1964
Comments: Powerful front runner, who has come up through the rank's

**RITC – Ritchie Andy**  Oldham Athletic  **Striker**  27  15  7   DL$........
Born: Manchester – 28/11/1960
Comments: Well travelled and experieced striker

**ROBG – Roberts Graham**  West Bromwich Albion  **Defender**  4  4  2   DL$........
Born: Southampton – 03/07/1959
Comments: A good pro, an excellent leader, automatic choice if younger

**ROIW – Roberts Iwan**  Huddersfield Town  **Striker**  2  14  30   DL$........
Born: Bangor – 26/06/1968
Comments: Iwan's been bang on target this season, recommended to all

**ROBM – Robins Mark**  Manchester United  **Striker**  10  4  2   DL$........
Born: Ashton-under-Lyme – 22/12/1969
Comments: Rarely seen these day's at Old Trafford

**ROCO – Robinson Colin**  Hereford  **Striker**  6  2  0   DL$........
Born: Birmingham – 15/05/1960
Comments: Near the sell-buy date it seems

**ROBI – Robinson David**  Peterborough United  **Defender**  5  2  3   DL$........
Born: Cleveland – 14/01/1965
Comments: Dave's coming back from serious injury

**ROBD – Robinson David**  Reading  **Striker**  1  3  0   DL$........
Born: Newcastle – 27/11/1969
Comments: Loan and wishes he was coming back from injury

**ROBJ – Robinson John**  Brighton & Hove A.  **Midfield**  0  0  7   DL$........
Born: Bulawayo, Rhodesia – 29/08/1971
Comments: Product of the Seagulls Youth policy

**ROLI – Robinson Liam**  Bury  **Striker**  17  4  10   DL$........
Born: Bradford – 29/12/1965
Comments: Has been the "Shaker's" top scorer for the past 3 seasons

**DREAM LEAGUE – CHAPTER 10**　　　　　　　　　　**90 91 92**

ROMA – **Robinson Mark**　Barnsley　　**Midfield**　0　1　2　**DL$........**
Born: Manchester – 21/11/1968
Comments: Midfielder who rarely troubles goalies

ROPA – **Robinson Paul**　Plymouth Argyle　　**Striker**　3　3　0　**DL$........**
Born: Nottingham – 21/02/1971
Comments: Paul's lost his touch around goal

ROPH – **Robinson Philip**　Notts County　　**Defender**　3　4　0　**DL$........**
Born: Stafford – 06/01/1967
Comments: A troubled 1992

RORO – **Robinson Ronnie** Peterborough United　**Defender**　1　0　2　**DL$........**
Born: Sunderland – 22/10/1966
Comments: Versatile player with good pace

ROBB – **Robson Bryan**　Manchester United　**Midfield**　4　1　5　**DL$........**
Born: Chester-le-Street – 11/01/1957
Comments: Captain Courageous must have injured most parts of his body

RGAR – **Robson Gary** West Bromwich Albion　**Midfield**　6　2　10　**DL$........**
Born: Durham – 06/07/1965
Comments: Runs till he drops, tackling midfielder just like his brother

RMAR – **Robson Mark**　Exeter City　　**Striker**　0　0　1　**DL$........**
Born: Newham – 22/05/1969
Comments: Loan

ROST – **Robson Stewart**　Coventry City　　**Midfield**　1　0　3　**DL$........**
Born: Billericary – 06/11/1964
Comments: Although not related he seems to suffer injuries all the same

ROCA – **Rocastle David**　Arsenal　　**Midfield**　4　2　3　**DL$........**
Born: Lewisham – 02/05/1967
Comments: Still trying to recapture his success of previous years. No luck so far

RODG – **Rodger Graham**　Grimsby Town　　**Defender**　0　2　0　**DL$........**
Born: Glasgow – 01/04/1967
Comments: Experience in defence

RODI – **Rodgerson Ian**　Birmingham City　　**Midfield**　4　2　11　**DL$........**
Born: Hereford – 09/04/1966
Comments: Exciting player, can also mend a dripping tap

RODW – **Rodwell Tony**　Blackpool　　**Striker**　0　7　10　**DL$........**
Born: Southport – 26/08/1962
Comments: Being groomed as Bamber's successor

ROED – **Roeder Glenn**　Leyton Orient　　**Defender**　3　1　0　**DL$........**
Born: Woodford – 13/12/1955
Comments: Struggling with injury

---

## Dream League Trivia

*Who holds the Littlewoods Cup record for the most goals in one game?*

Answer: Frank Bunn, 6 – Oldham

| PLAYER GUIDE | | | 90 | 91 | 92 | |
|---|---|---|---|---|---|---|
| ROGT – **Rogan Anthon** Sunderland | Defender | 0 | 1 | 1 | DL$........ |
| Born: Belfast – 25/03/1966 | | | | | |
| Comments: Got a good left peg, or is it the right | | | | | |
| ROGE – **Rogers Darren** West Bromwich Albion | Defender | 0 | 0 | 1 | DL$........ |
| Born: Birmingham – 09/04/1971 | | | | | |
| Comments: Nervous, needs Roberts behind him to boost morale | | | | | |
| ROSA – **Rosario Robert** Coventry City | Striker | 6 | 0 | 6 | DL$........ |
| Born: Hammersmith – 04/03/1966 | | | | | |
| Comments: So that's where he is | | | | | |
| ROSC – **Rose Colin** Crewe Alexandra | Midfield | 0 | 1 | 0 | DL$........ |
| Born: Winsford – 22/01/1972 | | | | | |
| Comments: Blooming midfielder | | | | | |
| ROSL – **Rosenior Leroy** Bristol City | Striker | 2 | 3 | 6 | DL$........ |
| Born: London – 24/03/1964 | | | | | |
| Comments: Rose of the night from the Hammer's | | | | | |
| ROSE – **Rosenthal Ronny** Liverpool | Striker | 7 | 5 | 3 | DL$........ |
| Born: Haifa, Israel – 11/10/1963 | | | | | |
| Comments: Usually found on the bench | | | | | |
| ROSW – **Rostron Wilf** Brentford | Midfield | 3 | 2 | 0 | DL$........ |
| Born: Sunderland – 29/09/1956 | | | | | |
| Comments: Age before anything else | | | | | |
| ROWB – **Rowbotham Darren** Birmingham City | Midfield | 31 | 3 | 8 | DL$........ |
| Born: Cardiff – 22/10/1966 | | | | | |
| Comments: Back from a serious knee injury | | | | | |
| ROWG – **Rowett Gary** Cambridge United | Striker | 0 | 0 | 2 | DL$........ |
| Born: Bromsgrove – 06/03/1974 | | | | | |
| Comments: Newcomer to Abby Stadium | | | | | |
| RUDD – **Ruddock Neil** Tottenham | Defender | 4 | 4 | 1 | DL$........ |
| Born: London – 09/05/1968 | | | | | |
| Comments: Experience and vision in defence | | | | | |
| RUMB – **Rumble Paul** Maidstone United | Defender | 2 | 1 | 0 | DL$........ |
| Born: Hemel Hempstead – 14/03/1969 | | | | | |
| Comments: Rumbles about at the back | | | | | |
| RUSD – **Rush David** Sunderland | Striker | 0 | 2 | 7 | DL$........ |
| Born: Sunderland – 15/05/1971 | | | | | |
| Comments: David's been rushing into the box | | | | | |
| RUSH – **Rush Ian** Liverpool | Striker | 26 | 26 | 7 | DL$........ |
| Born: St.Asaph – 20/10/1961 | | | | | |
| Comments: Seem's to have lost the goal scoring habit through injury | | | | | |
| RUSM – **Rush Matthew** West Ham United | Midfield | 0 | 0 | 2 | DL$........ |
| Born: Dalston – 06/08/1971 | | | | | |
| Comments: From Trainee | | | | | |
| RUSK – **Russell Kevin** Leicester City | Striker | 0 | 8 | 9 | DL$........ |
| Born: Portsmouth – 06/12/1966 | | | | | |
| Comments: Kev»s another Filbert Street traveller | | | | | |
| RUSL – **Russell Lee** Portsmouth | Defender | 0 | 1 | 0 | DL$........ |
| Born: Southampton – 03/09/1969 | | | | | |
| Comments: Not often seen on the park | | | | | |

DREAM LEAGUE - CHAPTER 10                90 91 92

> ## Dream League Trivia
> Which "full back" scored in the finals of the 1981 League Cup, 1981 European Cup, 1983 League Cup, plus the winner in a penalty shoot out in the 1984 European Cup?
>
> Answer: Alan Kennedy

RYAJ – **Ryan John**   Rochdale           **Defender**   4   0   4   DL$........
Born: Ashton – 18/02/1962
Comments: Would like to score five

RYAV – **Ryan Vaughan**   Wimbledon       **Midfield**   0   0   2   DL$........
Born: Westminster – 02/09/1968
Comments: Vaughan's a tough, reliable midfielder

SADD – **Saddington Nigel**   Carlisle United   **Defender**   10   0   0   DL$........
Born: Sunderland – 09/12/1965
Comments: Nigel was a promising goal scorer once

SAGE – **Sage Mel**   Derby County        **Defender**   0   1   0   DL$........
Born: Gillingham – 24/03/1964
Comments: Mel's stuck at the Baseball Ground

SALA – **Salako John**   Crystal Palace   **Striker**    4   8   2   DL$........
Born: Nigeria – 11/02/1969
Comments: International media star with dodgy knee

SALM – **Salman Danis**   Peterborough United   **Defender**   0   4   1   DL$........
Born: Cyprus – 12/03/1960
Comments: There's nothing rushdie about Danis.....Loan

SAMW – **Samways Vinny**   Tottenham Hotspur   **Midfield**   4   1   2   DL$........
Born: Bethnal Green – 27/10/1968
Comments: Best passer at the club, often left out because of the pitch

SANC – **Sanchez Lawrie**   Wimbledon     **Midfield**   1   0   3   DL$........
Born: Lambeth – 22/10/1959
Comments: Long time serving "Don"

SAND – **Sandeman Bradley**   Maidstone United   **Midfield**   1   1   7   DL$........
Born: Northampton – 24/02/1970
Comments: Certainly seems an 'andy man

SANL – **Sandford Lee**   Stoke City      **Defender**   2   2   0   DL$........
Born: Basingstoke – 22/04/1968
Comments: Lee's another who's back from injury

SANS – **Sansom Kenny**   Coventry City   **Defender**   2   0   0   DL$........
Born: Camberwell – 26/09/1958
Comments: In this team there's only one thin you do

SAUC – **Saunders Carl**   Bristol Rovers   **Striker**   5   16   16   DL$........
Born: Marston Green – 26/11/1964
Comments: Good close ball control, able to score goals from nothing

SAUN – **Saunders Dean**   Liverpool      **Striker**   18   20   14   DL$........
Born: Swansea – 21/06/1964
Comments: Now scoring as well in the league as cup competions

186

**PLAYER GUIDE**                                                               **90 91 92**

SAUW – **Saunders Wes**   Torquay United    **Defender**   9   4   2   **DL$**........
Born: Sunderland – 23/02/1963
Comments: Major peg in the Gulls defence

SAVI – **Saville Andrew**   Hartlepool United    **Striker**   3   12   6   **DL$**........
Born: Hull – 12/12/1964
Comments: Andy's recovering from a broken arm

SAYE – **Sayer Andy**   Leyton Orient    **Striker**   1   2   4   **DL$**........
Born: Brent – 06/06/1966
Comments: Could be a winner at Brisbane Road

SCAL – **Scales John**   Wimbledon    **Defender**   3   2   0   **DL$**........
Born: Harrogate – 04/07/1966
Comments: Has been known to pop up at set pieces to score

SCHO – **Schofield Jon**   Lincoln City    **Midfield**   2   3   3   **DL$**........
Born: Barnsley – 16/05/1965
Comments: Aggressive midfielder

SCOP – **Scope David**   Northampton Town    **Striker**   0   0   1   **DL$**........
Born: Newcastle – 10/05/1967
Comments: Plenty of scope to score more

SCOT – **Scott Ian**   Stoke City    **Midfield**   1   0   1   **DL$**........
Born: Radcliffe – 20/09/1967
Comments: Finding it hard to retain a first team place

SCKE – **Scott Kevin**   Newcastle United    **Defender**   4   0   1   **DL$**........
Born: Easington – 17/12/1966
Comments: Tall, strong, silent type (mute) should score more goals

SCOM – **Scott Martin**   Bristol City    **Midfield**   1   1   3   **DL$**........
Born: Sheffield – 07/01/1968
Comments: Midfielder who isn't afraid to score

SCPE – **Scott Peter**   Fulham    **Midfield**   6   2   1   **DL$**........
Born: London – 01/10/1963
Comments: If only the first team had got as many points as he's got

SCUL – **Scully Pat**   Southend United    **Defender**   1   0   3   **DL$**........
Born: Dublin – 23/06/1970
Comments: Tall, experienced defender

SEAG – **Seagraves Mark**   Bolton Wanderers    **Defender**   0   0   1   **DL$**........
Born: Bootle – 22/10/1966
Comments: Mark's made the long journey upfield to score

SEAT – **Sealy Tony**   Brentford    **Striker**   3   4   1   **DL$**........
Born: London – 07/05/1959
Comments: Loves number 12

SEAR – **Searle Damon**   Cardiff City    **Defender**   0   0   2   **DL$**........
Born: Cardiff – 26/10/1971
Comments: Another of the promising youngsters at Ninian Park

SEDG – **Sedgley Steve**   Tottenham Hotspur    **Midfield**   1   0   0   **DL$**........
Born: Enfield – 26/05/1968
Comments: Young shaver also defends

SELL – **Sellars Scott**   Blackburn Rovers    **Midfield**   15   1   8   **DL$**........
Born: Sheffield – 27/11/1965
Comments: Probably the most skilful Rover

**DREAM LEAGUE – CHAPTER 10**                              **90 91 92**

SEND – **Sendall Richard**   Carlisle United   **Striker**   **1  0  1**   **DL$........**
Born: Stamford – 10/07/1967
Comments: Bargain for the Cumbrians – free

SENS – **Senior Steve**   Preston North End   **Defender**   **0  2  2**   **DL$........**
Born: Sheffield – 15/05/1963
Comments: Tough tackling no-nonsense defender

SENI – **Senior Trevor**   Reading   **Striker**   **18 15  7**   **DL$........**
Born: Dorchester – 28/11/1961
Comments: The most prolific striker in the Royal's history

SHAK – **Shakespeare Craig** W. Bromwich Albion **Midfield**   **2  1 11**   **DL$........**
Born: Birmingham – 26/10/1963
Comments: Also likes to play in the middle.....but doesn't

SHAG – **Sharp Graeme**   Oldham Athletic   **Striker**   **7  8 15**   **DL$........**
Born: Glasgow – 16/10/1960
Comments: Razor goal getter

SHAL – **Sharpe Lee**   Manchester United   **Midfield**   **1  8  2**   **DL$........**
Born: Halesowen – 25/07/1971
Comments: Coming back into the picture after injury

SHGR – **Shaw Graham**   Preston North End   **Striker**   **9 11 16**   **DL$........**
Born: Stoke – 07/06/1967
Comments: Getting better and better

SHRI – **Shaw Richard**   Crystal Palace   **Defender**   **0  1  0**   **DL$........**
Born: Brentford – 11/09/1968
Comments: Michael Jackson double but no chimp

SHLA – **Shearer Alan**   Southampton   **Striker**   **5 12 18**   **DL$........**
Born: Newcastle – 13/08/1970
Comments: Alan hold's the all time scoring record for England U-21

SHEA – **Shearer Duncan**   Blackburn Rovers   **Striker**   **25 23 33**   **DL$........**
Born: Fort William – 28/08/1962
Comments: He certainly is not a one-off. Will he keep it up in the big time?

SHPE – **Shearer Peter**   AFC Bournemouth   **Striker**   **5  0  1**   **DL$........**
Born: Birmingham – 04/02/1967
Comments: If the name is anything to go by, his time will come

SHEE – **Sheedy Kevin**   Newcastle United   **Midfield**   **13  4  2**   **DL$........**
Born: Builth Wells – 21/10/1959
Comments: Don't bet against that trusty left foot

SHEL – **Shelton Gary**   Bristol City   **Midfield**   **9  8  3**   **DL$........**
Born: Nottingham – 21/03/1958
Comments: Team captain

---

## Dream League Trivia

*Arthur Wilkie scored twice against Halifax in August 1962. What position did he play and which team?*

Answer: Reading goalkeeper

| PLAYER GUIDE | | | 90 | 91 | 92 | |
|---|---|---|---|---|---|---|

SHEP – **Shepherd Tony**  Carlisle United  **Midfield**  3  6  0  DL$........
Born: Glasgow – 16/11/1966
Comments: Gathers his flock around the middle of the park

SHPA – **Shepstone Paul**  York City  **Midfield**  0  1  0  DL$........
Born: Coventry – 08/11/1970
Comments: Get down Shep....Loan

SHER – **Sheridan John**  Sheffield Wednesday  **Midfield**  2  12  7  DL$........
Born: Manchester – 01/10/1964
Comments: Scored the Wembley winner in 91 but in contract dispute

SHTE – **Sheringham Teddy**  Notts Forest  **Striker**  12  38  20  DL$........
Born: Highams Park – 02/04/1966
Comments: For once Clough's bought a striker who scores goals

SHEM – **Sheron Mike**  Manchester City  **Striker**  0  0  8  DL$........
Born: Liverpool – 11/01/1972
Comments: Risen through the rank's to first team status

SHET – **Sherwood Tim**  Blackburn Rovers  **Midfield**  3  8  0  DL$........
Born: Selby – 10/12/1953
Comments: Bit surprised if he crops up next season

SHIR – **Shirtliff Peter**  Sheffield Wednesday  **Defender**  3  4  0  DL$........
Born: Barnsley – 06/04/1961
Comments: Popular wtih the Hillsborough faithful

SHOR – **Short Chris**  Notts County  **Defender**  1  1  1  DL$........
Born: Munster – 09/05/1970
Comments: Very promising young defender

SHOC – **Short Craig**  Notts County  **Defender**  3  1  2  DL$........
Born: Bridlington – 25/06/1968
Comments: A bit more prolific around goal than brother Chris

SHOM – **Shotton Malcolm**  Hull City  **Defender**  2  0  0  DL$........
Born: Newcastle – 16/02/1957
Comments: True professional, what ever that means

SHOW – **Showler Paul**  Barnet  **Striker**  0  0  9  DL$........
Born: Doncaster – 10/10/1966
Comments: Prolific striker from Non-league football

SHUT – **Shutt Carl**  Leeds United  **Striker**  2  10  2  DL$........
Born: Sheffield – 10/10/1961
Comments: Carl's open to score more goals

SIMF – **Simpson Fitzroy**  Manchester City  **Midfield**  2  4  5  DL$........
Born: Trowbridge – 26/02/1970
Comments: Fitzroy's one to watch

SIMP – **Simpson Paul**  Derby County  **Striker**  12  18  17  DL$........
Born: Carlisle – 26/07/1966
Comments: Prolific striker

SINF – **Sinclair Frank**  Chelsea  **Defender**  0  0  2  DL$........
Born: Lambeth – 03/12/1971
Comments: Doesn't need a C5 to get around the park

SITR – **Sinclair Trevor**  Blackpool  **Midfield**  0  1  4  DL$........
Born: Dulwich – 02/03/1973
Comments: Useful product from the Youth Scheme at Bloomfield Road

# Dream League Trivia

*John Murray's hat trick for Bury against Doncaster in 1973 was 'different', why?*

Answer: He got sent off after the third goal

**SING – Singleton Martin**  Walsall   **Midfield**   0  1  0   DL$........
Born: Banbury – 02/08/1963
Comments: Lives up to his name

**SINN – Sinnott Lee**  Crystal Palace   **Defender**   2  1  0   DL$........
Born: Pelsall – 12/07/1965
Comments: Not so Saintly Sinnott, Bradford reject

**SINT – Sinton Andy**  Queens Park Rangers   **Midfield**   8  3  3   DL$........
Born: Newcastle – 19/03/1966
Comments: Midfielder who likes to pop in the odd goal or three

**SKIN – Skinner Justin**  Bristol Rovers   **Midfield**   6  5  3   DL$........
Born: London – 30/01/1969
Comments: Tall midfielder, who likes to push forward

**SLAT – Slater Stuart**  West Ham United   **Striker**   9  3  0   DL$........
Born: Sudbury – 27/03/1969
Comments: Can be blindingly quick down the wings

**SLAV – Slaven Bernie**  Middlesbrough   **Striker**   25  19  18   DL$........
Born: Paisley – 13/11/1960
Comments: Another of the Boro's prolific scorers

**SLAW – Slawson Steve**  Notts County   **Striker**   0  0  1   DL$........
Born: Nottingham – 13/11/1972
Comments: Trainee

**SMAL – Small Mike**  West Ham United   **Striker**   0  18  18   DL$........
Born: Birmingham – 02/03/1962
Comments: Impressive striker with an eye for goal

**SMAM – Smalley Mark**  Maidstone United   **Defender**   1  1  2   DL$........
Born: Newark – 02/01/1965
Comments: Mark's steady at the back for the Stones

**SMAJ – Smart Jason**  Crewe Alexandra   **Defender**   2  0  0   DL$........
Born: Rochdale – 15/02/1969
Comments: Not too clever scoring

**SMIL – Smillie Neil**  Brentford   **Striker**   5  3  7   DL$........
Born: Barnsley – 19/07/1958
Comments: Only Bee to have played in a FA Cup Final

**SMIT – Smith Alan**  Arsenal   **Striker**   13  28  13   DL$........
Born: Birmingham – 21/11/1962
Comments: The Gunner's top scorer since 87/88 season

**SDAV – Smith David**  Coventry City   **Midfield**   6  1  4   DL$........
Born: Gloucester – 29/03/1968
Comments: Reliable and must be near top of their score charts

# PLAYER GUIDE

**90 91 92**

SMDA – **Smith David A**   Plymouth Argyle   **Striker**   5   6   5   DL$........
Born: Sidcup – 25/06/1961
Comments: Might be in his element in Division 3

SMIK – **Smith Kevan**   Darlington   **Defender**   0   4   2   DL$........
Born: Eaglescliffe – 13/12/1959
Comments: On current form will guarantee you a single return

SMMA – **Smith Mark**   Barnsley   **Defender**   4   6   1   DL$........
Born: Sheffield – 21/03/1960
Comments: Big tough tackling defender

SITH – **Smith Mark**   Grimsby Town   **Striker**   8   2   4   DL$........
Born: Sheffield – 19/12/1961
Comments: Smithy's done the rounds in the lower divisions

SMIM – **Smith Mark A**   Shrewsbury Town   **Striker**   0   0   2   DL$........
Born: Bell Hill – 16/12/1964
Comments: One of Mr Clough's rejects

SMIC – **Smith Mick**   Hartlepool United   **Defender**   5   1   0   DL$........
Born: Sunderland – 28/10/1958
Comments: Not troubled the scoring card this season

SMIN – **Smith Neil**   Gillingham   **Midfield**   0   0   4   DL$........
Born: Warley – 10/02/1970
Comments: Neil's a recent addition to the Gills squad

SMNI – **Smith Nigel**   Bury   **Midfield**   0   0   3   DL$........
Born: Leeds – 21/12/1969
Comments: Impressive young winger

SMIP – **Smith Paul**   Lincoln City   **Defender**   5   6   3   DL$........
Born: Rotherham – 09/11/1964
Comments: Plays at right back

SMPA – **Smith Paul**   Torquay United   **Striker**   6   5   0   DL$........
Born: London – 05/10/1967
Comments: Dazzles everyone with his runs down the wing

SPAU – **Smith Paul**   Southend United   **Striker**   1   0   0   DL$........
Born: Lenham – 18/09/1971
Comments: Another of Roots Hall's youngsters

SMIR – **Smith Richard**   Leicester City   **Defender**   0   0   2   DL$........
Born: Leicester – 03/10/1970
Comments: Youth product showing potential

SORR – **Sorrell Tony**   Maidstone United   **Midfield**   3   5   0   DL$........
Born: London – 17/10/1966
Comments: Quiet 91/92 season with lots to prove

SOUN – **Southall Nicky**   Hartlepool United   **Striker**   0   0   3   DL$........
Born: Teeside – 28/01/1972
Comments: Very promising youngster

SPEA – **Spearing Tony**   Plymouth Argyle   **Defender**   1   0   0   DL$........
Born: Romford – 07/10/1964
Comments: Sound strong tackling full back

SPEE – **Speed Gary**   Leeds United   **Midfield**   3   10   10   DL$........
Born: Hawarden – 08/09/1969
Comments: Outstanding product of the Elland Road youth policy

| DREAM LEAGUE – CHAPTER 10 | | 90 91 92 | |
|---|---|---|---|

**SPED – Speedie David**  Blackburn Rovers  **Striker**  9  6  26  DL$........
Born: Glenrothes – 20/02/1960
Comments: If only he could keep his gob shut and avoid the fans

**SPID – Spink Dean**  Shrewsbury Town  **Striker**  5  7  1  DL$........
Born: Birmingham – 22/01/1967
Comments: Was a big name in non-league football

**SPON – Spooner Nicky**  Bolton Wanderers  **Defender**  0  0  1  DL$........
Born: Manchester – 05/06/1971
Comments: Usually found on the bench

**SPOO – Spooner Steve**  Mansfield Town  **Midfield**  9  1  3  DL$........
Born: London – 25/01/1961
Comments: Don't write this journeyman off yet

**STPA – Stancliffe Paul**  York City  **Defender**  2  0  1  DL$........
Born: Sheffield – 05/05/1958
Comments: "Battleaxe". Stalwart saunters into battle, then gets injured

**STAR – Stanislaus Roger**  Bury  **Defender**  1  2  4  DL$........
Born: Hammersmith – 02/11/1968
Comments: Defender with an eye for goal

**STPH – Stant Phil**  Mansfield Town  **Striker**  7  11  28  DL$........
Born: Bolton – 13/10/1962
Comments: Will it be the net or the stanchions next season

**STAP – Stapleton Frank**  Bradford  **Striker**  4  10  1  DL$........
Born: Dublin – 10/07/1956
Comments: I'm a Wanda, the wanderer, I travel...

**SPHI – Starbuck Phillip**  Huddersfield Town  **Striker**  0  1  18  DL$........
Born: Nottingham – 24/11/1968
Comments: Twinkles infront of goal

**STAU – Staunton Steve**  Aston Villa  **Defender**  3  2  4  DL$........
Born: Drogheda – 19/01/1969
Comments: Cost £1.1m. from Liverpool

**STEB – Stebbing Gary**  Maidstone United  **Defender**  0  1  4  DL$........
Born: Croydon – 11/08/1965
Comments: Gary's gettinb better

**STEE – Steel Jim**  Tranmere Rovers  **Striker**  7  8  7  DL$........
Born: Dumfries – 04/12/1959
Comments: Tall, strong experienced striker

**STET – Steele Tim**  Stoke City  **Striker**  1  3  5  DL$........
Born: Coventry – 01/02/1967
Comments: Loan

---

## Dream League Trivia

*Which continental side scored 6 at Wembley and 7 at home in two internationals against England?*

Answer: Hungary

| PLAYER GUIDE | | | 90 | 91 | 92 | |
|---|---|---|---|---|---|---|

**STBR – Stein Brian**   Luton Town   **Striker**   9   0   3   DL$........
Born: S.Africa – 19/10/1957
Comments: Veteran sticker, now lacking a little in pace

**STEI – Stein Mark**   Stoke City   **Striker**   9   8   18   DL$........
Born: S Africa – 28/01/1966
Comments: Prolific goal scorer

**SEPH – Stephenson Paul**   Millwall   **Striker**   2   3   3   DL$........
Born: Wallsend – 02/01/1968
Comments: Steady striker

**STER – Sterland Mel**   Leeds United   **Defender**   5   6   7   DL$........
Born: Sheffield – 01/10/1961
Comments: Strong in defence, menacing infront of goal

**STEW – Sterling Worrell**   Peterborough United   **Midfield**   7   11   7   DL$........
Born: Bethnal Green – 08/06/1965
Comments: Worrell's a winger

**STEV – Stevens Gary**   Portsmouth   **Defender**   1   0   0   DL$........
Born: Hillingdon – 30/03/1962
Comments: One time golden boy of English football

**STIA – Stevens Ian**   Bury   **Striker**   0   0   17   DL$........
Born: Malta – 21/10/1966
Comments: Prolific scorer, recently anyway

**STEK – Stevens Keith**   Millwall   **Defender**   0   1   0   DL$........
Born: Merton – 21/06/1964
Comments: "Rhino" is a firm favourite at The Den

**STVE – Stevenson Andy**   Doncaster Rovers   **Midfield**   1   0   0   DL$........
Born: Scunthorpe – 29/09/1967
Comments: Has talent, should concentrate on thumping the ball -On Loan

**STMA – Stewart Marcus**   Bristol Rovers   **Striker**   0   0   5   DL$........
Born: Bristol – 07/11/1972
Comments: Now a firm fixture in the first team

**STEP – Stewart Paul**   Tottenham Hotspur   **Midfield**   9   9   6   DL$........
Born: Manchester – 07/10/1964
Comments: Powerhouse of a midfielder

**STIL – Stiles John**   Rochdale   **Midfield**   2   0   0   DL$........
Born: Manchester – 06/05/1964
Comments: Loan

**STIM – Stimson Mark**   Newcastle United   **Defender**   1   2   0   DL$........
Born: Plaistow – 27/12/1967
Comments: "Stimson out, Stimson Out"

**STOC – Stockwell Mike**   Ipswich Town   **Midfield**   3   6   2   DL$........
Born: Chelmsford – 14/02/1965
Comments: Mr. Utility. Can play almost anywhere on the park

**STOK – Stoker Gareth**   Hull City   **Striker**   0   0   2   DL$........
Born: Bishop Auckland – 22/02/1973
Comments: One of a batch of promising young tigers

**STON – Stoneman Paul**   Blackpool   **Defender**   0   0   1   DL$........
Born: Whitley Bay – 26/02/1973
Comments: Stone me, Paul's scored

# DREAM LEAGUE – CHAPTER 10

---

> # Dream League Trivia
>
> Which team has had two players score hat tricks in the same game six times?
>
> Answer: Sheffield United

**STOR** – **Storer Stuart**   Bolton Wanderers   **Striker**   4   6   0   DL$........
Born: Harborough – 16/01/1967
Comments: Another Trotter whose lost his touch

**STOU** – **Stoutt Stephen**   Lincoln City   **Defender**   0   1   0   DL$........
Born: Halifax – 05/04/1964
Comments: If you don't know nor do we

**STRA** – **Strachan Gordon**   Leeds United   **Midfield**   1   9   4   DL$........
Born: Edinburgh – 09/02/1957
Comments: Needs bananas these day's

**STRI** – **Stringfellow Ian**   Mansfield Town   **Striker**   6   2   3   DL$........
Born: Nottingham – 08/05/1969
Comments: There's always the nightclub

**STRO** – **Strodder Gary**   W. Bromwich Albion   **Defender**   0   0   4   DL$........
Born: Leeds – 01/04/1965
Comments: Powerful stopper, happy at high balls being aimed at him

**STUA** – **Stuart Graham**   Chelsea   **Striker**   1   5   1   DL$........
Born: Tooting, London – 24/10/1970
Comments: One of many youngster's at the Bridge

**STUM** – **Stuart Mark**   Bradford   **Striker**   2   2   3   DL$........
Born: Hammersmith – 15/12/1966
Comments: 22 or 23 and then we are talking the business

**STUB** – **Stubbs Alan**   Bolton Wanderers   **Defender**   0   0   1   DL$........
Born: Kirkby – 06/10/1971
Comments: Product of the youth team

**STUR** – **Sturridge Simon**   Birmingham City   **Striker**   11   7   11   DL$........
Born: Birmingham – 09/12/1969
Comments: Product of the youth team at St. Andrews

**SUMM** – **Summerbee Nicky**   Swindon Town   **Striker**   0   0   1   DL$........
Born: Altrincham – 26/08/1971
Comments: Running out of time

**SUMK** – **Summerfield Kevin**   Shrewsbury T.   **Midfield**   0   5   11   DL$........
Born: Walsall – 07/01/1959
Comments: His first goal for the "Shrew's" was his 50th league goal

**SUSS** – **Sussex Andy**   Southend United   **Striker**   13   16   4   DL$........
Born: Enfield – 23/11/1964
Comments: Andy's often overshadowed by the other strikers

**SUTT** – **Sutton Chris**   Norwich City   **Striker**   0   0   5   DL$........
Born: Nottingham – 10/03/1973
Comments: From trainee to...

| PLAYER GUIDE | | 90 91 92 |

SWAK – **Swain Kenny**   Crewe Alexandra   **Defender**   1   0   0   DL$........
Born: Gateshead – 28/01/1952
Comments: No longer highly recommended

SWAN – **Swan Peter**   Port Vale   **Striker**   11  13  3   DL$........
Born: Leeds – 29/09/1966
Comments: Pete's no ugly duckling

SWAG – **Swann Gary**   Preston North End   **Midfield**   8   7   8   DL$........
Born: York – 11/04/1962
Comments: Consistent scorer

SYMO – **Symons Kit**   Portsmouth   **Defender**   0   0   1   DL$........
Born: Basingstoke – 08/03/1971
Comments: From Trainee

TAGG – **Taggart Gerry**   Barnsley   **Defender**   3   2   3   DL$........
Born: Belfast – 18/10/1970
Comments: Consistent around goal

TAIT – **Tait Mick**   Darlington   **Midfield**   5   2   0   DL$........
Born: Wallsend – 30/09/1956
Comments: Experience in the middle of the park

TAIP – **Tait Paul**   Birmingham City   **Midfield**   2   0   0   DL$........
Born: Sutton Coldfield – 31/01/1971
Comments: Coming back after 8 months out through injury

TANK – **Tankard Allen**   Wigan Athletic   **Defender**   1   1   0   DL$........
Born: Fleet – 21/05/1969
Comments: Dependable young mug,who can score the odd spectacular goal

TANN – **Tanner Nick**   Liverpool   **Defender**   0   0   1   DL$........
Born: Bristol – 24/05/1965
Comments: Another winning a regular senior place through injury

TAYB – **Taylor Bob**   West Bromwich Albion   **Striker**   35  11  12   DL$........
Born: Horden – 03/02/1967
Comments: Beginning to show his previous prolific form

TAYC – **Taylor Colin**   Wigan Athletic   **Striker**   0   2   2   DL$........
Born: Liverpool – 25/12/1971
Comments: Loan

TAYL – **Taylor John**   Bristol Rovers   **Striker**   22  19  13   DL$........
Born: Norwich – 24/10/1964
Comments: Worth a dollar or two maybe

TAYK – **Taylor Kevin**   Scunthorpe United   **Midfield**   10  0   0   DL$........
Born: Wakefield – 22/01/1961
Comments: Somebody from Scunthorpe, please advise

TAYM – **Taylor Mark**   Wrexham   **Midfield**   0   3   2   DL$........
Born: Hartlepool – 20/11/1964
Comments: Adding strength to the Robin's midfield.

TAMA – **Taylor Mark**   Shrewsbury Town   **Midfield**   0   2   2   DL$........
Born: Walsall – 22/02/1966
Comments: Another refugee from Hillsborough

TAYR – **Taylor Robert**   Leyton Orient   **Striker**   0   1   1   DL$........
Born: Norwich – 30/04/1971
Comments: Getting over the disappointment of Norwich releasing him

| | | 90 | 91 | 92 | |
|---|---|---|---|---|---|
| TAYS – **Taylor Scott**   Reading<br>Born: Portsmouth – 23/11/1970<br>Comments: Young, classy product of the Royal's youth Scheme | Midfield | 2 | 1 | 3 | DL$........ |
| TASH – **Taylor Shaun**   Swindon Town<br>Born: Plymouth – 26/03/1963<br>Comments: Police Five or what? | Defender | 5 | 4 | 5 | DL$........ |
| TEAL – **Teale Shaun**   Aston Villa<br>Born: Southport – 10/03/1964<br>Comments: A fairly recent arrival, who is now permanent in defence | Defender | 0 | 5 | 1 | DL$........ |
| TELF – **Telfer Paul**   Luton Town<br>Born: Edinburgh – 21/10/1971<br>Comments: Constantly on the move for the whole 90 minutes | Midfield | 0 | 0 | 1 | DL$........ |
| TERR – **Terry Steve**   Northampton Town<br>Born: Clapton – 14/06/1962<br>Comments: Regular at the back for the Cobblers | Defender | 2 | 6 | 3 | DL$........ |
| TEST – **Tester Paul**   Hereford<br>Born: Stroud – 10/03/1959<br>Comments: Consistently downhill on the goal front | Striker | 6 | 3 | 0 | DL$........ |
| THAC – **Thackeray Andy**   Wrexham<br>Born: Huddersfield – 13/02/1968<br>Comments: Andy's wacking them in | Midfield | 7 | 2 | 4 | DL$........ |
| THEO – **Theodosious Andy**   Hereford<br>Born: Stoke Newington – 30/10/1970<br>Comments: Tall, powerful defender | Defender | 0 | 0 | 2 | DL$........ |
| THOD – **Thomas Dean**   Notts County<br>Born: Manchester – 05/08/1964<br>Comments: Dean's spent time playing in europe | Defender | 2 | 3 | 1 | DL$........ |
| THOM – **Thomas Geoff**   Crystal Palace<br>Born: Manchester – 05/08/1964<br>Comments: Best left-footed albino in England | Midfield | 4 | 6 | 7 | DL$........ |
| THOG **Thomas Glen**   Fulham<br>Born: Hackney – 06/10/1967<br>Comments: Has added to his repertoire by going upfield with the ball | Defender | 1 | 1 | 2 | DL$........ |
| THGW – **Thomas Gwyn**   Carlisle United<br>Born: Swansea – 26/09/1957<br>Comments: Gwyn has not been the most prolific scorer | Midfield | 0 | 0 | 1 | DL$........ |
| THOJ – **Thomas John**   Hartlepool United<br>Born: Wednesbury – 05/08/1958<br>Comments: Who needs to say anything, with a name like that | Striker | 6 | 1 | 4 | DL$........ |

## Dream League Trivia

*Who was the first Colchester United player to score a hat trick in the Football League?*

Answer: Vic Keeble

| PLAYER GUIDE | | | 90 | 91 | 92 | |
|---|---|---|---|---|---|---|

TMIC – **Thomas Michael**  Liverpool  **Midfield**  5  3  6  **DL$**........
Born: Lambeth – 24/08/1967
Comments: Began his career at full-back but watch out

THMI – **Thomas Mickey**  Wrexham  **Midfield**  0  7  3  **DL$**........
Born: Mochdre – 07/07/1954
Comments: If he's not in the cells maybe worth a shout

TMIT – **Thomas Mitchell**  West Ham United  **Defender**  1  0  3  **DL$**........
Born: Luton – 02/10/1964
Comments: Another "Hammer" who can play full-back or midfield

THRO – **Thomas Rod**  Gillingham  **Striker**  6  1  1  **DL$**........
Born: London – 10/10/1970
Comments: Loan

THOT – **Thomas Tony**  Tranmere Rovers  **Defender**  2  3  3  **DL$**........
Born: Liverpool – 12/07/1971
Comments: Refuses to score more than three a season

TAND – **Thompson Andy**  Wolverhampton W.  **Midfield**  4  3  0  **DL$**........
Born: Carnock – 09/11/1967
Comments: Very quiet season on the goalscoring front

THDA – **Thompson David**  Preston North End  **Midfield**  7  2  2  **DL$**........
Born: Manchester – 27/05/1962
Comments: Here's the speedman of Preston

TDAV – **Thompson David**  Millwall  **Defender**  2  3  1  **DL$**........
Born: Ashington – 20/11/1968
Comments: Nearly a 'dusty bin'

THGA – **Thompson Garry**  Queens Park Rangers  **Striker**  2  2  4  **DL$**........
Born: Birmingham – 07/10/1959
Comments: Seasoned vet,who is much travelled around the League

THLE – **Thompson Les**  Maidstone United  **Striker**  0  2  1  **DL$**........
Born: Cleethorpes – 23/09/1968
Comments: Overshadowed by the other Stones strikers

THON – **Thompson Neil**  Ipswich Town  **Defender**  3  6  6  **DL$**........
Born: Beverley – 02/10/1963
Comments: Deadly from the set ball

THOS – **Thompson Simon**  Scarborough  **Striker**  0  0  3  **DL$**........
Born: Sheffield – 27/02/1970
Comments: Alway's gives 100% effort

THST – **Thompson Steve**  Leicester City  **Midfield**  1  6  4  **DL$**........
Born: Oldham – 02/11/1964
Comments: Recent arrival at Filbert Street

THOI – **Thompstone Ian**  Exeter City  **Midfield**  0  0  3  **DL$**........
Born: Manchester – 17/01/1971
Comments: Recent addition to the club

THAN – **Thorn Andy**  Crystal Palace  **Defender**  2  1  2  **DL$**........
Born: Carshalton – 12/11/1966
Comments: A prick in the side

TSTE – **Thornber Stephen**  Swansea City  **Midfield**  1  0  6  **DL$**........
Born: Dewsbury – 11/10/1965
Comments: Signed as a forward,plays at left back

# DREAM LEAGUE – CHAPTER 10    90 91 92

---

## Dream League Trivia

*Which team was the first to score 100 goasl in the Football League?*

Answer: Sunderland

---

**THAD – Thorpe Adrian**  Northampton Town   **Striker**   3  1  3   DL$........
Born: Chesterfield – 20/11/1963
Comments: Well travelled front man at the County Ground

**THJE – Thorpe Jeffrey**  Carlisle United   **Midfield**   0  0  1   DL$........
Born: Whitehaven – 17/11/1972
Comments: Product of the Youth policy at Brunton Park

**TILE – Tiler Carl**  Nottingham Forest   **Defender**   1  2  1   DL$........
Born: Sheffield – 11/02/1970
Comments: Dependable central defender

**TILL – Tillson Andy**  Queens Park Rangers   **Defender**   3  2  0   DL$........
Born: Huntingdon – 30/06/1966
Comments: Flair in defence

**TILS – Tilson Steve**  Southend United   **Striker**   0  8  7   DL$........
Born: Essex – 27/07/1966
Comments: Steady local lad

**TINK – Tinkler John**  Hartlepool United   **Midfield**   2  2  2   DL$........
Born: Trimdon – 24/08/1968
Comments: Tenacious in midfield, likes to tinker about as a striker

**TINN – Tinnion Brian**  Bradford   **Defender**   6  4  11   DL$........
Born: Stanley – 23/02/1968
Comments: Very popular in Dream Leagues last season

**TITT – Titterton David**  Hereford   **Midfield**   0  0  1   DL$........
Born: Hatton – 25/09/1971
Comments: Just starting so be patient

**TODM – Todd Mark**  Rotherham United   **Midfield**   1  0  3   DL$........
Born: Belfast – 04/12/1967
Comments: Might prove a good buy for some

**TOLS – Tolson Neil**  Oldham Athletic   **Striker**   0  0  2   DL$........
Born: – 25/10/1973
Comments: Promising younster

**TOMA – Toman Andy**  Darlington   **Midfield**   1  5  5   DL$........
Born: Northallerton – 07/03/1962
Comments: Another who is fairly accurate from long range

**TIML – Tomlinson Michael**  Leyton Orient   **Striker**   0  1  0   DL$........
Born: Lambeth – 15/09/1972
Comments: Room for improvement

**TORS – Torpey Stephen**  Bradford   **Striker**   0  7  10   DL$........
Born: Islington – 08/12/1970
Comments: Coming into form. Will he fulfill potential

| PLAYER GUIDE | | | 90 | 91 | 92 | |
|---|---|---|---|---|---|---|

TOWN – **Townsend Andy**  Chelsea        Midfield     3   5   7    DL$........
Born: Maidstone – 23/07/1963
Comments: Back to fitness after injury

TREA – **Treacy Darren**  Bradford        Striker      0   2   0    DL$........
Born: Lambeth – 06/09/1970
Comments: One of the youngest at Valley Parade

TREV – **Trevitt Simon**  Huddersfield Town   Defender    0   0   1    DL$........
Born: Dewsbury – 20/12/1967
Comments: Back to form after missing most of the 90/91 season injured

TROT – **Trotter Michael**  Leicester City    Defender    0   2   0    DL$........
Born: Hartlepool – 27/10/1969
Comments: Mick's still looking for his Reliant

TUPL – **Tupling Steve**  Hartlepool United   Midfield    1   2   0    DL$........
Born: Wensleydale – 11/07/1964
Comments: Steve's been about in the lower divisions

TURN – **Turnbull Lee**  Chesterfield       Midfield    12  9   7    DL$........
Born: Teesside – 27/09/1967
Comments: Due an upturn in goal stats

TURP – **Turner Phil**  Notts County        Midfield    6   1   2    DL$........
Born: Sheffield – 12/02/1962
Comments: Good club man

TURR – **Turner Robert**  Plymouth Argyle    Striker     9   14  4    DL$........
Born: Durham – 18/09/1966
Comments: Rob's a burly striker, who the opposition find difficult

TUTI – **Tutill Steve**  York City           Defender    0   0   1    DL$........
Born: Derwent – 01/10/1969
Comments: Competes with Atkin in the longest, highest ball competition

TWEN – **Twentyman Geoff**  Preston North End  Defender   3   1   1    DL$........
Born: Liverpool – 10/03/1959
Comments: We will avoid stating the obvious

TYNA – **Tynan Tommy**  Doncaster Rovers    Striker     18  15  1    DL$........
Born: Liverpool – 17/11/1955
Comments: Will he live to fight another day?

ULLA – **Ullathorne Robert**  Norwich City    Defender    0   0   3    DL$........
Born: Wakefield – 11/10/1971
Comments: Now holding a first team place

UNDA – **Unsworth David**  Leeds United     Striker     0   0   1    DL$........
Born: Preston – 16/10/1973
Comments: Scored on his debut against Spurs

VALE – **Valentine Peter**  Bury            Defender    0   3   3    DL$........
Born: Huddersfield – 16/06/1963
Comments: Centre-half who is popular with the fan's at Gigg Lane

VANL – **Van Der Laan Robin**  Port Vale    Striker     0   4   6    DL$........
Born: Schiedam – 05/09/1968
Comments: Bustling striker, one of the favourites at Vale Park

VARA – **Varadi Imre**  Luton Town          Striker     2   1   1    DL$........
Born: Paddington – 08/07/1959
Comments: Loan

# DREAM LEAGUE – CHAPTER 10   90 91 92

VAUN – **Vaughan Nigel**   Hereford   **Midfield**   0   0   1   **DL$**........
Born: Caerleon – 20/05/1959
Comments: Veteran who's made it for United

VENI – **Venison Barry**   Liverpool   **Defender**   0   0   1   **DL$**........
Born: Consett – 16/08/1964
Comments: Often found on the bench checking the highlights

VENU – **Venus Mark**   Wolverhampton W.   **Defender**   2   0   1   **DL$**........
Born: Hartlepool – 06/04/1967
Comments: Usually found lost in space

VERV – **Verveer Etienne**   Millwall   **Midfield**   0   0   3   **DL$**........
Born: Surinam – 22/09/1967
Comments: YOung midfield player who's been places

VICK – **Vickers Steve**   Tranmere Rovers   **Defender**   4   3   1   **DL$**........
Born: Bishop Auckland – 13/10/1967
Comments: Occasionally scores

VIVE – **Viveash Adrian**   Swindon Town   **Striker**   0   1   0   **DL$**........
Born: Swindon – 30/09/1969
Comments: Youngster with a weird name

WADG – **Waddock Gary**   Swindon Town   **Midfield**   0   2   0   **DL$**........
Born: Alperton – 17/03/1962
Comments: Loan

WADE – **Wade Bryan**   Brighton & Hove A.   **Striker**   1   6   3   **DL$**........
Born: Bath – 25/06/1963
Comments: Likes to score the odd goal

WALA – **Walker Alan**   Gillingham   **Defender**   1   4   5   **DL$**........
Born: Mossley – 17/12/1959
Comments: Long time server at Priestfield

WAND – **Walker Andy**   Bolton Wanderers   **Striker**   6   0   18   **DL$**........
Born: Glasgow – 06/04/1965
Comments: Could be the buy of the season

WACL – **Walker Clive**   Brighton & Hove A.   **Striker**   15   3   3   **DL$**........
Born: Oxford – 26/05/1957
Comments: Usually plays for London teams

WAIA – **Walker Ian**   Swansea City   **Midfield**   0   0   2   **DL$**........
Born: Watford – 31/10/1971
Comments: Figures in the defensive line up

WALK – **Walker Ray**   Port Vale   **Midfield**   1   7   2   **DL$**........
Born: North Shields – 28/09/1963
Comments: Has been parading silky skills at Vale Park for years

---

## Dream League Trivia

Who holds the record for the most hat tricks, for a British team in European football?

Answer: Denis Law – 5

# PLAYER GUIDE  90 91 92

**WALD – Wallace Danny**  Manchester United  **Striker**  6  4  0  DL$........
Born: London – 21/01/1964
Comments: Danny's not troubled the goal sheet this season

**WALL – Wallace Rod**  Leeds United  **Striker**  3  18  13  DL$........
Born: Lewisham – 02/10/1969
Comments: Rod's certainly no plonker around goal

**WADV – Waller David**  Chesterfield  **Striker**  18  0  0  DL$........
Born: Urmston – 20/12/1963
Comments: CID better investigate this sudden loss of form

**WDEN – Walling Dean**  Carlisle United  **Striker**  3  0  5  DL$........
Born: Leeds – 17/04/1969
Comments: Up, down, up – what next?

**WDAV – Walmsley David**  Hull City  **Striker**  0  1  1  DL$........
Born: Hull – 23/11/1972
Comments: Time to improve

**WALC – Walsh Colin**  Charlton Athletic  **Midfield**  3  1  5  DL$........
Born: Hamilton – 22/07/1962
Comments: Culture in midfield. Exquisite left foot, dodgy left knee

**WALS – Walsh Paul**  Portsmouthr  **Striker**  3  7  4  DL$........
Born: Plumstead – 01/10/1962
Comments: Often found living on the bench, smarting. Now living on beach

**WAST – Walsh Steve**  Leicester City  **Defender**  3  3  8  DL$........
Born: Fulwood – 03/11/1964
Comments: Likes to get forward and score

**WALT – Walters Mark**  Liverpool  **Striker**  5  0  5  DL$........
Born: Birmingham – 12/01/1961
Comments: Sometime's brilliant, sometimes non-existent

**WSTE – Walters Steve**  Crewe Alexandra  **Striker**  2  0  4  DL$........
Born: Plymouth – 09/01/1972
Comments: Either 8 or nothing, take your pick

**WARB – Warburton Ray**  York City  **Defender**  4  4  0  DL$........
Born: Rotherham – 07/10/1967
Comments: Another Bootham hero

**WAAS – Ward Ashley**  Leicester City  **Striker**  0  2  0  DL$........
Born: Manchester – 24/11/1970
Comments: Seems to have a phobia of the oppositions area

**WARD – Ward Mark**  Everton  **Midfield**  3  11  4  DL$........
Born: Prescot – 10/10/1962
Comments: Twice cost £1m in transfer deals

**WAMI – Ward Mitch**  Sheffield United  **Defender**  0  0  2  DL$........
Born: Sheffield – 18/06/1971
Comments: Trainee with a good squad

**WAPA – Ward Paul**  Lincoln City  **Midfield**  4  0  1  DL$........
Born: Sedgefield – 15/09/1963
Comments: Searching for his earlier form

**WARP – Ward Peter**  Stockport County  **Striker**  6  5  1  DL$........
Born: Durham – 15/10/1964
Comments: Oh dear! Oh dear!

# Dream League Trivia

*Who holds the record for the most own goals?*

Answer: Danny Malloy 14 at Cardiff

**WARE – Ware Paul** Stoke City    **Midfield**   0   2   3   DL$........
Born: Congleton – 07/11/1970
Comments: Skilful product from the youth team

**WARH – Warhurst Paul** Sheffield Wednesday    **Defender**   1   1   0   DL$........
Born: Stockport – 26/09/1969
Comments: Defender with a very quick turn of speed

**WARK – Wark John** Ipswich Town    **Midfield**   10   2   3   DL$........
Born: Glasgow – 04/08/1957
Comments: Portman Road old boy returns

**WARR – Warren Lee** Hull City    **Midfield**   0   1   1   DL$........
Born: Manchester – 28/02/1969
Comments: Good, solid midfielder

**WARZ – Warzycha Robert** Everton    **Striker**   0   2   3   DL$........
Born: Poland – 20/06/1963
Comments: Struggling to find a regular first team place

**WATK – Watkin Steve** Wrexham    **Striker**   0   1   13   DL$........
Born: Wrexham – 16/06/1971
Comments: Great prospect

**WATA – Watson Alex** AFC Bournemouth    **Defender**   0   3   1   DL$........
Born: Liverpool – 05/04/1968
Comments: Ever present "Cherry"

**WAAN – Watson Andy** Carlisle United    **Striker**   11   1   15   DL$........
Born: Huddersfield – 01/04/1967
Comments: Popular choice for your Dream Team

**WATD – Watson Dave** Everton    **Defender**   1   4   3   DL$........
Born: Liverpool – 20/11/1961
Comments: Long time server at Goodison Park

**WATJ – Watson John** Newcastle United    **Midfield**   0   0   1   DL$........
Born: South Shields – 14/04/1974
Comments: Youngster not often seen

**WATS – Watson Tommy** Grimsby Town    **Midfield**   2   9   2   DL$........
Born: Liverpool – 29/09/1969
Comments: Skilful product of the Youth policy

**WATT – Watts Julian** Rotherham United    **Defender**   0   0   1   DL$........
Born: Sheffield – 17/03/1971
Comments: Promising young defender

**WEBB – Webb Neil** Manchester United    **Midfield**   3   4   3   DL$........
Born: Reading – 30/07/1963
Comments: Another Devil coming back from injury, possibly on the move

| PLAYER GUIDE | | | 90 | 91 | 92 | |
|---|---|---|---|---|---|---|
| WEBS – **Webster Simon** Charlton Athletic<br>Born: Earl Shilton – 20/01/1964<br>Comments: Captain Fantastic.Solid oak at our end,Pele at theirs | **Defender** | 0 | 0 | 5 | DL$........ |
| WEGE – **Wegerle Roy** Blackburn Rovers<br>Born: S.Africa – 19/03/1964<br>Comments: Kenny must know something | **Striker** | 11 | 19 | 7 | DL$........ |
| WEIR – **Weir Billy** Shrewsbury Town<br>Born: Ballieston – 11/04/1968<br>Comments: One of the products of the Youth scheme at Gay Meadow | **Striker** | 0 | 1 | 0 | DL$........ |
| WEST – **West Colin** West Bromwich Albion<br>Born: Wallsend – 13/11/1962<br>Comments: Erratic,not to clever in the air | **Striker** | 4 | 0 | 3 | DL$........ |
| WESD – **West Dean** Lincoln City<br>Born: Wakefield – 05/12/1972<br>Comments: Impressive young Imp | **Midfield** | 0 | 1 | 3 | DL$........ |
| WESG – **West Gary** Lincoln City<br>Born: Scunthorpe – 25/08/1964<br>Comments: Skilful centre-half | **Defender** | 0 | 0 | 1 | DL$........ |
| WESS – **Westley Shane** Wolverhampton W.<br>Born: Canterbury – 16/06/1965<br>Comments: Tall, tough tackling defender | **Defender** | 1 | 1 | 0 | DL$........ |
| WHEE – **Wheeler Paul** Stockport County<br>Born: Caerphilly – 03/01/1965<br>Comments: Wheels in the goals | **Striker** | 8 | 4 | 6 | DL$........ |
| WHEP – **Whelan Paul** Ipswich Town<br>Born: Stockport – 07/08/1972<br>Comments: Giant central defender | **Defender** | 0 | 0 | 2 | DL$........ |
| WHEL – **Whelan Ronnie** Liverpool<br>Born: Dublin – 25/09/1961<br>Comments: Talented midfielder,recently struck down by injury | **Midfield** | 2 | 1 | 1 | DL$........ |
| WHIP – **Whiston Peter** Exeter City<br>Born: Widnes – 04/01/1968<br>Comments: Pete's improving | **Striker** | 1 | 1 | 3 | DL$........ |
| WHIA – **Whitbread Adrian** Leyton Orient<br>Born: Epping – 22/10/1971<br>Comments: Adrian's no half pint | **Defender** | 0 | 0 | 1 | DL$........ |
| WHID – **White David** Manchester City<br>Born: Manchester – 30/10/1967<br>Comments: Producing the goods in the six yard box | **Striker** | 10 | 16 | 21 | DL$........ |
| WHDE – **White Devon** Cambridge United<br>Born: Nottingham – 02/03/1964<br>Comments: One of United's potent strike force | **Striker** | 12 | 11 | 13 | DL$........ |
| WHIJ – **White Jason** Scunthorpe United<br>Born: Birmingham – 19/10/1971<br>Comments: Lumberer, not a pretty sight but knows where the goal is | **Striker** | 0 | 0 | 12 | DL$........ |
| WHIS – **White Steve** Swindon Town<br>Born: Chipping Sodbury – 02/01/1959<br>Comments: Glenda knows a bargain | **Striker** | 23 | 11 | 13 | DL$........ |

WHIW – **White Winston**  W. Bromwich Albion  **Midfield**  9  0  0  DL$........
Born: Leicester – 26/10/1958
Comments: Another tried at full back

WSTV – **Whitehall Steve**  Rochdale  **Striker**  0  0  10  DL$........
Born: Bromborough – 08/12/1966
Comments: Crowd favourite at Spotland

WHDA – **Whitehouse Dane**  Sheffield United  **Midfield**  1  0  8  DL$........
Born: Sheffield – 14/10/1970
Comments: Product of the Youth policy at Bramall Lane

WHIB – **Whitehurst Billy**  Crewe Alexandra  **Striker**  2  1  3  DL$........
Born: Thurnscoe – 10/06/1959
Comments: Loan

WHMI – **Whitlow Mike**  Leicester City  **Midfield**  1  1  1  DL$........
Born: Northwich – 13/01/1968
Comments: Mr. Consistency. One a season

WHIT – **Whittingham Guy**  Portsmouth  **Striker**  24  20  13  DL$........
Born: Evesham – 10/11/1964
Comments: Prolific scorer and the fans favourite, Fratton Park

WHST – **Whitton Steve**  Ipswich Town  **Striker**  5  2  10  DL$........
Born: East Ham – 04/12/1960
Comments: Can also play in midfield

WHYT – **Whyte Chris**  Leeds United  **Defender**  6  4  1  DL$........
Born: London – 02/09/1961
Comments: Chris has travelled far and near

WHYD – **Whyte David**  Charlton Athletic  **Striker**  0  0  4  DL$........
Born: London – 20/04/1971
Comments: Loan

WIGL – **Wigley Steve**  Portsmouth  **Striker**  4  5  3  DL$........
Born: Ashton – 15/10/1961
Comments: Dependable striker

WILC – **Wilcox Jason**  Blackburn Rovers  **Striker**  0  0  4  DL$........
Born: Bolton – 15/07/1971
Comments: Product of the Youth policy at Ewood Park

WILR – **Wilcox Russel**  Hull City  **Defender**  3  1  5  DL$........
Born: Hemsworth – 25/03/1964
Comments: Russel loves to get forward

WICH – **Wilder Chris**  Leyton Orient  **Defender**  0  0  1  DL$........
Born: Wortley – 23/09/1967
Comments: Loan

# Dream League Trivia

*Who was the last player to score a hat trick against Liverpool at Anfield?*

Answer: Terry Allcock – Norwich 1962

**PLAYER GUIDE**                    **90 91 92**

WIKE – **Wilkin Kevin**   Northampton Town   **Striker**   0  4  0   DL$........
Born: Cambridge – 01/10/1967
Comments: Been dogged by injury while at the County Ground

WILD – **Wilkins Dean**   Brighton & Hove A.   **Midfield**   7  7  0   DL$........
Born: Hillingdon – 12/07/1962
Comments: Dean's missed the goal this season

WIRA – **Wilkins Ray**   Queens Park Rangers   **Midfield**   3  2  2   DL$........
Born: Hillingdon – 14/09/1956
Comments: The old timer's suffered a bit from injury this season

WIRI – **Wilkins Richard**   Cambridge United   **Midfield**   4  3  4   DL$........
Born: London – 28/05/1965
Comments: Dicky's a regular scorer from midfield

WILK – **Wilkinson Paul**   Middlesbrough   **Striker**   15 18 22   DL$........
Born: Louth – 30/10/1964
Comments: Well travelled and experienced striker

WIST – **Wilkinson Steve**   Mansfield Town   **Striker**   16 12 14   DL$........
Born: Louth – 30/10/1964
Comments: Steve's nearly always first on the score sheet

WILA – **Williams Adrian**   Reading   **Defender**   2  0  6   DL$........
Born: Reading – 16/08/1971
Comments: Strong and very difficult to play against

WIAN – **Williams Andy**   Notts County   **Midfield**   2  0  1   DL$........
Born: Birmingham – 29/07/1962
Comments: Can sing a bit to

WILB – **Williams Bill**   Stockport County   **Defender**   0  1  2   DL$........
Born: Rochdale – 07/10/1960
Comments: Good solid club man

WIGE – **Williams Geraint**   Derby County   **Midfield**   0  0  3   DL$........
Born: Treorchy – 05/01/1962
Comments: Longest serving current player at the Baseball Ground

WIJO – **Williams John**   Cardiff City   **Defender**   2  0  0   DL$........
Born: Liverpool – 03/10/1960
Comments:

WIJN – **Williams John**   Swansea City   **Striker**   0  0  11   DL$........
Born: Birmingham – 11/05/1968
Comments: Prolific goal poacher

WILN – **Williams Neil**   Preston North End   **Midfield**   3  0  1   DL$........
Born: Waltham Abbey – 23/10/1964
Comments: Can either play in the middle or at full back

WILL – **Williams Paul**   West Bromwich Albion   **Striker**   0 14  6   DL$........
Born: Sheffield – 08/09/1963
Comments: Supposed to knock down balls for his partners, seldom does

WILP – **Williams Paul**   Sheffield Wednesday   **Striker**   12 17 10   DL$........
Born: London – 16/08/1965
Comments: Could be good with the books

WPAL – **Williams Paul**   Derby County   **Midfield**   0  4 14   DL$........
Born: Burton – 26/03/1971
Comments: The Rams goal getter

**DREAM LEAGUE – CHAPTER 10**

## Dream League Trivia

*Who scored six goals at Wembley in the 1960/61 season all at the same end (opposite end to the tunnel)?*

Answer: Bobby Smith – Spurs

**WWPA – Williams Paul R** Stockport County **Striker** 0 2 1 DL$........
Born: Leicester – 11/09/1969
Comments: Struggles to keep first team place

**WWVE – Williams Steve** Exeter City **Midfield** 1 0 0 DL$........
Born: London – 12/07/1958
Comments: Steve's player, assistant manager

**WISV – Williams Steven** Chesterfield **Midfield** 1 4 0 DL$........
Born: Mansfield – 18/07/1970
Comments: Lost the scoring touch

**WIBO – Williamson Bobby** Rotherham United **Striker** 20 6 0 DL$........
Born: Glasgow – 13/08/1961
Comments: Where did he go?

**WIJI – Willis Jimmy** Bradford **Defender** 0 2 3 DL$........
Born: Liverpool – 12/07/1968
Comments: Loan

**WROG – Willis Roger** Barnet **Striker** 0 0 12 DL$........
Born: Sheffield – 17/06/1967
Comments: "Harry" is a member of the "Barnet Exiles Club"

**WICL – Wilson Clive** Queens Park Rangers **Midfield** 0 1 2 DL$........
Born: Manchester – 13/11/1961
Comments: Can play either left side of midfield or left-back

**WDAN – Wilson Danny** Sheffield Wednesday **Midfield** 8 7 3 DL$........
Born: Wigan – 01/01/1960
Comments: Well travelled in the midfield role

**WRRE – Wilson Darren** Bury **Defender** 0 0 1 DL$........
Born: Cheadle – 30/09/1971
Comments: Can either play at right-back or midfield

**WWDA – Wilson David** Bristol Rovers **Midfield** 0 2 0 DL$........
Born: Burnley – 20/03/1969
Comments: Dave's missing the onion bag

**WILE – Wilson Eugene** Crewe Alexandra **Defender** 0 0 1 DL$........
Born: Manchester – 11/04/1963
Comments: Rarely troubles the oppositions defence

**WILS – Wilson Kevin** Notts County **Striker** 16 9 4 DL$........
Born: Banbury – 18/04/1961
Comments: One of Ken's clearout's

**WWUL – Wilson Paul** Halifax Town **Defender** 0 3 6 DL$........
Born: Bradford – 02/08/1968
Comments: Brought into bolster the defence, bonus goalscorer

| PLAYER GUIDE | | 90 | 91 | 92 | |
|---|---|---|---|---|---|

**WIUL – Wilson Paul**  Barnet  **Defender**  0  0  1  DL$........
Born: London – 26/09/1964
Comments: Like a rock in defence

**WIRO – Wilson Robert**  Rotherham United  **Midfield**  8  2  3  DL$........
Born: Kensington – 05/06/1961
Comments: Faded goal scorer

**WILT – Wilson Terry**  Newcastle United  **Midfield**  0  4  0  DL$........
Born: Broxburn – 08/02/1969
Comments: Loan

**WIMB – Wimbleton Paul**  Exeter City  **Midfield**  2  2  4  DL$........
Born: Havant – 13/11/1964
Comments: Busy midfielder, who likes a pop at goal

**WIND – Windass Dean**  Hull City  **Midfield**  0  0  6  DL$........
Born: Hull – 01/04/1969
Comments: Another of the promising youth at Boothferry

**WINS – Winstanley Mark**  Bolton Wanderers  **Defender**  1  0  0  DL$........
Born: St.Helens – 22/01/1968
Comments: Product of the youth scheme, coming back after injury

**WINI – Winterburn Nigel**  Arsenal  **Defender**  0  0  1  DL$........
Born: Nuneaton – 11/12/1963
Comments: One of the League's best Left-backs. Likes a challenge, legal and otherwise

**WISE – Wise Dennis**  Chelsea  **Striker**  8  12  13  DL$........
Born: Kensington – 15/12/1966
Comments: One of the many Wimbledon refugees at Stamford Bridge

**WITH – Withe Chris**  Watford  **Striker**  1  0  1  DL$........
Born: Liverpool – 25/09/1962
Comments: Rarely troubles, opposition goalie's

**WITT – Witter Tony**  Plymouth Argyle  **Defender**  0  0  1  DL$........
Born: London – 12/08/1965
Comments: Loan

**WOAN – Woan Ian**  Nottingham Forest  **Midfield**  0  3  5  DL$........
Born: Wirrall – 14/12/1967
Comments: Holding his place in midfield

**WOOP – Wood Paul**  AFC Bournemouth  **Striker**  3  0  10  DL$........
Born: Middlesbrough – 01/11/1964
Comments: Much needed bolster to the Cherries attack

**WOOS – Wood Steve**  Southampton  **Defender**  0  0  1  DL$........
Born: Bracknell – 02/02/1963
Comments: Another newcomer to The Dell

**WOON – Woods Neil**  Grimsby Town  **Striker**  2  12  8  DL$........
Born: York – 30/07/1966
Comments: Tall, productive striker

**WOOR – Woods Ray**  Coventry City  **Striker**  0  1  0  DL$........
Born: Birkenhead – 07/06/1965
Comments: Rarely seen in the sky blue strip

**WOOC – Woodthorpe Colin**  Norwich City  **Defender**  1  0  1  DL$........
Born: Ellesmere Port – 13/01/1969
Comments: Struggling to find a first team place

**DREAM LEAGUE – CHAPTER 10**  **90 91 92**

WORB – **Worboys Gavain**   Notts County   **Striker**   0   0   2   **DL$**........
Born: Doncaster – 14/07/1974
Comments: One to watch

WORS – **Worsley Graeme**   Shrewsbury Town   **Defender**   0   1   1   **DL$**........
Born: Liverpool – 04/01/1969
Comments: Attacking full back

WORT – **Worthington Gary**   Wigan Athletic   **Striker**   12  13  18   **DL$**........
Born: Cleethorpes – 10/11/1966
Comments: Latest in the Worthington dynasty

WORN – **Worthington Nigel**   Sheffield Wed   **Defender**   2   1   5   **DL$**........
Born: Ballymena – 04/11/1961
Comments: Long serving and popular at Hillsborough

WRIA – **Wright Alan**   Blackburn Rovers   **Midfield**   0   0   1   **DL$**........
Born: Ashton-under-Lyme – 28/09/1971
Comments: Recent arrival at Ewood Park

WRIG – **Wright Ian**   Arsenal   **Striker**   4  19  31   **DL$**........
Born: Woolwich – 03/11/1963
Comments: Not missing Bright. Second best in North London 91/92

WRIM – **Wright Mark**   Liverpool   **Defender**   6   0   0   **DL$**........
Born: Dorchester – 01/08/1963
Comments: One of the best central defenders in the league

WRTO – **Wright Tommy**   Leicester City   **Striker**   3   7  12   **DL$**........
Born: Dumfermline – 10/01/1966
Comments: Tiny Tony's a prolific scorer

WRIJ – **Wrightson Jeff**   Preston North End   **Defender**   0   3   2   **DL$**........
Born: Newcastle – 18/05/1968
Comments: Highly rated in defence

YATE – **Yates Dean**   Notts County   **Defender**   6   4   2   **DL$**........
Born: Leicester – 26/10/1967
Comments: A skilful product of the youth policy at Meadow Lane

YATM – **Yates Mark**   Burnley   **Midfield**   2   1   1   **DL$**........
Born: Birmingham – 24/01/1970
Comments: Steady scorer from midfield

YAST – **Yates Steve**   Burnley   **Defender**   0   0   1   **DL$**........
Born: Bristol – 29/01/1970
Comments: Steve just made the long journey upfield to score

YORK – **Yorke Dwight**   Aston Villa   **Striker**   0   2  16   **DL$**........
Born: Tobago – 03/12/1971
Comments: Yorkie's Villa's leading scorer, good from halfway line

## Dream League Trivia

*How many goals did Enbland score in the 1966 World Cup Finals?*

Answer: 11

| PLAYER GUIDE | | | 90 | 91 | 92 | |

YOUD – **Youds Edward**   Ipswich Town   **Defender**   2   0   0   **DL$........**
Born: Liverpool – 03/05/1970
Comments: Yet to make his mark due to injury

YOUN – **Young Eric**   Crystal Palace   **Defender**   5   4   1   **DL$........**
Born: Singapore – 25/03/1960
Comments: Mutant ninja Welshman from the far east

YOUR – **Young Richard**   Exeter City   **Striker**   7   0   0   **DL$........**
Born: Nottingham – 31/12/1968
Comments: Where did he go?

YOUS – **Young Stewart**   Hull City   **Striker**   0   0   3   **DL$........**
Born: Hull – 16/12/1972
Comments: Stewart has a lot of ability

## ADDITIONAL PLAYERS

Name:..................................Club ............................................ **DL$........**

Name:..................................Club ............................................ **DL$........**

Name:..................................Club ............................................ **DL$........**

Name:..................................Club ............................................ **DL$........**

Name:..................................Club ............................................ **DL$........**

Name:..................................Club ............................................ **DL$........**

Name:..................................Club ............................................ **DL$........**

Name:..................................Club ............................................ **DL$........**

Name:..................................Club ............................................ **DL$........**

Name:..................................Club ............................................ **DL$........**

Name:..................................Club ............................................ **DL$........**

| Name:................................................Club................................................. | **DL$........** |
|---|---|
| Name:................................................Club................................................. | **DL$........** |
| Name:................................................Club................................................. | **DL$........** |
| Name:................................................Club................................................. | **DL$........** |
| Name:................................................Club................................................. | **DL$........** |
| Name:................................................Club................................................. | **DL$........** |
| Name:................................................Club................................................. | **DL$........** |
| Name:................................................Club................................................. | **DL$........** |
| Name:................................................Club................................................. | **DL$........** |
| Name:................................................Club................................................. | **DL$........** |
| Name:................................................Club................................................. | **DL$........** |
| Name:................................................Club................................................. | **DL$........** |
| Name:................................................Club................................................. | **DL$........** |
| Name:................................................Club................................................. | **DL$........** |
| Name:................................................Club................................................. | **DL$........** |
| Name:................................................Club................................................. | **DL$........** |

# GOALIE GUIDE

ARS – **Arsenal**  44 32 59  DL$........
SEAM – **Seaman David**
Born: Rotherham – 19/09/1963
Comments: Hold's the transfer record for a British goalie, £1.3 million.
Deputies:

AST – **Aston Villa**  47 66 51  DL$........
SPIN – **Spink Nigel**
Born: Chelmsford – 08/08/1958
Comments: Not bad for reserve goalie
Deputies: Mark Bosnich, Les Sealey

BAR – **Barnsley**  47 66 60  DL$........
BLEE – **Butler Lee**
Born: Sheffield – 30/05/1966
Comments: The Tyke's no.1 goalie
Deputies: Scott Thomson

BIR – **Birmingham City**  66 54 63  DL$........
WDEA – **Williams Dean**
Born: Lichfield – 05/01/1972
Comments: First team scholar
Deputies:

BLR – **Blackburn Rovers**  58 73 62  DL$........
MIMM – **Mimms Bobby**
Born: York – 12/10/1963
Comments: Experience and skill between the posts didn't tell in 1992
Deputies: Terry Gennoe, Darren Collier

BLA – **Blackpool**  72 53 55  DL$........
MCIL – **McIlhargey Steve**
Born: Ferryhill – 28/08/1963
Comments: Crowd favourite at Bloomfield Road
Deputies: Russell Hoult, Jason Kearton

BOU – **AFC Bournemouth**  65 65 62  DL$........
BARV – **Bartram Vince**
Born: London – 07/08/1968
Comments: Promising young keeper
Deputies: Peter Guthrie

BOL – **Bolton Wanderers**  62 65 75  DL$........
FELG – **Felgate David**
Born: Blaenau Ffestiniog – 04/03/1960
Comments: Long time favourite at Burnden Park
Deputies:

BRA – **Bradford**  77 63 71  DL$........
TOMP – **Tomlinson Paul**
Born: Brierley Hill – 22/02/1964
Comments: The Bantam's No. 1 in goal
Deputies: Mark Evans

| DREAM LEAGUE – CHAPTER 10 | 90 91 92 | |
|---|---|---|

BRE – **Brentford**     65 59 76   DL$........
BENS – **Benstead Graham**
Born: Aldershot – 20/08/1963
Comments: Jim Robinson of Neighbours look-alike
Deputies: Lawrence Batty

BRI – **Brighton & Hove Albion**     79 84 85   DL$........
DIGW – **Digweed Perry**
Born: London – 26/10/1959
Comments: The Seagulls No. 1 often found digging the ball out
Deputies: Mark Beeney, Brian McKenna

BRC – **Bristol City**     54 81 82   DL$........
LEAN – **Leaning Andy**
Born: York – 18/05/1963
Comments: No leaning on the post for Andy, he's alway's to busy
Deputies: Keith Welch

BRR – **Bristol Rovers**     40 64 73   DL$........
PARK – **Parkin Brian**
Born: Birkenhead – 12/10/1965
Comments: Involved in the Nigel Martyn £1 million transfer deal
Deputies: Gavin Kelly

BUN – **Burnley**     64 61 56   DL$........
WIDA – **Williams David**
Born: Liverpool – 18/09/1968
Comments: Capable No. 2 at Turf Moor
Deputies: Mark Kendall, Andrew Marriott

BUR – **Bury**     54 64 78   DL$........
KELG – **Kelly Gary**
Born: Fulwood – 03/08/1966
Comments: Reliable No.1 for the "Shaker's"
Deputies:

CAM – **Cambridge United**     79 54 61   DL$........
VAUG – **Vaughan John**
Born: Isleworth – 26/06/1964
Comments: United's No. 1 stopper
Deputies:

CAR – **Cardiff City**     74 60 62   DL$........
HANS – **Hansbury Roger**
Born: Barnsley – 26/01/1955
Comments: Experience and strength in the Bluebirds goal
Deputies: John Priestley, Gavin Ward

CAU – **Carlisle United**     68 95 83   DL$........
OHAN – **O'Hanlon Kelham**
Born: Saltburn – 16/05/1962
Comments: Kel's the Cumbrians No. 1
Deputies:

CHA – **Charlton Athletic**     61 66 60   DL$........
BOLD – **Bolder Bob**
Born: Dover – 02/10/1958
Comments: Good reflex keeper, rooted to his line, reliable
Deputies:

| GOALIE GUIDE | 90 91 92 | |
|---|---|---|

**CHE – Chelsea**         58 81 67    DL$........
**BEAS – Beasant Dave**
Born: Willesden – 20/03/1959
Comments: Best remembered for penalty save v Liverpool FA Cup in 88
Deputies: Kevin Hitchcock

**CHC – Chester City**         67 74 71    DL$........
**STBI – Stewart Billy**
Born: Liverpool – 01/01/1965
Comments: Deputy to the ageing Mr.Siddall
Deputies: Barry Siddall

**CHF – Chesterfield**         58 72 67    DL$........
**LEOM – Leonard Mick**
Born: Carshalton – 09/05/1959
Comments: They say things get better with age
Deputies: Michael Allison

**COV – Coventry**         66 62 50    DL$........
**OGRI – Ogrizovic Steve**
Born: Mansfield – 12/09/1957
Comments: Shropshire cricket club's most famous son
Deputies: Clive Baker

**CRE – Crewe Alexandra**         58 93 72    DL$........
**GRED – Greygoose Dean**
Born: Thetford – 18/12/1964
Comments: Watch out Dean when the shooting starts
Deputies: Paul Edwards, Andy Gorton

**CRY – Crystal Palace**         82 49 72    DL$........
**MART – Martyn Nigel**
Born: St Austell – 11/08/1966
Comments: A million pounds plus goals galore against equals England keeper
Deputies:

**DAR – Darlington**         67 45 97    DL$........
**PRUD – Prudhoe Mark**
Born: Washington – 08/11/1963
Comments: The Quaker's main man between the posts
Deputies: Matt Coddington

**DER – Derby County**         57 65 64    DL$........
**SUTS – Sutton Steve**
Born: Hartington – 16/04/1961
Comments: Couldn't handle all those shredded wheat
Deputies: Martin Taylor

**DON – Doncaster Rovers**         56 58 76    DL$........
**CRIC – Crichton Paul**
Born: Pontefract – 03/10/1968
Comments: Anyone for Red Dwarf
Deputies:

**EVE – Everton**         56 54 58    DL$........
**SOUT – Southall Neville**
Born: Llandudno – 16/09/1958
Comments: Nev's been the "Toffee's" No.1 goalie for the past 8 year's
Deputies: Gerry Payton

| | | |
|---|---|---|
| DREAM LEAGUE – CHAPTER 10 | | 90 91 92 |

EXE – **Exeter City**     66 56 88   **DL$**........
MIKE – **Miller Kevin**
Born: Falmouth – 15/03/1969
Comments: Long time Grecian shot stopper

FUL – **Fulham**     79 63 60   **DL$**........
STAN – **Stannard Jim**
Born: London – 06/10/1962
Comments: "Big Jim" one of the best stoppers in the lower divisions
Deputies:

GIL – **Gillingham**     58 64 66   **DL$**........
LIMH – **Lim Harvey**
Born: Halesworth – 30/08/1967
Comments: Always out on a limb is Harvey
Deputies: Ron Hillyard

GRI – **Grimsby Town**     56 40 69   **DL$**........
REEP – **Reece Paul**
Born: Nottingham – 16/07/1968
Comments: Useful between the posts
Deputies: Steve Sherwood

HAL – **Halifax Town**     78 80 89   **DL$**........
BRAL – **Bracey Lee**
Born: Ashford – 11/09/1968
Comments: Shaymen's No. 1 shot stopper
Deputies: David Brown, Jonathan Gould

HAR – **Hartlepool United**     79 60 79   **DL$**........
COXB – **Cox Brian**
Born: Sheffield – 07/05/1961
Comments: Brians a busy boy
Deputies:

HER – **Hereford**     70 63 65   **DL$**........
ELTO – **Elliott Tony**
Born: Nuneaton – 30/11/1969
Comments: Experience between the posts
Deputies: Alan Judge

HUD – **Huddersfield Town**     73 59 53   **DL$**........
CLAT – **Clarke Tim**
Born:
Comments: Dream League sensation 92/93?
Deputies: Lee Martin, Steve Hardwick

HUL – **Hull City**     68 94 65   **DL$**........
WIVE – **Wilson Steve**
Born: Hull – 24/04/1974
Comments: Product of the Youth scheme at Boothferry Park
Deputies: Alan Fettis

IPS – **Ipswich Town**     70 74 56   **DL$**........
FORR – **Forrest Craig**
Born: Vancouver – 20/09/1967
Comments: Tall, commanding keeper. Canadian international
Deputies: Phil Parkes

LEE – **Leeds United**     57 56 43   **DL$**........

**GOALIE GUIDE**                                           **90 91 92**

LUKI – **Lukic John**
Born: Chesterfield – 11/12/1960
Comments: Usually Mr.Reliable
Deputies: Mervyn Day

LEI – **Leicester City**                  85 89 62    DL$........
MUGG – **Muggleton Carl**
Born: Leicester – 13/09/1968
Comments: Not many chances to prove himself
Deputies: Kevin Pole, Martin Hodge

LEY – **Leyton Orient**                 56 64 64    DL$........
TURC – **Turner Chris**
Born: Sheffield – 15/09/1958
Comments: Excellent veteran goalie
Deputies:

LIN – **Lincoln City**                   54 67 58    DL$........
BOWL – **Bowling Ian**
Born: Sheffield – 27/07/1965
Comments: Fighting for his first team place
Deputies: Mark Wallington

LIV – **Liverpool**                       47 56 53    DL$........
GROB – **Grobbelaar Bruce**
Born: Durban – 06/10/1957
Comments: Often brilliant, often not
Deputies: Mike Hooper

LUT – **Luton Town**                    69 70 80    DL$........
CHAM – **Chamberlain Alec**
Born: Glasgow – 31/10/1963
Comments: Suffers from Dracula syndrome – afraid of crosses
Deputies:

MAI – **Maidstone United**            68 94 67    DL$........
HESF – **Hesford Iain**
Born: Zambia – 04/03/1960
Comments: Tall, impressive goalie. Can score goals
Deputies:

MAC – **Manchester City**             61 59 54    DL$........
COTO – **Coton Tony**
Born: Tamworth – 19/05/1961
Comments: One of a rare breed, a £1m goalie
Deputies: Martyn Margetson

MAU – **Manchester United**         61 59 39    DL$........
SCHM – **Schmeichel Peter**
Born: TBA
Comments: Possibly the best!
Deputies: Gary Walsh

MAT – **Mansfield Town**              79 70 62    DL$........
PEJA – **Pearcey Jason**
Born: Leamington Spa – 02/07/1971
Comments: Number 1 at Quarry Lane
Deputies: Andy Beasley

**DREAM LEAGUE – CHAPTER 10**   **90 91 92**

MID – **Middlesbrough**   67 58 53   DL$........
PEST – **Pears Steve**
Born: Brandon – 22/01/1962
Comments: Now back to form after injury
Deputies:

MIL – **Millwall**   58 64 78   DL$........
DAAI – **Davison Aidan**
Born: Sedgefield – 11/05/1968
Comments: The Lion's No. 1 shot stopper
Deputies:

NEW – **Newcastle United**   68 68 90   DL$........
WRIT – **Wright Tommy**
Born: Belfast – 29/08/1963
Comments: No. 1
Deputies: Pavel Srnicek

NOT – **Northampton Town**   85 65 67   DL$........
RICB – **Richardson Barry**
Born: Willington Key – 05/08/1969
Comments: Capable goalie
Deputies:

NOR – **Norwich City**   50 50 70   DL$........
GUNN – **Gunn Bryan**
Born: Thurso – 22/12/1963
Comments: Long time serving "Canary"
Deputies: Mark Walton

NOF – **Nottingham Forest**   57 65 68   DL$........
CROS – **Crossley Mark**
Born: Barnsley – 16/06/1969
Comments: Now established between the post's
Deputies:

NOC – **Notts County**   58 67 70   DL$........
CHER – **Cherry Steve**
Born: Nottingham – 05/08/1960
Comments: Well travelled veteran goalie
Deputies:

OLD – **Oldham Athletic**   75 61 76   DL$........
HALL – **Hallworth Jon**
Born: Stockport – 26/10/1965
Comments: Long time serving Latic
Deputies: John Keeley

OXF – **Oxford United**   73 75 78   DL$........
KEEP – **Kee Paul**
Born: Belfast – 08/11/1969
Comments: Paul's the key to the 'U's' success
Deputies: Ken Veysey

PET – **Peterborough United**   77 74 69   DL$........
BARF – **Barber Fred**
Born: Ferryhill – 26/08/1963
Comments: Well travelled and experienced between the post's
Deputies: Paul Bradshaw

**GOALIE GUIDE**                                           **90 91 92**

PLY – **Plymouth Argyle**                         **50 81 72**   DL$........
SHIL – **Shilton Peter**
Born: Leicester – 18/09/1949
Comments: Player manager and ex-England keeper, so be careful
Deputies: Rhys Wilmot, David Walter

POR – **Portsmouth**                              **71 78 63**   DL$........
KNIG – **Knight Alan**
Born: Balham – 03/06/1961
Comments: Won't have to deal with John Barnes free-kicks
Deputies: Andy Gosney, Tony Lange

POV – **Port Vale**                               **72 71 72**   DL$........
GREW – **Grew Mark**
Born: Bilston – 15/02/1958
Comments: Long time "Valiant"
Deputies: Trevor Wood

PRE – **Preston North End**                       **54 73 82**   DL$........
FARN – **Farnsworth Simon**
Born: Chorley – 28/10/1963
Comments: Simons the Lillywhites star between the posts
Deputies: Alan Kelly

QPR – **Queens Park Rangers**                     **52 61 53**   DL$........
STEJ – **Stejskal Jan**
Born: Czechoslavakia – 15/01/1962
Comments: The original bouncing Czech
Deputies: Tony Roberts

REA – **Reading**                                 **76 71 72**   DL$........
FRST – **Francis Steve**
Born: Billericay – 29/05/1964
Comments: Previous winner of the Royal's player of the year award
Deputies:

ROC – **Rochdale**                                **62 65 62**   DL$........
ROSK – **Rose Kevin**
Born: Evesham – 23/11/1960
Comments: Using his experience well at Willbutts Lane
Deputies: Gareth Gray

ROT – **Rotheram United**                         **68 95 47**   DL$........
MERC – **Mercer William**
Born: Liverpool – 22/05/1969
Comments: Very capable, shows a lot of potential. New investment opportunity
Deputies:

SCA – **Scarborough**                             **67 58 83**   DL$........
IROI – **Ironside Ian**
Born: Sheffield – 08/03/1964
Comments: Loan
Deputies: Philip Hughes

SCU – **Scunthorpe United**                       **66 74 70**   DL$........
MUSS – **Musselwhite Paul**
Born: Portsmouth – 22/12/1968
Comments: Well known quick bowler in local cricket leagues
Deputies: Peter Litchfield, Chris Marples

| DREAM LEAGUE – CHAPTER 10 | 90 91 92 | |
|---|---|---|
| SHU – **Sheffield United**<br>TRAC – **Tracey Simon**<br>Born: Woolwich – 09/12/1967<br>Comments: No. 1 choice for the Blades<br>Deputies: Paul Kite, Mel Rees | 65 62 69 | DL$........ |
| SHW – **Sheffield Wednesday**<br>WOCH – **Woods Chris**<br>Born: Boston – 14/11/1959<br>Comments: Sell before visit to Highbury<br>Deputies: Kevin Pressman | 54 54 54 | DL$........ |
| SHR – **Shrewsbury Town**<br>HUGK – **Hughes Ken**<br>Born: Barmouth – 09/01/1966<br>Comments: Courageous shot stopper<br>Deputies: Steve Perks | 66 76 81 | DL$........ |
| SOU – **Southampton**<br>FLOW – **Flowers Tim**<br>Born: Kenilworth – 03/02/1967<br>Comments: "Saint's" regular shot stopper, even from behind the line?<br>Deputies: Ian Andrews | 65 62 69 | DL$........ |
| SND – **Southend United**<br>SANP – **Sansome Paul**<br>Born: N.Addington – 06/10/1961<br>Comments: Lomg time serving Shrimper<br>Deputies: | 56 67 67 | DL$........ |
| STC – **Stockport County**<br>EDWN – **Edwards Neil**<br>Born: Aberdare – 05/12/1970<br>Comments: Busy keeper<br>Deputies: David Redfern, Tony Pennock | 57 56 61 | DL$........ |
| STO – **Stoke City**<br>SINC – **Sinclair Ron**<br>Born: Stirling – 19/11/1964<br>Comments: Reliable and steady between the post's<br>Deputies: Peter Fox, Daniel Nobel | 54 81 59 | DL$........ |
| SUN – **Sunderland**<br>NORM – **Norman Tony**<br>Born: Mancot – 24/02/1958<br>Comments: Even the car park attendant doesn't recognize him<br>Deputies: | 78 70 79 | DL$........ |
| SWA – **Swansea City**<br>FRER – **Freestone Roger**<br>Born: Newport – 19/08/1968<br>Comments: No.1 at Vetch Field<br>Deputies: | 78 81 75 | DL$........ |
| SWI – **Swindon Town**<br>DIGB – **Digby Fraser**<br>Born: Sheffield – 23/04/1967<br>Comments: Lomg time goalie for Robins<br>Deputies: Nicky Hammond | 74 81 65 | DL$........ |

**GOALIE GUIDE**                                  90 91 92

TOR – **Torquay United**                          74 60 84   DL$........
HOWG – **Howells Gareth**
Born: Guildford – 13/06/1970
Comments: Saved a penalty, scored the winner in 1991 Play-Off final
Deputies:

TOT – **Tottenham Hotspur**                       58 61 70   DL$........
THOR – **Thorstvedt Eric**
Born: Stravanger – 28/10/1962
Comments: Tall Norwegian international, would like to communicate with a back four
Deputies: Ian Walker

TRA – **Tranmere Rovers**                         62 55 72   DL$........
NIXO – **Nixon Eric**
Born: Manchester – 04/10/1962
Comments: A real 'rover'
Deputies: Paul Collings

WAL – **Walsall**                                 68 44 64   DL$........
MCKN – **McKnight Allen**
Born: Antrim – 27/01/1964
Comments: No 1 for Walsall
Deputies: Ron Green

WAT – **Watford**                                 66 68 55   DL$........
JAME – **James David**
Born: Welwyn – 01/08/1970
Comments: Sound, commands his area well
Deputies: Tony Meola, Keith Waugh

WBA – **West Bromwich Albion**                    81 68 55   DL$........
NAYL – **Naylor Stuart**
Born: Wetherby – 06/12/1962
Comments: Can be good, can be outstanding. Rarely shouts-made captain
Deputies:

WES – **West Ham United**                         68 44 69   DL$........
MIKL – **Miklosko Ludek**
Born: Ostrava – 09/12/1961
Comments: Only ever present member of the promotion winning side 90/91
Deputies: Tony Parks

WIG – **Wigan Athletic**                          74 57 72   DL$........
ADKI – **Adkins Nigel**
Born: Birkenhead – 11/03/1965
Comments: Dependable long time server for the Latic's
Deputies: Giuseppe Paladino

WIM – **Wimbledon**                               45 51 59   DL$........
SEGE – **Segers Hans**
Born: Eindhoven – 30/10/1961
Comments: Very popular with the fan's at Selhurst Park
Deputies: Neil Sullivan

WOV – **Wolverhampton Wanderers**                 88 65 63   DL$........
STOW – **Stowell Mike**
Born: Preston – 19/04/1965
Comments: Top class keeper who needs a defence
Deputies:

**DREAM LEAGUE – CHAPTER 10**　　　　　**90 91 92**

WRE – **Wrexham**　　　　　　　　　　**75 88 82   DL$........**
OKEE – **O'Keefe Vince**
Born: Birmingham – 02/04/1957
Comments: Ageing, tall keeper
Deputies: Mark Morris

YOR – **York City**　　　　　　　　　　**62 63 66   DL$........**
KIEL – **Kiely Dean**
Born: Manchester – 10/10/1970
Comments: Young goalkeeper
Deputies:

## GOALIE NOTES

# QUICK REFERENCE 91/92
# GOALS CONCEDED BY GOALIES

| Name | Club | Goals | Name | Club | Goals |
|---|---|---|---|---|---|
| Schmeichel Peter | Manchester United | 39 | Sutton Steve | Derby County | 64 |
| Lukic John | Leeds United | 43 | Turner Chris | Leyton Orient | 64 |
| Mercer William | Rotherham United | 47 | McKnight Allen | Walsall | 64 |
| Seaman David | Arsenal | 50 | Elliott Tony | Hereford | 65 |
| Ogrizovic Steve | Coventry City | 50 | Fettis Alan | Hull City | 65 |
| Spink Nigel | Aston Villa | 51 | Digby Fraser | Swindon Town | 65 |
| Clarke Tim | Huddersfield T | 53 | Harrison Lee | Gillingham | 66 |
| Grobbelaar Bruce | Liverpool | 53 | Kiely Dean | York City | 66 |
| Pears Steve | Middlesbrough | 53 | Beasant Dave | Chelsea | 67 |
| Stejskal Jan | QPR | 53 | Leonard Mick | Chesterfield | 67 |
| Coton Tony | Manchester City | 54 | Hesford Iain | Maidstone United | 67 |
| Woods Chris | Sheffield Wed | 54 | Richardson Barry | Northampton T | 67 |
| McIlhargey Steve | Blackpool | 55 | Sansome Paul | Southend United | 67 |
| James David | Watford | 55 | Crossley Mark | Notts Forest | 68 |
| Naylor Stuart | W.B.A. | 55 | Reece Paul | Grimsby Town | 69 |
| Williams David | Burnley | 56 | Barber Fred | Peterborough Utd | 69 |
| Forrest Craig | Ipswich Town | 56 | Tracey Simon | Sheffield Utd | 69 |
| Southall Neville | Everton | 58 | Flowers Tim | Southampton | 69 |
| Bowling Ian | Lincoln City | 58 | Miklosko Ludek | West Ham Utd | 69 |
| Sinclair Ron | Stoke City | 59 | Cherry Steve | Notts County | 70 |
| Segers Hans | Wimbledon | 59 | Gunn Bryan | Norwich City | 70 |
| Butler Lee | Barnsley | 60 | Samways Mark | Scunthorpe Utd | 70 |
| Bolder Bob | Charlton Athletic | 60 | Thorstvedt Eric | Tottenham | 70 |
| Stannard Jim | Fulham | 60 | Tomlinson Paul | Bradford | 71 |
| Vaughan John | Cambridge Utd | 61 | Stewart Billy | Chester City | 71 |
| Edwards Neil | Stockport County | 61 | Greygoose Dean | Crewe Alexandra | 72 |
| Mimms Bobby | Blackburn Rovers | 62 | Martyn Nigel | Crystal Palace | 72 |
| Bartram Vince | AFC Bournemouth | 62 | Shilton Peter | Plymouth Argyle | 72 |
| Hansbury Roger | Cardiff City | 62 | Grew Mark | Port Vale | 72 |
| Muggleton Carl | Leicester City | 62 | Francis Steve | Reading | 72 |
| Pearcey Jason | Mansfield Town | 62 | Nixon Eric | Tranmere Rovers | 72 |
| Rose Kevin | Rochdale | 62 | Adkins Nigel | Wigan Athletic | 72 |
| Dearden Kevin | Birmingham City | 63 | Parkin Brian | Bristol Rovers | 73 |
| Knight Alan | Portsmouth | 63 | Pape Andrew | Barnet | 75 |
| Stowell Mike | Wolverhampton W. | 63 | Felgate David | Bolton Wanderers | 75 |

## DREAM LEAGUE – CHAPTER 10

| | | | | | | |
|---|---|---|---|---|---|---|
| Freestone Roger | Swansea City | 75 | Leaning Andy | Bristol City | 82 |
| Benstead Graham | Brentford | 76 | Farnworth Simon | Preston North End | 82 |
| Crichton Paul | Doncaster Rovers | 76 | O'Keefe Vince | Wrexham | 82 |
| Hallworth Jon | Oldham Athletic | 76 | O'Hanlon Kelham | Carlisle United | 83 |
| Kelly Gary | Bury | 78 | Ironside Ian | Scarborough | 83 |
| Davison Aidan | Millwall | 78 | Howells Gareth | Torquay United | 84 |
| Kee Paul | Oxford | 78 | Digweed Perry | Brighton & Hove A. | 85 |
| Cox Brian | Hartlepool United | 79 | Miller Kevin | Exeter City | 88 |
| Norman Tony | Sunderland | 79 | Bracey Lee | Halifax Town | 89 |
| Day Mervyn | Luton Town | 80 | Wright Tommy | Newcastle United | 90 |
| Hughes Ken | Shrewsbury Town | 81 | Prudhoe Mark | Darlington | 97 |

## QUICK REFERENCE 91/92 GOALS SCORED BY DEFENDERS

| | | | | | |
|---|---|---|---|---|---|
| Gannon Jim | Stockport County | 17 | Matthewson Trevor | Birmingham City | 6 |
| Eli Roger | Burnley | 12 | Thompson Neil | Ipswich Town | 6 |
| Tinnion Brian | Bradford | 11 | Williams Adrian | Reading | 6 |
| Darby Julian | Bolton Wanderers | 10 | Wilson Paul | Halifax Town | 6 |
| Abel Graham | Chester City | 9 | Barr Billy | Halifax Town | 5 |
| Evans Terry | Brentford | 9 | Barras Tony | Stockport County | 5 |
| Newman Rob | Norwich City | 9 | Curle Keith | Manchester City | 5 |
| Blake Nathan | Cardiff City | 8 | Dicks Julian | West Ham United | 5 |
| Elliot Matthew | Scunthorpe United | 8 | Drysdale Jason | Watford | 5 |
| Pearce Stuart | Nottingham Forest | 8 | Fee Greg | Mansfield Town | 5 |
| Walsh Steve | Leicester City | 8 | Hall Richard | Southampton | 5 |
| Barnsley Andy | Carlisle United | 7 | Heathcote Mike | Cambridge United | 5 |
| Eckhardt Jeff | Fulham | 7 | Hendry Colin | Blackburn Rovers | 5 |
| Sterland Mel | Leeds United | 7 | Horner Philip | Blackpool | 5 |
| Alexander Graham | Scunthorpe United | 6 | Howard Terence | Leyton Orient | 5 |
| Atkins Mark | Blackburn Rovers | 6 | Kelly Tom | Exeter City | 5 |
| Bruce Steve | Manchester United | 6 | Meyer Adrian | Scarborough | 5 |
| Butler Barry | Chester City | 6 | Palmer Carlton | Sheffield Wednesday | 5 |
| Calderwood Colin | Swindon Town | 6 | Phillips Wayne | Wrexham | 5 |
| Cunnington Shaun | Grimsby Town | 6 | Taylor Shaun | Swindon Town | 5 |
| Greenall Colin | Preston North End | 6 | Walker Alan | Gillingham | 5 |
| Johnson Gavin | Ipswich Town | 6 | Webster Simon | Charlton Athletic | 5 |
| Lee David | Plymouth Argyle | 6 | Wilcox Russel | Hull City | 5 |

## QUICK REFERENCE 91/92

| | | | | | | |
|---|---|---|---|---|---|---|
| **Worthington Nigel** | Sheffield Wednesday | 5 | **Comyn Andy** | Derby County | 3 |
| **Anderson Viv** | Sheffield Wednesday | 4 | **Cranson Ian** | Stoke City | 3 |
| **Babb Phil** | Bradford | 4 | **Daniels Scott** | Exeter City | 3 |
| **Bowen Mark** | Norwich City | 4 | **Dorigo Tony** | Leeds United | 3 |
| **Chapman Ian** | Brighton & Hove A. | 4 | **Elliott Paul** | Chelsea | 3 |
| **Coleman Chris** | Crystal Palace | 4 | **Fairclough Wayne** | Mansfield Town | 3 |
| **Dixon Lee** | Arsenal | 4 | **Gatting Steve** | Charlton Athletic | 3 |
| **Flynn Mike** | Preston North End | 4 | **Gibson Colin** | Leicester City | 3 |
| **Gayle Brian** | Sheffield United | 4 | **Hardyman Paul** | Sunderland | 3 |
| **Gooding Mick** | Reading | 4 | **Hewitt Jamie** | Chesterfield | 3 |
| **Green Richard** | Gillingham | 4 | **Hirst Lee** | Scarborough | 3 |
| **Harris Mark** | Swansea City | 4 | **Horton Duncan** | Barnet | 3 |
| **Hill Andy** | Manchester City | 4 | **Howell David** | Barnet | 3 |
| **Humphries Glenn** | Scunthorpe United | 4 | **Jobson Richard** | Oldham Athletic | 3 |
| **Hutchings Chris** | Rotherham United | 4 | **Le Saux Graeme** | Chelsea | 3 |
| **Irwin Denis** | Manchester United | 4 | **Linighan David** | Ipswich Town | 3 |
| **Johnson Alan** | Wigan Athletic | 4 | **McGugan Paul** | Chesterfield | 3 |
| **Melville Andy** | Oxford | 4 | **Moran Kevin** | Blackburn Rovers | 3 |
| **Mills Simon** | Port Vale | 4 | **Morgan Simon** | Fulham | 3 |
| **Osborne Lawrence** | Gillingham | 4 | **Newson Mark** | Fulham | 3 |
| **Patterson Darren** | Wigan Athletic | 4 | **O'Reilly Gary** | Brighton & Hove A. | 3 |
| **Ryan John** | Rochdale | 4 | **Ormsby Brendan** | Doncaster Rovers | 3 |
| **Stanislaus Roger** | Bury | 4 | **Overson Vince** | Stoke City | 3 |
| **Staunton Steve** | Aston Villa | 4 | **Pender John** | Burnley | 3 |
| **Stebbing Gary** | Maidstone United | 4 | **Price Chris** | Blackburn Rovers | 3 |
| **Strodder Gary** | West Bromwich Albion | 4 | **Ramsey Paul** | Cardiff City | 3 |
| **Walters Steve** | Crewe Alexandra | 4 | **Reeves Alan** | Rochdale | 3 |
| **Adams Mick** | Southampton | 3 | **Robinson David** | Peterborough United | 3 |
| **Bennett Gary** | Sunderland | 3 | **Scully Pat** | Southend United | 3 |
| **Bond Kevin** | AFC Bournemouth | 3 | **Swan Peter** | Port Vale | 3 |
| **Bradley Russell** | Halifax Town | 3 | **Taggart Gerry** | Barnsley | 3 |
| **Brown Kenny** | West Ham United | 3 | **Terry Steve** | Northampton Town | 3 |
| **Brown Phil** | Bolton Wanderers | 3 | **Thomas Tony** | Tranmere Rovers | 3 |
| **Barratt Tony** | York City | 3 | **Thomas Mitchell** | West Ham United | 3 |
| **Burrows Adrian** | Plymouth Argyle | 3 | **Ullathorne Robert** | Norwich City | 3 |
| **Butters Guy** | Portsmouth | 3 | **Watson Dave** | Everton | 3 |
| **Butler John** | Stoke City | 3 | **West Dean** | Lincoln City | 3 |
| **Carr Darren** | Crewe Alexandra | 3 | **Whiston Peter** | Exeter City | 3 |
| **Chapple Phil** | Cambridge United | 3 | **Willis Jimmy** | Bradford | 3 |

## DREAM LEAGUE – CHAPTER 10

| | | | | | | |
|---|---|---|---|---|---|---|
| Adams Tony | Arsenal | 2 | Methven Colin | Walsall | 2 |
| Angus Terry | Northampton Town | 2 | Morgan Steve | Plymouth Argyle | 2 |
| Austin Dean | Southend United | 2 | Minto Scott | Charlton Athletic | 2 |
| Barrett Earl | Aston Villa | 2 | Mohan Nicky | Middlesbrough | 2 |
| Barlow Andy | Oldham Athletic | 2 | Morrell Paul | AFC Bournemouth | 2 |
| Bates Jamie | Brentford | 2 | Newsome Jon | Leeds United | 2 |
| Beesley Paul | Sheffield United | 2 | O'Shea Danny | Cambridge United | 2 |
| Bennett Tom | Wolverhampton W. | 2 | Osman Russell | Bristol City | 2 |
| Bradley Darren | West Bromwich Albion | 2 | Patterson Mark | Derby County | 2 |
| Breacker Tim | West Ham United | 2 | Pearce Andy | Coventry City | 2 |
| Brown Grant | Lincoln City | 2 | Pearson Nigel | Sheffield Wednesday | 2 |
| Bryant Matthew | Bristol City | 2 | Pejic Mel | Wrexham | 2 |
| Burgess Daryl | West Bromwich Albion | 2 | Phillips Jimmy | Middlesbrough | 2 |
| Callaghan Aaron | Crewe Alexandra | 2 | Pike Martin | Fulham | 2 |
| Cooper Colin | Millwall | 2 | Pitcher Darren | Charlton Athletic | 2 |
| Cross Steve | Bristol Rovers | 2 | Ratcliffe Simon | Brentford | 2 |
| Curran Chris | Scarborough | 2 | Richardson Neil | Rotherham United | 2 |
| Davis Darren | Maidstone United | 2 | Roberts Graham | West Bromwich Albion | 2 |
| Davies Steve | Burnley | 2 | Robinson Ronnie | Peterborough United | 2 |
| Day Keith | Leyton Orient | 2 | Saunders Wes | Torquay United | 2 |
| Downs Greg | Hereford | 2 | Searle Damon | Cardiff City | 2 |
| Dreyer John | Luton Town | 2 | Senior Steve | Preston North End | 2 |
| Edmondson Darren | Carlisle United | 2 | Short Craig | Notts County | 2 |
| Fairclough Chris | Leeds United | 2 | Sinclair Frank | Chelsea | 2 |
| Forsyth Mike | Derby County | 2 | Smalley Mark | Maidstone United | 2 |
| Foster Steve | Oxford | 2 | Smith Kevan | Darlington | 2 |
| Gill Gary | Cardiff City | 2 | Smith Richard | Leicester City | 2 |
| Harvey Richard | Luton Town | 2 | Thorn Andy | Crystal Palace | 2 |
| Holdsworth David | Watford | 2 | Theodosious Andy | Hereford | 2 |
| Holmes Paul | Birmingham City | 2 | Thomas Glen | Fulham | 2 |
| Hopkins Tony | Aldershot | 2 | Ward Mitch | Sheffield United | 2 |
| Hughes Darren | Port Vale | 2 | Whelan Paul | Ipswich Town | 2 |
| Jeffels Simon | Carlisle United | 2 | Williams Bill | Stockport County | 2 |
| Johnson Nigel | Rotherham United | 2 | Wrightson Jeff | Preston North End | 2 |
| Joyce Joe | Scunthorpe United | 2 | Yates Dean | Notts County | 2 |
| Kerr Dylan | Blackpool | 2 | | | |
| Lambert Matthew | Preston North End | 2 | | | |
| Mabbutt Gary | Tottenham Hotspur | 2 | | | |
| McCarthy Mick | Millwall | 2 | | | |

# QUICK REFERENCE 91/92
# GOALS SCORED BY MIDFIELDERS

| Player | Club | Goals |
|---|---|---|
| Gleghorn Nigel | Birmingham City | 22 |
| Peacock Gavin | Newcastle United | 20 |
| Hignett Craig | Crewe Alexandra | 17 |
| Dozzell Jason | Ipswich Town | 15 |
| Preece Andy | Stockport County | 15 |
| Dalton Paul | Hartlepool United | 14 |
| Williams Paul | Derby County | 14 |
| Kerr Paul | Millwall | 13 |
| Magilton John | Oxford | 13 |
| Rae Alex | Millwall | 13 |
| Groves Paul | Blackpool | 12 |
| Keane Roy | Nottingham Forest | 12 |
| Armstrong Gordon | Sunderland | 11 |
| Castle Steve | Leyton Orient | 11 |
| Rodgerson Ian | Birmingham City | 11 |
| Shakespeare Craig | West Bromwich Albion | 11 |
| Summerfield Kevin | Shrewsbury Town | 11 |
| Ashdjian John | Scarborough | 10 |
| Birch Paul | Wolverhampton W. | 10 |
| Gemmill Scot | Nottingham Forest | 10 |
| Houghton Ray | Liverpool | 10 |
| Narbett Jon | Hereford | 10 |
| Robson Gary | West Bromwich Albion | 10 |
| Speed Gary | Leeds United | 10 |
| Benjamin Ian | Southend United | 9 |
| Bowden Jon | Rochdale | 9 |
| Bryson Ian | Sheffield United | 9 |
| Burns Christopher | Portsmouth | 9 |
| Legg Andy | Swansea City | 9 |
| Porter Gary | Watford | 9 |
| Richardson Nick | Halifax Town | 9 |
| Atkinson Graeme | Hull City | 8 |
| Barker Simon | Queens Park Rangers | 8 |
| Beresford John | Portsmouth | 8 |
| Charles Steve | Mansfield Town | 8 |
| Cook Paul | Wolverhampton W. | 8 |
| Halsall Mick | Peterborough United | 8 |
| Kanchelskis Andrej | Manchester United | 8 |
| Milton Simon | Ipswich Town | 8 |
| Rowbotham Darren | Birmingham City | 8 |
| Sellars Scott | Blackburn Rovers | 8 |
| Swann Gary | Preston North End | 8 |
| Whitehouse Dane | Sheffield United | 8 |
| Beadle Peter | Gillingham | 7 |
| Clarkson Phil | Crewe Alexandra | 7 |
| Codner Robert | Brighton & Hove A. | 7 |
| Dobbin Jim | Grimsby Town | 7 |
| Goodwin Shaun | Rotherham United | 7 |
| Gray Andy | Tottenham Hotspur | 7 |
| Hazard Mike | Swindon Town | 7 |
| Henry Nick | Oldham Athletic | 7 |
| Hodge Steve | Leeds United | 7 |
| Joyce Warren | Preston North End | 7 |
| Mills Gary | Leicester City | 7 |
| Owen Gareth | Wrexham | 7 |
| Painter Robert | Burnley | 7 |
| Puttnam David | Lincoln City | 7 |
| Robinson John | Brighton & Hove A. | 7 |
| Sandeman Bradley | Maidstone United | 7 |
| Sheridan John | Sheffield Wednesday | 7 |
| Sterling Worrell | Peterborough United | 7 |
| Thomas Geoff | Crystal Palace | 7 |
| Townsend Andy | Chelsea | 7 |
| Turnbull Lee | Chesterfield | 7 |
| Beagrie Peter | Everton | 6 |
| Black Kingsley | Nottingham Forest | 6 |
| Canham Tony | York City | 6 |
| Cockerill Glenn | Southampton | 6 |
| Cusack Nick | Darlington | 6 |
| Deary John | Burnley | 6 |
| Duxbury Lee | Bradford | 6 |
| Holland Paul | Mansfield Town | 6 |

# DREAM LEAGUE – CHAPTER 10

| | | | | | | |
|---|---|---|---|---|---|---|
| Honour Brian | Hartlepool United | 6 | Walsh Colin | Charlton Athletic | 5 |
| Jones Keith | Southend United | 6 | Woan Ian | Nottingham Forest | 5 |
| Lovell Stuart | Reading | 6 | Atkinson Brian | Sunderland | 4 |
| Mardenborough S. | Darlington | 6 | Barrow Graham | Chester City | 4 |
| Morrissey John | Tranmere Rovers | 6 | Barlow Martin | Plymouth Argyle | 4 |
| Olsson Paul | Hartlepool United | 6 | Barber Philip | Millwall | 4 |
| Richardson Kevin | Aston Villa | 6 | Bell Michael | Northampton Town | 4 |
| Thomas Michael | Liverpool | 6 | Bishop Eddie | Crewe Alexandra | 4 |
| Thornber Stephen | Swansea City | 6 | Blackmore Clayton | Manchester United | 4 |
| Windass Dean | Hull City | 6 | Brennan Mark | Manchester City | 4 |
| Allen Paul | Tottenham Hotspur | 5 | Brock Kevin | Newcastle United | 4 |
| Beeston Carl | Stoke City | 5 | Cartwright Lee | Preston North End | 4 |
| Bernard Paul | Oldham Athletic | 5 | Chard Phil | Northampton Town | 4 |
| Clark Lee | Newcastle United | 5 | Cooper Graham | Halifax Town | 4 |
| Cooper Gary | Peterborough United | 5 | Cook Mitch | Blackpool | 4 |
| Cooper Mark | Birmingham City | 5 | Flore Mark | Plymouth Argyle | 4 |
| Falconer Willie | Middlesbrough | 5 | Fitzpatrick Paul | Leicester City | 4 |
| Frain John | Birmingham City | 5 | Frain David | Stockport County | 4 |
| Gayle Marcus | Brentford | 5 | Hall Wayne | York City | 4 |
| Gormley Eddie | Doncaster Rovers | 5 | Hopkins Robert | Shrewsbury Town | 4 |
| Hill David | Scunthorpe United | 5 | Horne Barry | Southampton | 4 |
| Holden Rick | Oldham Athletic | 5 | James Martin | Preston North End | 4 |
| Holmes Micky | Carlisle United | 5 | Jones Tommy | Swindon Town | 4 |
| Hoyland Jamie | Sheffield United | 5 | Jones Vinny | Chelsea | 4 |
| Kelly Tony | Hull City | 5 | Kuhl Martin | Portsmouth | 4 |
| Lake Michael | Sheffield United | 5 | Lewis Mickey | Oxford | 4 |
| Lightfoot Chris | Chester City | 5 | Lillis Jason | Maidstone United | 4 |
| McAllister Gary | Leeds United | 5 | McKearney David | Crewe Alexandra | 4 |
| Mockler Andrew | Scarborough | 5 | Milligan Mike | Oldham Athletic | 4 |
| Newton Edward | Chelsea | 5 | Molby Jan | Liverpool | 4 |
| Ntamark Charlie | Walsall | 5 | Morrison Andy | Plymouth Argyle | 4 |
| O'Regan Kieran | Huddersfield Town | 5 | Mundee Denny | AFC Bournemouth | 4 |
| Otto Ricky | Leyton Orient | 5 | Myers Chris | Torquay United | 4 |
| Pickering Nick | Darlington | 5 | O'Brien Liam | Newcastle United | 4 |
| Philpott Lee | Cambridge United | 5 | Owers Gary | Sunderland | 4 |
| Rankine Mark | Wolverhampton W. | 5 | Peer Dean | Birmingham City | 4 |
| Redfearn Neil | Barnsley | 5 | Pembridge Mark | Luton Town | 4 |
| Robson Bryan | Manchester United | 5 | Pepper Nigel | York City | 4 |
| Simpson Fitzroy | Manchester City | 5 | Reece Andy | Bristol Rovers | 4 |
| Toman Andy | Darlington | 5 | Rennie David | Birmingham City | 4 |

| | | | | | | |
|---|---|---|---|---|---|---|
| Smith David | Coventry City | 4 | Onwere Udo | Fulham | 3 |
| Sinclair Trevor | Blackpool | 4 | Parker Garry | Aston Villa | 3 |
| Smith Neil | Gillingham | 4 | Parkinson Joe | Wigan Athletic | 3 |
| Strachan Gordon | Leeds United | 4 | Patterson Mark | Bolton Wanderers | 3 |
| Thackeray Andy | Wrexham | 4 | Pilling Andy | Wigan Athletic | 3 |
| Thompson Steve | Leicester City | 4 | Preece David | Luton Town | 3 |
| Ward Mark | Everton | 4 | Reid Wesley | Scottish League | 3 |
| Wimbleton Paul | Exeter City | 4 | Rocastle David | Arsenal | 3 |
| Wilkins Richard | Cambridge United | 4 | Robson Stewart | Coventry City | 3 |
| Anderson Colin | Walsall | 3 | Sanchez Lawrie | Wimbledon | 3 |
| Beavon Stuart | Northampton Town | 3 | Schofield Jon | Lincoln City | 3 |
| Brady Kieron | Sunderland | 3 | Scott Martin | Bristol City | 3 |
| Cork David | Darlington | 3 | Shelton Gary | Bristol City | 3 |
| Cheetham Michael | Cambridge United | 3 | Sinton Andy | Queens Park Rangers | 3 |
| Childs Gary | Grimsby Town | 3 | Skinner Justin | Bristol Rovers | 3 |
| Chappell Shaun | Swansea City | 3 | Smith Nigel | Bury | 3 |
| Comstive Paul | Chester City | 3 | Spooner Steve | Mansfield Town | 3 |
| Crosby Gary | Nottingham Forest | 3 | Taylor Scott | Reading | 3 |
| Dillon Kevin | Reading | 3 | Thomas Mickey | Wrexham | 3 |
| Dyche Sean | Chesterfield | 3 | Thompstone Ian | Exeter City | 3 |
| Elsey Karl | Gillingham | 3 | Todd Mark | Rotherham United | 3 |
| Farrell Andy | Burnley | 3 | Verveer Etienne | Millwall | 3 |
| Ford Gary | Mansfield Town | 3 | Ware Paul | Stoke City | 3 |
| Gilbert David | Grimsby Town | 3 | Wark John | Ipswich Town | 3 |
| Gynn Mick | Coventry City | 3 | Wilson Danny | Sheffield Wednesday | 3 |
| Halpin John | Rochdale | 3 | Williams Darren | Non League Team | 3 |
| Harkes John | Sheffield Wednesday | 3 | Webb Neil | Manchester United | 3 |
| Holmes Matt | AFC Bournemouth | 3 | Williams Geraint | Derby County | 3 |
| Ince Paul | Manchester United | 3 | Wilson Robert | Rotherham United | 3 |
| Kelly Tony G | Bolton Wanderers | 3 | Alexander Ian | Bristol Rovers | 2 |
| Lowe Kenny | Barnet | 3 | Allen Martin | West Ham United | 2 |
| Luscombe Lee | Brentford | 3 | Atteveld Ray | Bristol City | 2 |
| Martin Dean | Scunthorpe United | 3 | Banks Ian | Barnsley | 2 |
| McGoldrick Eddie | Crystal Palace | 3 | Barham Mark | Brighton & Hove A. | 2 |
| McLoughlin Alan | Portsmouth | 3 | Batty David | Leeds United | 2 |
| McMinn Ted | Derby County | 3 | Blake Mark | Aston Villa | 2 |
| Mortimer Paul | Crystal Palace | 3 | Bodin Paul | Swindon Town | 2 |
| Mustoe Robbie | Middlesbrough | 3 | Booker Bob | Brentford | 2 |
| O'Connor Mark | Gillingham | 3 | Carr Franz | Newcastle United | 2 |
| O'Hara Steve | Walsall | 3 | Carr Cliff | Shrewsbury Town | 2 |

227

## DREAM LEAGUE – CHAPTER 10

| | | | | | | |
|---|---|---|---|---|---|---|
| **Coleman Simon** | Derby County | 2 | **Morris David** | AFC Bournemouth | 2 |
| **Connelly Dean** | Barnsley | 2 | **Norton David** | Hull City | 2 |
| **Cowans Gordon** | Blackburn Rovers | 2 | **Oakes Scott** | Luton Town | 2 |
| **Dempsey Mark** | Gillingham | 2 | **Osborn Simon** | Crystal Palace | 2 |
| **Dennis Tony** | Cambridge United | 2 | **Pardew Alan** | Charlton Athletic | 2 |
| **Doling Stuart** | Portsmouth | 2 | **Phillips David** | Norwich City | 2 |
| **Doble Mark** | Torquay United | 2 | **Poole Gary** | Barnet | 2 |
| **Draper Mark** | Notts County | 2 | **Proctor Mark** | Middlesbrough | 2 |
| **Ebdon Marcus** | Peterborough United | 2 | **Putney Trevor** | Watford | 2 |
| **Fereday Wayne** | West Bromwich Albion | 2 | **Randall Adrian** | Burnley | 2 |
| **Flynn Sean** | Coventry City | 2 | **Reddish Shane** | Doncaster Rovers | 2 |
| **Fox Ruel** | Norwich City | 2 | **Robinson Mark** | Barnsley | 2 |
| **Gouck Andy** | Blackpool | 2 | **Rush Matthew** | West Ham United | 2 |
| **Hamilton Gary** | Darlington | 2 | **Ryan Vaughan** | Wimbledon | 2 |
| **Hawke Warren** | Chesterfield | 2 | **Samways Vinny** | Tottenham Hotspur | 2 |
| **Hessenthaler Andy** | Watford | 2 | **Sharpe Lee** | Manchester United | 2 |
| **Houghton Scott** | Tottenham Hotspur | 2 | **Sheedy Kevin** | Newcastle United | 2 |
| **Howey Steve** | Newcastle United | 2 | **Stockwell Mike** | Ipswich Town | 2 |
| **James Julian** | Luton Town | 2 | **Taylor Mark** | Shrewsbury Town | 2 |
| **Jobling Kevin** | Grimsby Town | 2 | **Taylor Mark** | Wrexham | 2 |
| **Jones Mark** | Cardiff City | 2 | **Thompson David** | Preston North End | 2 |
| **Jones Philip** | Wigan Athletic | 2 | **Tinkler John** | Hartlepool United | 2 |
| **Langley Kevin** | Wigan Athletic | 2 | **Turner Phil** | Notts County | 2 |
| **Lynch Tommy** | Shrewsbury Town | 2 | **Walker Ian** | Swansea City | 2 |
| **Matthews Mike** | Hull City | 2 | **Walker Ray** | Port Vale | 2 |
| **May Andy** | Bristol City | 2 | **Watson Tommy** | Grimsby Town | 2 |
| **McGrath Lloyd** | Coventry City | 2 | **Wilson Clive** | Queens Park Rangers | 2 |
| **McNally Bernard** | West Bromwich Albion | 2 | **Wilkins Ray** | Queens Park Rangers | 2 |
| **Micklewhite Gary** | Derby County | 2 | | | |

# QUICK REFERENCE 91/92
## GOALS SCORED BY STRIKERS

| | | | | | | |
|---|---|---|---|---|---|---|
| **Bamber Dave** | Blackpool | 34 | **Fleck Robert** | Norwich City | 19 |
| **Aldridge John** | Tranmere Rovers | 33 | **Dublin Dion** | Cambridge United | 18 |
| **Holdsworth Dean** | Brentford | 33 | **Flounders Andy** | Rochdale | 18 |
| **Lineker Gary** | Tottenham Hotspur | 33 | **Gabbiadini Marco** | Derby County | 18 |
| **Shearer Duncan** | Blackburn Rovers | 33 | **Norris Steve** | Chesterfield | 18 |
| **Wright Ian** | Arsenal | 31 | **Philliskirk Tony** | Bolton Wanderers | 18 |
| **Roberts Iwan** | Huddersfield Town | 30 | **Shearer Alan** | Southampton | 18 |
| **Carter Mark** | Barnet | 29 | **Slaven Bernie** | Middlesbrough | 18 |
| **Conroy Mike** | Burnley | 28 | **Small Mike** | West Ham United | 18 |
| **Stant Phil** | Mansfield Town | 28 | **Starbuck Phillip** | Huddersfield Town | 18 |
| **Bull Gary** | Barnet | 26 | **Stein Mark** | Stoke City | 18 |
| **Speedie David** | Blackburn Rovers | 26 | **Walker Andy** | Bolton Wanderers | 18 |
| **Biggins Wayne** | Stoke City | 24 | **Worthington Gary** | Wigan Athletic | 18 |
| **Naylor Tony** | Crewe Alexandra | 24 | **Deane Brian** | Sheffield United | 17 |
| **Bull Steve** | Wolverhampton W. | 23 | **Francis Kevin** | Stockport County | 17 |
| **Crown David** | Gillingham | 23 | **Kiwomya Chris** | Ipswich Town | 17 |
| **Dale Carl** | Cardiff City | 23 | **Lovell Steve** | Gillingham | 17 |
| **McClair Brian** | Manchester United | 23 | **Nugent Kevin** | Plymouth Argyle | 17 |
| **Quinn Jimmy** | AFC Bournemouth | 23 | **Simpson Paul** | Derby County | 17 |
| **Charlery Ken** | Peterborough United | 22 | **Stevens Ian** | Bury | 17 |
| **Pike Chris** | Cardiff City | 22 | **Baker Paul** | Hartlepool United | 16 |
| **Wilkinson Paul** | Middlesbrough | 22 | **Brazil Gary** | Fulham | 16 |
| **Angell Brett** | Southend United | 21 | **Gall Mark** | Brighton & Hove A. | 16 |
| **Bright Mark** | Crystal Palace | 21 | **Maskell Craig** | Reading | 16 |
| **Byrne John** | Sunderland | 21 | **Saunders Carl** | Bristol Rovers | 16 |
| **Chapman Lee** | Leeds United | 20 | **Shaw Graham** | Preston North End | 16 |
| **Fashanu John** | Wimbledon | 20 | **Yorke Dwight** | Aston Villa | 16 |
| **Goodman Don** | Sunderland | 20 | **Adcock Tony** | Peterborough United | 15 |
| **Hirst David** | Sheffield Wednesday | 20 | **Brain Simon** | Hereford | 15 |
| **McDonald Rod** | Walsall | 20 | **Foyle Martin** | Port Vale | 15 |
| **Moran Steve** | Exeter City | 20 | **Harford Mick** | Luton Town | 15 |
| **Sheringham Teddy** | Nottingham Forest | 20 | **Johnson Tommy** | Derby County | 15 |
| **White David** | Manchester City | 20 | **McCarthy Sean** | Bradford | 15 |
| **Beardsley Peter** | Everton | 19 | **Quinn Niall** | Manchester City | 15 |
| **Bissett Gary** | Brentford | 19 | **Rimmer Stuart** | Chester City | 15 |
| **Cunningham Tony** | Rotherham United | 19 | **Sharp Graeme** | Oldham Athletic | 15 |

## DREAM LEAGUE – CHAPTER 10

| | | | | | | |
|---|---|---|---|---|---|---|
| Watson Andy | Carlisle United | 15 | Berry Greg | Leyton Orient | 11 |
| Claridge Steve | Cambridge United | 14 | Blackstone Ian | York City | 11 |
| Daley Phillip | Wigan Athletic | 14 | Cole Andrew | Bristol City | 11 |
| Earle Robbie | Wimbledon | 14 | Ekoko Efan | AFC Bournemouth | 11 |
| Helliwell Ian | Scunthorpe United | 14 | Ellison Lee | Darlington | 11 |
| Leaburn Carl | Charlton Athletic | 14 | Farrell Sean | Fulham | 11 |
| Marshall Dwight | Plymouth Argyle | 14 | Hunt Andy | Newcastle United | 11 |
| Milner Andy | Rochdale | 14 | Lyne Neil | Shrewsbury Town | 11 |
| Saunders Dean | Liverpool | 14 | McManaman Steven | Liverpool | 11 |
| Wilkinson Steve | Mansfield Town | 14 | Mehew David | Bristol Rovers | 11 |
| Wright Tommy | Leicester City | 14 | Mooney Tommy | Scarborough | 11 |
| Allen Clive | West Ham United | 13 | Noteman Kevin | Mansfield Town | 11 |
| Anderton Darren | Portsmouth | 13 | Ormondroyd Ian | Leicester City | 11 |
| Barnes Bobby | Peterborough United | 13 | Payton Andy | Middlesbrough | 11 |
| Bennett Gary | Chester City | 13 | Reeves David | Bolton Wanderers | 11 |
| Campbell Kevin | Arsenal | 13 | Regis Cyrille | Aston Villa | 11 |
| Davison Bobby | Sheffield United | 13 | Riley David | Peterborough United | 11 |
| Kelly David | Newcastle United | 13 | Sturridge Simon | Birmingham City | 11 |
| Kitson Paul | Derby County | 13 | Williams John | Swansea City | 11 |
| Merson Paul | Arsenal | 13 | Beauchamp Joey | Oxford | 10 |
| Newell Mike | Blackburn Rovers | 13 | Beckford Darren | Norwich City | 10 |
| Onuora Iffy | Huddersfield Town | 13 | Daws Tony | Scunthorpe United | 10 |
| Page Don | Rotherham United | 13 | Eyres David | Blackpool | 10 |
| Smith Alan | Arsenal | 13 | Fashanu Justin | Torquay United | 10 |
| Taylor John | Bristol Rovers | 13 | Ferdinand Les | Queens Park Rangers | 10 |
| Wallace Rod | Leeds United | 13 | Francis John | Burnley | 10 |
| Watkin Steve | Wrexham | 13 | Gallacher Kevin | Coventry City | 10 |
| White Devon | Cambridge United | 13 | Hamilton Ian | Scunthorpe United | 10 |
| White Steve | Swindon Town | 13 | Irons Kenny | Tranmere Rovers | 10 |
| Whittingham Guy | Portsmouth | 13 | Lancashire Graham | Burnley | 10 |
| Wise Dennis | Chelsea | 13 | Marshall Ian | Oldham Athletic | 10 |
| Blissett Luther | Watford | 12 | Mutch Andy | Wolverhampton W. | 10 |
| Hughes Mark | Manchester United | 12 | Nogan Lee | Watford | 10 |
| Lee Robert | Charlton Athletic | 12 | Rodwell Tony | Blackpool | 10 |
| Meade Raphael | Brighton & Hove A. | 12 | Robinson Liam | Bury | 10 |
| Taylor Bob | West Bromwich Albion | 12 | Torpey Stephen | Bradford | 10 |
| White Jason | Scunthorpe United | 12 | Whitton Steve | Ipswich Town | 10 |
| Willis Roger | Barnet | 12 | Williams Paul | Sheffield Wednesday | 10 |
| Allison Wayne | Bristol City | 11 | Wood Paul | AFC Bournemouth | 10 |
| Bailey Dennis | Queens Park Rangers | 11 | Whitehall Steve | Rochdale | 10 |

# QUICK REFERENCE 91/92

| | | | | | | |
|---|---|---|---|---|---|---|
| Ansah Andy | Southend United | 9 | Cooper Mark | Leyton Orient | 7 |
| Bartlett Kevin | Notts County | 9 | Daley Tony | Aston Villa | 7 |
| Connelly Karl | Wrexham | 9 | Gardiner Mark | Crewe Alexandra | 7 |
| Cottee Tony | Everton | 9 | Giggs Ryan | Manchester United | 7 |
| Dowie Iain | Southampton | 9 | Henry Tony | Shrewsbury Town | 7 |
| Durie Gordon | Tottenham Hotspur | 9 | Harper Steve | Burnley | 7 |
| Edwards Robert | Crewe Alexandra | 9 | Johnston Maurice | Everton | 7 |
| Gilligan Jimmy | Swansea City | 9 | Jones Andy | Leyton Orient | 7 |
| Goater Shaun | Rotherham United | 9 | Lee Jason | Lincoln City | 7 |
| Heritage Peter | Hereford | 9 | McAvennie Frank | West Ham United | 7 |
| Jenkinson Leigh | Hull City | 9 | Paskin John | Wrexham | 7 |
| Jules Mark | Scarborough | 9 | Quinn Mick | Newcastle United | 7 |
| Loram Mike | Stockport County | 9 | Rammell Andy | Barnsley | 7 |
| Lormor Tony | Lincoln City | 9 | Ritchie Andy | Oldham Athletic | 7 |
| McCarthy Jon | York City | 9 | Rush David | Sunderland | 7 |
| Russell Kevin | Leicester City | 9 | Rush Ian | Liverpool | 7 |
| Showler Paul | Barnet | 9 | Senior Trevor | Reading | 7 |
| Butler Steve | Watford | 8 | Smillie Neil | Brentford | 7 |
| Cecere Michele | Walsall | 8 | Steel Jim | Tranmere Rovers | 7 |
| Chalmers Paul | Swansea City | 8 | Tilson Steve | Southend United | 7 |
| Clough Nigel | Nottingham Forest | 8 | Wegerle Roy | Blackburn Rovers | 7 |
| Cooke John | Chesterfield | 8 | Archdeacon Owen | Barnsley | 6 |
| Currie David | Barnsley | 8 | Aspinall Warren | Portsmouth | 6 |
| Durnin John | Oxford | 8 | Aylott Trevor | Oxford | 6 |
| Griffiths Carl | Shrewsbury Town | 8 | Buckley John | Scunthorpe United | 6 |
| Hazel Desmond | Rotherham United | 8 | Davenport Peter | Sunderland | 6 |
| Henry Liburd | Maidstone United | 8 | Dziekanowski Dariuz | Bristol City | 6 |
| Lancaster Dave | Chesterfield | 8 | Evans Stewart | Crewe Alexandra | 6 |
| Le Tissier Matthew | Southampton | 8 | Futcher Ron | Crewe Alexandra | 6 |
| McGinlay John | Millwall | 8 | Fyfe Tony | Carlisle United | 6 |
| McLoughlin Paul | Mansfield Town | 8 | Garner Andy | Blackpool | 6 |
| Mitchell David | Swindon Town | 8 | Gee Phil | Leicester City | 6 |
| Naylor Glenn | York City | 8 | Godfrey Kevin | Brentford | 6 |
| Powell Gary | Wigan Athletic | 8 | Gray Philip | Luton Town | 6 |
| Puckett David | AFC Bournemouth | 8 | Griffiths Bryan | Wigan Athletic | 6 |
| Sheron Mike | Manchester City | 8 | Haag Kelly | Fulham | 6 |
| Woods Neil | Grimsby Town | 8 | Jeffrey Micheal | Doncaster Rovers | 6 |
| Bazeley Darren | Watford | 7 | Jewell Paul | Bradford | 6 |
| Carmichael Matt | Lincoln City | 7 | Kimble Garry | Peterborough United | 6 |
| Clarke Colin | Portsmouth | 7 | Nelson Garry | Charlton Athletic | 6 |

# DREAM LEAGUE – CHAPTER 10

| | | | | | | |
|---|---|---|---|---|---|---|
| Powell Darryl | Portsmouth | 6 | Penney David | Oxford | 5 |
| Rosario Robert | Coventry City | 6 | Penrice Gary | Queens Park Rangers | 5 |
| Rosenior Leroy | Bristol City | 6 | Rees Tony | Grimsby Town | 5 |
| Saville Andrew | Hartlepool United | 6 | Smith David A | Plymouth Argyle | 5 |
| Stewart Paul | Tottenham Hotspur | 6 | Steele Tim | Stoke City | 5 |
| Van Der Laan Robin | Port Vale | 6 | Stewart Marcus | Bristol Rovers | 5 |
| Wheeler Paul | Stockport County | 6 | Sutton Chris | Norwich City | 5 |
| Williams Paul | West Bromwich Albion | 6 | Walters Mark | Liverpool | 5 |
| Adams Neil | Oldham Athletic | 5 | Walling Dean | Carlisle United | 5 |
| Agana Tony | Leeds United | 5 | Barnes John | Liverpool | 4 |
| Allen Bradley | Queens Park Rangers | 5 | Chapman Gary | Exeter City | 4 |
| Allen Malcolm | Millwall | 5 | Clarke Andy | Wimbledon | 4 |
| Armstrong Chris | Millwall | 5 | Colquhoun John | Millwall | 4 |
| Ashcroft Lee | Preston North End | 5 | Cork Alan | Sheffield United | 4 |
| Barnett Gary | Huddersfield Town | 5 | Davies Gordon | Wrexham | 4 |
| Bannister Gary | Oxford | 5 | Evans Nicky | Barnet | 4 |
| Borthwick John | Darlington | 5 | Falco Mark | Millwall | 4 |
| Cadette Richard | Scottish League | 5 | France Darren | Hull City | 4 |
| Dixon Kerry | Chelsea | 5 | Fry Chris | Hereford | 4 |
| Dobson Paul | Lincoln City | 5 | Gabbiadini Ricardo | Scarborough | 4 |
| Ellis Tony | Stoke City | 5 | Gavin Pat | Peterborough United | 4 |
| Fletcher Andrew | Scarborough | 5 | Goddard Paul | Ipswich Town | 4 |
| Furlong Paul | Coventry City | 5 | Greenwood Nigel | Preston North End | 4 |
| Garner Simon | Blackburn Rovers | 5 | Hilaire Vince | Exeter City | 4 |
| Gordon Colin | Leicester City | 5 | Houchen Keith | Port Vale | 4 |
| Hendrie John | Middlesbrough | 5 | Hulme Kevin | Bury | 4 |
| Himsworth Gary | Scarborough | 5 | Johnrose Lenny | Hartlepool United | 4 |
| Jemson Nigel | Sheffield Wednesday | 5 | Jones Murray | Grimsby Town | 4 |
| Jepson Ron | Preston North End | 5 | Kabia Jason | Lincoln City | 4 |
| Jones Lee | Liverpool | 5 | Kernaghan Alan | Middlesbrough | 4 |
| Juryeff Ian | Halifax Town | 5 | Limpar Anders | Arsenal | 4 |
| Malkin Chris | Tranmere Rovers | 5 | Lowndes Steve | Hereford | 4 |
| McClean Christian | Northampton Town | 5 | Lyons Darren | Bury | 4 |
| McGhee Mark | Reading | 5 | Marshall Gary | Exeter City | 4 |
| Morgan Nicky | Bristol City | 5 | Mendonca Clive | Grimsby Town | 4 |
| Morley Trevor | West Ham United | 5 | Oldfield David | Leicester City | 4 |
| Muir Ian | Tranmere Rovers | 5 | Ripley Stuart | Middlesbrough | 4 |
| Murphy Frank | Barnet | 5 | Sayer Andy | Leyton Orient | 4 |
| O'Connell Brendan | Barnsley | 5 | Smith Mark | Grimsby Town | 4 |
| Palmer Roger | Oldham Athletic | 5 | Sussex Andy | Southend United | 4 |

## QUICK REFERENCE 91/92

| | | | | | | |
|---|---|---|---|---|---|---|
| Thompson Garry | Queens Park Rangers | 4 | Rideout Paul | Scottish League | 3 |
| Thomas John | Hartlepool United | 4 | Rosenthal Ronny | Liverpool | 3 |
| Turner Robert | Plymouth Argyle | 4 | Stephenson Paul | Millwall | 3 |
| Walsh Paul | Tottenham Hotspur | 4 | Smith Paul | Lincoln City | 3 |
| Whyte David | Charlton Athletic | 4 | Southall Nicky | Hartlepool United | 3 |
| Wilcox Jason | Blackburn Rovers | 4 | Stein Brian | Luton Town | 3 |
| Wilson Kevin | Notts County | 4 | Stringfellow Ian | Mansfield Town | 3 |
| Ampadu Kwame | West Bromwich Albion | 3 | Stuart Mark | Bradford | 3 |
| Arnott Sandy | Gillingham | 3 | Thorpe Adrian | Northampton Town | 3 |
| Barnes Paul | Stoke City | 3 | Thompson Simon | Scarborough | 3 |
| Beaumont Chris | Stockport County | 3 | Walker Clive | Brighton & Hove A. | 3 |
| Bent Junior | Stoke City | 3 | Wade Bryan | Brighton & Hove A. | 3 |
| Bertschin Keith | Aldershot | 3 | Warzycha Robert | Everton | 3 |
| Bradshaw Carl | Sheffield United | 3 | West Colin | West Bromwich Albion | 3 |
| Brown Steve | Northampton Town | 3 | Whitehurst Billy | Crewe Alexandra | 3 |
| Burke Mark | Wolverhampton W. | 3 | Wigley Steve | Portsmouth | 3 |
| Campbell Greg | Northampton Town | 3 | Young Stewart | Hull City | 3 |
| Cantona Eric | Leeds United | 3 | Achampong Kenny | Leyton Orient | 2 |
| Fletcher Steve | Hartlepool United | 3 | Allon Joe | Port Vale | 2 |
| Francis Trevor | Sheffield Wednesday | 3 | Beckford Jason | Birmingham City | 2 |
| Gaynor Tommy | Nottingham Forest | 3 | Bennett Dave | Shrewsbury Town | 2 |
| Goodman Jon | Millwall | 3 | Billy Chris | Huddersfield Town | 2 |
| Gorman Paul | Charlton Athletic | 3 | Bremner Kevin | Shrewsbury Town | 2 |
| Green Scott | Bolton Wanderers | 3 | Brown Mike | Bolton Wanderers | 2 |
| Hall Paul | Torquay United | 3 | Burnham Jason | Northampton Town | 2 |
| Hodges Glyn | Sheffield United | 3 | Byrne David | Fulham | 2 |
| Howard Jonathan | Rotherham United | 3 | Caffrey Henry | Hereford | 2 |
| James Robbie | Bradford | 3 | Carter Danny | Leyton Orient | 2 |
| Jeffers John | Port Vale | 3 | Cascarino Tony | Chelsea | 2 |
| Johnson David A | Sheffield Wednesday | 3 | Chalk Martyn | Derby County | 2 |
| Kilner Andy | Rochdale | 3 | Connor Terry | Bristol City | 2 |
| Ling Martin | Swindon Town | 3 | Cooper David | Plymouth Argyle | 2 |
| Lowe David | Port Vale | 3 | Collymore Stan | Crystal Palace | 2 |
| Lund Gary | Notts County | 3 | Darby Dwayne | Torquay United | 2 |
| Matthews Rob | Notts County | 3 | Donowa Lou | Birmingham City | 2 |
| MacDonald Kevin | Walsall | 3 | Donovan Kevin | Halifax Town | 2 |
| McGee Paul | Wimbledon | 3 | Drinkell Kevin | Coventry City | 2 |
| Morris Andy | Chesterfield | 3 | Edwards Dean | Northampton Town | 2 |
| Pounder Tony | Bristol Rovers | 3 | Finney Kevin | Lincoln City | 2 |
| Proudlock Paul | Carlisle United | 3 | Gibbins Roger | Cardiff City | 2 |

# DREAM LEAGUE - CHAPTER 10

| | | | | | | |
|---|---|---|---|---|---|---|
| Glover Lee | Nottingham Forest | 2 | Olney Ian | Aston Villa | 2 |
| Harmon Darren | Shrewsbury Town | 2 | Donaldson O Neill | Shrewsbury Town | 2 |
| Heath Adrian | Stoke City | 2 | Pascoe Colin | Sunderland | 2 |
| Heaney Neil | Cambridge United | 2 | Paterson Jamie | Halifax Town | 2 |
| Hendry John | Tottenham Hotspur | 2 | Payne Mark | Rochdale | 2 |
| Henry Charlie | Non League Team | 2 | Pearson John | Barnsley | 2 |
| Howells David | Tottenham Hotspur | 2 | Ramage Craig | Derby County | 2 |
| Kennedy Andy | Watford | 2 | Raynor Paul | Cambridge United | 2 |
| Lemon Paul | Chesterfield | 2 | Regis Dave | Plymouth Argyle | 2 |
| Leonard Mark | Rochdale | 2 | Richards Carl | Maidstone United | 2 |
| Lillis Mark | Stockport County | 2 | Robins Mark | Manchester United | 2 |
| McCarrison Dugald | Darlington | 2 | Rowett Gary | Cambridge United | 2 |
| Millar Paul | Cardiff City | 2 | Salako John | Crystal Palace | 2 |
| Miller Paul | Wimbledon | 2 | Shutt Carl | Leeds United | 2 |
| Morton Neil | Chester City | 2 | Smith Mark A | Shrewsbury Town | 2 |
| Ndlovu Peter | Coventry City | 2 | Stoker Gareth | Hull City | 2 |
| Nevin Pat | Everton | 2 | Taylor Colin | Wigan Athletic | 2 |
| Nicholson Max | Doncaster Rovers | 2 | Tolson Neill | Oldham Athletic | 2 |
| Nogan Kurt | Luton Town | 2 | Ward Peter | Stockport County | 2 |
| Norbury Mick | Cambridge United | 2 | Worboys Gavain | Notts County | 2 |